COMMUNICATION IN THE 2020s

This book provides an inside look at the discipline of Communication. In this collection of chapters, top scholars from a wide range of subfields discuss how they have experienced and how they study crucial issues of our time.

The 2020s opened with a series of events with massive implications for the ways we communicate, from the COVID-19 pandemic, a summer of protests for social justice, and climate change-related natural disasters, to one of the most contentious presidential elections in modern U.S. history. The chapters in this book provide snapshots of many of these issues as seen through the eyes of specialists in the major subfields of Communication, including interpersonal, organizational, strategic, environmental, religious, social justice, risk, sport, health, family, instructional, and political communication. Written in an informal style that blends personal narrative with accessible explanation of basic concepts, the book is ideal for introducing students to the range and practical applications of the Communication discipline.

This book comprises a valuable companion text for Introduction to Communication courses as well as a primary resource for Capstone and Introduction to Graduate Studies courses. Further, this collection provides meaningful insights for Communication scholars as we look ahead to the remainder of the 2020s and beyond.

Christina S. Beck is Professor of Communication Studies at Ohio University and Past President of the National Communication Association and the Central States Communication Association.

COMMUNICATION IN THE 2020s

Viewing Our World Through the Eyes of Communication Scholars

Edited by Christina S. Beck

Routledge
Taylor & Francis Group

NEW YORK AND LONDON

Cover image: Thodsapol Thongdeekhieo/EveEm

First published 2022
by Routledge
605 Third Avenue, New York, NY 10158

and by Routledge
4 Park Square, Milton Park, Abingdon, Oxon, OX14 4RN

Routledge is an imprint of the Taylor & Francis Group, an informa business

Library of Congress Cataloging-in-Publication Data
A catalog record for this book has been requested

ISBN: 978-1-032-11563-4 (hbk)
ISBN: 978-1-032-11160-5 (pbk)
ISBN: 978-1-003-22046-6 (ebk)

DOI: 10.4324/9781003220466

Typeset in Bembo
by Apex CoVantage, LLC

CONTENTS

FIGURES

CONTRIBUTORS

Dr. Pat Arneson (Ph.D., Ohio University) is Professor Emerita in the Department of Communication and Rhetorical Studies at Duquesne University. She examines issues of human communication from various philosophical perspectives. Her current research interests include civil rights, free and responsible speech, political rhetoric, and communication ethics. Pat is the author of *Communicative Engagement and Social Liberation: Justice Will Be Made* (Fairleigh Dickinson University Press, 2014) and co-author (with Ronald C. Arnett) of *Dialogic Civility in a Cynical Age: Community, Hope, and Interpersonal Relationships* (SUNY Press, 1999). She is editor of *Perspectives on Philosophy of Communication* (Purdue University Press, 2007) and *Exploring Communication Ethics: Interviews With Influential Scholars in the Field* (Peter Lang, 2007) and co-editor (with Žilvinas Svigaris) of *Preeminence of Myth and the Decline of Instrumental Reason* (Nova Science Publishers, 2020) and (with Ronald C. Arnett) of *Philosophy of Communication Ethics: Alterity and the Other* (Fairleigh Dickinson University Press, 2014). She has published over 50 book chapters, journal articles, encyclopedia entries, or research reports in journals including *Empedocles: European Journal for the Philosophy of Communication, Integrative Explorations: Journal of Culture and Consciousness, International Journal of Listening, Women's Studies in Communication, Free Speech Yearbook, Communication Law Review, Communication Studies, The Review of Communication, The Electronic Journal of Communication/La Revue Electronique de Communication*, and *Journal of the Association for Communication Administration.*

Dr. Ahmet Atay (Ph.D., Southern Illinois University) is Associate Professor of Communication at the College of Wooster. His research focuses on diasporic experiences and cultural identity formations; political and social complexities of city life such as immigrant and queer experiences; the usage of new media technologies in different settings; and the notion of home; representation of gender, sexuality, and ethnicity in media; queer and immigrant experiences in cyberspace, and critical communication pedagogies. He is the author of *Globalization's Impact on Identity Formation: Queer Diasporic Males in Cyberspace* (2015) and the co-editor of several books. His scholarship appeared in a number of journals and edited books.

Dr. Christina S. Beck (Ph.D., University of Oklahoma) is Professor in the School of Communication Studies at Ohio University and Past President of the National Communication Association and Central States Communication Association, past-editor of *Communication Yearbook* (volumes 30–33), and past-book review editor for *Journal of Health Communication: International Perspectives*. Beck's current work lies at the intersection of health communication, mediated communities, and fan studies. In addition to numerous book chapters, journal articles, and conference presentations, Beck has published four award-winning books in the areas of health communication and gender: *The Lynching of Language: Gender, Politics, and Power in the Hill-Thomas Hearings* (co-edited with Sandra Ragan, Lynda Kaid, and Dianne Bystromm, University of Illinois Press), *Partnership for Health: Building Relationships Between Women and Health Caregivers* (co-authored with Sandra Ragan and Athena DuPre, Erlbaum), *Communicating for Better Health: A Guide Through the Medical Mazes* (Allyn & Bacon), and *Narrative, Health, and Healing: Communication Theory, Research, and Practice* (co-edited with Lynn Harter and Phyllis Japp, Erlbaum). Released in 2015, Beck's book, *Celebrity Health Narratives and the Public Health* (with co-authors Nate Simmons, Stellina Chapman, Kelly Tenzek, and Stephanie Ruhl, McFarland) bridges her work in health communication, popular culture, fandom, and media audiences. Her co-edited book with Richard West, the *Routledge Handbook of Communication and Bullying*, extended from her NCA Presidential Initiative that included founding the NCA Anti-Bullying Project and received the 2020 NCA Applied Communication Division Distinguished Edited Book Award.

Dr. Laura W. Black (Ph.D., University of Washington) is Professor in the School of Communication Studies at Ohio University, where she holds the endowed Stocker Professorship in Interpersonal Communication. Dr. Black is an engaged communication scholar who is dedicated to democracy and community. She uses qualitative and discourse-based methods to conduct research that helps groups address difficult, divisive issues through collaboration, dialogue, and deliberation. Dr. Black's scholarship focuses on three overarching questions: How do groups discursively construct community and difference? How do communication practices enable and constrain group members' efforts to address difficult collective problems? How can communication be designed to challenge oppressive structures and promote ethical decision making in diverse groups? She has published in outlets such as the *Journal of Applied Communication Research*, *Communication Theory*, *Western Journal of Communication*, *Small Group Research*, and *Social Science*

Quarterly. She is the former editor of the *Journal of Public Deliberation* and one of the founding members of the Public Dialogue and Deliberation division of the National Communication Association.

Dr. Dawn O. Braithwaite (Ph.D., University of Minnesota) is a Willa Cather Professor in the Department of Communication Studies at the University of Nebraska-Lincoln. Dr. Braithwaite studies how people in personal and family relationships communicate and negotiate family change and challenges. Her research centers on communication in understudied and changing families, communication rituals, and dialectics of relating in stepfamilies and among voluntary (fictive) kin. Dr. Braithwaite has authored over 130 articles and is co-author or co-editor of six books including *Family Communication: Cohesion and Change and Engaging Theories in Interpersonal Communication*. She received the National Communication Association's Brommel Award for Outstanding Contributions in Family Communication and the NCA Becker Distinguished Service Award. She received outstanding book awards from the NCA Family Communication Division and the Interpersonal Communication Division. She was awarded the UNL College of Arts and Sciences Award for Outstanding Research in Social Science. Dr. Braithwaite was named a Distinguished Scholar of the National Communication Association in 2020 and of the Western States Communication Association in 2014. Dr. Braithwaite is a Past President of the Western States Communication Association and a Past President of the National Communication Association.

Dr. Michael L. Butterworth (Ph.D., Indiana University, Bloomington) is Director of the Center for Sports Communication and Media, the Governor Ann W. Richards Chair for the Texas Program in Sports and Media, and Professor in the Department of Communication Studies at the University of Texas at Austin. His research explores the connections between rhetoric, democracy, and sport, with particular interests in national identity, militarism, and public memory. He is the author of *Baseball and Rhetorics of Purity: The National Pastime and American Identity During the War on Terror*, co-author of *Communication and Sport: Surveying the Field*, editor of *Sport and Militarism: Contemporary Global Perspectives*, and co-editor of *Sport, Rhetoric, and Political Struggle* and *Rhetorics of Democracy in the Americas*. Dr. Butterworth's essays have appeared in journals such as *Communication and Critical/Cultural Studies, Communication and Sport, Communication, Culture & Critique, Critical Studies in Media Communication*, the *International Review for the Sociology of Sport*, the *Journal of Communication*, the *Journal of Sport & Social Issues*, the *Quarterly Journal of Speech*, and *Rhetoric & Public Affairs*. Dr. Butterworth serves as vice chair of the Sports Communication Interest Group for the International Communication Association. He previously served as the chair of the Communication and Sport Division for the National Communication Association and was the founding executive director of the International Association for Communication and Sport.

Dr. Sarah M. DeIuliis (Ph.D., Duquesne University) is Assistant Professor in the Department of Communication and Rhetorical Studies at Duquesne University. She serves as an undergraduate program director, recruitment coordinator, and the faculty co-advisor for the Duquesne Debating Society. Dr. DeIuliis has published in journals such as *Atlantic Journal of Communication, Communication Research Trends, Listening/Journal of Communication Ethics, Religion and Culture,* and *Journal of the Association for Communication Administration.* She is the co-author of *Corporate Communication Crisis Leadership: Advocacy and Ethics.*

Dr. Elizabeth Desnoyers-Colas (Ph.D., Regent University) is a Communication and Africana Studies scholar and graduate faculty member at Georgia Southern University, Armstrong Campus. Dr. Desnoyers-Colas' academic research interests include narrative and storytelling about the African Diaspora. She directs plays written by African American women playwrights and those which feature black women as protagonists/antagonists. She is a retired military United States Air Force Major who served in Operation Desert Storm in Saudi Arabia in 1991. She conducts research about African Americans in the military, past and present.

Dr. Leandra Hinojosa Hernández (Ph.D., Texas A&M University) is Assistant Professor in the Department of Communication Studies at Utah Valley University. Dr. Hernández enjoys teaching health communication, gender studies, and media studies courses. She utilizes Chicana feminist and qualitative approaches to explore Latina/o/x cultural health experiences, Latina/o/x journalism and media representations, and reproductive justice and gendered violence contexts. Her teaching philosophy is informed by social justice approaches, and she is passionate about mentoring undergraduate students through diverse and inclusive research projects.

Dr. Ashley Noel Mack (Ph.D., University of Texas at Austin) is Assistant Professor of Rhetoric and Cultural Studies at Louisiana State University in the Department of Communication Studies and an affiliate faculty member in African and African American Studies as well as Women's, Gender, and Sexuality Studies. Mack is an interdisciplinary rhetoric and cultural critic, and a justice-driven teacher of communication, rhetoric, media, and cultural studies. Their research explores how differences and disparities are communicated and naturalized through media in contemporary U.S. culture, and also how communication is wielded by historically marginalized bodies and communities as a resource for creating a more just and equitable world. Their writing has been published in *Departures in Critical Qualitative Research, Journal of Communication Inquiry, Women's Studies in Communication, Quarterly Journal of Speech, Communication and Critical/Cultural Studies,* and *Journal of Homosexuality.*

Dr. Diana Isabel Martínez (Ph.D., University of Texas at Austin) is Associate Professor of Communication in the Communication Division at Seaver College of Pepperdine University. Her research explores physical and psychological borderlands, a term coined by Gloria Anzaldúa to describe spaces of social, political, and cultural struggle. She is working on archival research with the Gloria Anzaldúa collection, and she is also interested in issues surrounding social movements, intercultural dialogue, public memory, and visual rhetoric. Her recent published research has appeared in journals such as *Western Journal of Communication, Communication Quarterly*, and *The Journal of Multimodal Rhetorics* as well as edited books. She co-edited the monograph *Latina/o Communication Studies: Theories, Methods, and Practice* and teaches courses in rhetoric and leadership, communication studies, and culture.

Dr. Jennifer Scott Mobley (Ph.D., Ohio University) serves as Director of Mentoring and Professional Development and Professor of Communication at Grove City College. Dr. Mobley is an award-winning educator, researcher, and Gallup-certified executive coach. Informed by more than 15 years of progressive experience as a higher education leader, she uses strengths-based and design thinking approaches to support leaders and teams in the successful pursuit of strategic initiatives and flourishing cultures. Clients include New York University, University of Tennessee, Microsoft, GE Aviation, and the Tennessee Higher Education Commission, among many others. Mobley is passionate about identifying and developing future leaders, and she is the founder of the Early Career Women Collective, a global leadership development community for young professional women. Her forthcoming book on early career women's leadership development will be published by Forbes Books/Advantage Media in 2023. Throughout her career, she has led several award-winning grant initiatives to enrich the intellectual and theological exploration of calling and vocation among undergraduate students. Her work has been featured in several journals including the *International Journal of Appreciative Inquiry, Communication Studies*, and the *Journal of Applied Communication Research*.

Beatriz Nieto-Fernandez (Ph.D., University of South Florida) situates her research at the intersection of media and organizations and examines corporate media use in the context of bio-capitalism. Her current research investigates the ways in which direct-to-consumer genetic testing organizations use different types of media and discursive strategies to sell ideas of ancestry, race, and health advocacy to their customers. In particular, she explores the ways in which the phenomenon of genetic testing frames ideas of racial identification, ethnicity, and belonging to the nation as ethno-commodities for profit. Her research has been presented at the National Communication Association, the International Communication Association, the World Congress of Semiotics, and the Doctoral Honors Seminar. Her work has been published in *The Routledge International Handbook of Organizational Autoethnography* and is forthcoming in *Management Communication Quarterly* and *The Encyclopedia of Health Humanities: Future Trends in Health Advocacy*. She can be contacted at beatriznieto@usf.edu.

Dr. Mahuya Pal (Ph.D., Purdue University) is Associate Professor in the Department of Communication at the University of South Florida. A critical organizational communication scholar, she examines organizing of power and resistance within the contexts of marginality, poverty, human rights, and social justice. She is particularly invested in challenging Eurocentric bases of communication theories and explores local knowledges anchored in the cartographies of the Global South. Her research has been published in *Human Relations, Communication Monographs, Communication Theory, Communication Yearbook, Communication, Culture & Critique,* and elsewhere. She is currently the chair of the Organizational Communication Division of National Communication Association and Associate Editor of *Journal of Applied Communication Research.* She can be contacted at mpal@usf.edu.

Dr. Trevor Parry-Giles (Ph.D., Indiana University) is Professor in the Department of Communication and Associate Dean for Diversity, Equity, and Inclusion in the College of Arts and Humanities at the University of Maryland. Dr. Parry-Giles's research and teaching focus on the historical and contemporary relationships between rhetoric, politics, law, and popular culture. He is the award-winning author or editor of four books and his research has appeared in the *Quarterly Journal of Speech, Rhetoric & Public Affairs, Presidential Studies Quarterly, Critical Studies in Mass Communication,* the *Journal of Popular Film and Television,* the *Journal of Communication,* and elsewhere. Dr. Parry-Giles is a Distinguished Research Fellow and a Distinguished Teaching Fellow of the Eastern Communication Association, and in 2020, received ECA's Distinguished Service Award. In addition, Parry-Giles is a recipient of the University of Maryland's Graduate Faculty Mentor of the Year Award.

Dr. Phaedra C. Pezzullo (M.A. and Ph.D., University of North Carolina, B.S. and B.A., University of Massachusetts) is Associate Professor in the Department of Communication at the University of Colorado, Boulder, USA. She is an internationally known interdisciplinary expert, focusing on environmental communication, environmental and climate justice, social movements, qualitative methods, and public advocacy. In addition to over 30 articles and chapters, Pezzullo authored *Toxic Tourism: Rhetorics of Travel, Pollution and Environmental Justice* (University of Alabama Press, 2007), which won four book awards, including the Jane Jacobs Urban Communication Book Award and the Christine L. Oravec Research Award in Environmental Communication. Pezzullo also has co-authored three editions of the award-winning textbook, *Environmental Communication and the Public Sphere* (Sage, 2016, 2018, 2021), co-edited *Green Communication and China* (MSU Press, 2020), co-edited *Environmental Justice and Environmentalism* (MIT Press, 2007), and edited *Cultural Studies and the Environment, Revisited* (Routledge, 2010). She serves on multiple editorial boards including *Environmental Communication.* Pezzullo has lectured throughout the United States and internationally, such as at the *Grand amphithéâtre de la Sorbonne, Université de Paris-Sorbonne* and

Fudan University in Shanghai, China. She co-edits a book series with University of California Press, *Environmental Communication, Power, and Culture*. Pezzullo serves as a founding co-director of C3BC (the Center for Creative Climate Communication and Behavior Change) and the Just Transition Collaborative. Committed to public engagement, Pezzullo has worked with many civic organizations, including the American Bar Association, the Sierra Club, the University Cooperation for Atmospheric Research, and government planning departments.

Dr. Prashant Rajan (Ph.D., Purdue University) is Assistant Professor in the School of Communication Studies at Ohio University. Dr. Rajan investigates the design and use of technology in low-income and low-literacy environments. His research interests include informal entrepreneurship and innovation in the Global South, and development and sustainability rhetorics. His work has appeared in *Journal of Business & Technical Communication*, *Technical Communication Quarterly*, *Information Technologies and International Development*, and *Studies in Symbolic Interaction*.

Dr. Amy Aldridge Sanford (Ph.D., University of Iowa) is a scholar-activist who uses qualitative methods to explore the role of communication in leadership, gender, activism, pedagogy, and privilege. She presents her work at academic conferences and to community groups and is published in peer-reviewed journals, books, newspapers, and newsletters. Her book *From Thought to Action: Developing a Social Justice Orientation* was published in 2020. A first-generation college graduate, Amy earned a Ph.D. in Communication Studies from the University of Iowa. She has spent the last decade in administrative roles, including department chair and associate provost, and is a Past President of the Central States Communication Association. Her honors include Corpus Christi Under 40, YWCA's Y Women in Careers, University Communication Educator of the Year in both Texas (2018) and Oklahoma (2008), and Outstanding Administrator from the National States Advisory Council of the National Communication Association.

Dr. Kristina M. Scharp (Ph.D., University of Iowa) is Assistant Professor in the Department of Communication at the University of Washington. She received her graduate degrees from the University of Iowa where she specialized in interpersonal, family, and health communication. Dr. Scharp primarily researches difficult family transitions and the ways in which families cope with the major disruptions to their lives. The research that she conducts on distressing family transitions manifests in a variety of contexts such as parent–child estrangement, (foster) adoption, undergraduate student parents, and disability diagnoses such as hearing loss. She is also expressly interested in the ways family members resist being marginalized through related processes such as identity (re)construction, social support-seeking, information/uncertainty management, and meaning-making. Her research on communication in family contexts has garnered attention from outlets such as the *New York Times*, NPR, PBS, *U.S. News & World*

Report, the *Washington Post*, and the *Wall Street Journal*. She also writes her own blog about interpersonal and family relationships for *Psychology Today*. Dr. Scharp is a director of the Family Communication and Relationships Lab that is housed at both the University of Washington and Michigan State University.

Dr. Julie-Ann Scott-Pollock (Ph.D., University of Maine) is Professor of Communication Studies and Director of the UNCW Performance Studies program at the University of North Carolina-Wilmington. Dr. Scott-Pollock's scholarship focuses on performance studies, performance ethnography, personal narrative, identity and difference, disability studies, and qualitative research methodology. She teaches courses in performance studies, storytelling, and qualitative research methods. Dr. Scott-Pollock's research explores personal narratives of embodiment and identity. Projects include personal narrative and performance ethnographic research of physical disability, eating disorders, and aging and memory. She also directs the UNCW Storytellers, Hawk Tale Players, and Just Us: Performance Troupe for Social Justice.

Dr. Deanna D. Sellnow (Ph.D., University of North Dakota) is Professor of Strategic Communication in the Nicholson School of Communication and Media at the University of Central Florida. Dr. Sellnow's research focuses on strategic instructional communication in a variety of contexts including risk, crisis, health, and online settings. She has conducted funded research for the United States Geological Survey, Department of Homeland Security, and Centers for Disease Control and Protection. She has also collaborated with agencies such as the International Food Information Council about food security across the globe. She has published her work in numerous refereed articles in national and international journals, as well as authored or co-authored several textbooks including *Effective Speaking in a Digital Age*, *Communicate!*, and *The Rhetorical Power of Popular Culture*.

Dr. Timothy L. Sellnow (Ph.D., Wayne State University) joined the University of Central Florida in 2015 as Professor at the Nicholson School of Communication and Media. Dr. Sellnow's research focuses on bioterrorism, pre-crisis planning, and strategic communication for risk management and mitigation in organizational and health settings. He has conducted funded research for the Department of Homeland Security, the United States Department of Agriculture, the Centers for Disease Control and Prevention, the Environmental Protection Agency, and the United States Geological Survey. He has also served in an advisory role for the National Academy of Sciences and the World Health Organization. He has published numerous refereed journal articles on risk and crisis communication and has co-authored five books on risk and crisis communication. Dr. Sellnow's most recent book is titled *Theorizing Crisis Communication*.

Dr. Stephanie A. Tikkanen (Ph.D., University of California, Santa Barbara) studies interpersonal communication—particularly processes of social support and self-disclosure—in mediated settings. Her work has been published in *Journal of Communication*, *Communication Studies*, and *Health Communication*, among others. She was most recently an Adjunct Professor at Santa Clara University and previously worked as Assistant Professor at Ohio University.

Dr. Tiffany R. Wang (Ph.D., University of Nebraska-Lincoln) is Associate Professor of Communication Studies and basic course coordinator at the University of Montevallo and the Executive Director of the Central States Communication Association. She holds a Ph.D. in Communication Studies from the University of Nebraska-Lincoln and a M.S. and B.S. in Communication Studies from Texas Christian University. Tiffany enjoys teaching and advising students in the Department of Communication and mentoring undergraduate researchers through the Honors and TRIO McNair Scholars Programs. She is also an active trainer and speaker providing training and guest lectures for nonprofit organizations and educational institutions. Tiffany's research interests include instructional communication, communication education, and family communication. Her research has appeared in numerous academic journals and edited books. In recognition of her research, teaching, and service, Tiffany has received international, national, and regional awards including the International Communication Association Instructional and Developmental Communication Division Dissertation and Outstanding Graduate Teaching Awards, National Communication Association Lambda Pi Eta Thomas L. Veenendall Advisor of the Year Award, National Communication Association Family Communication Division Distinguished Article Award, and Central States Communication Association Outstanding New Teacher Award. In her leisure time, Tiffany enjoys traveling, reading, baking, and spending time with her Cavalier King Charles Spaniel London.

ACKNOWLEDGMENTS

Over the past 11 months, I have enjoyed an incredibly meaningful and gratifying journey with a tremendous group of scholars. Together, we produced a collection with snapshots from our own experiences through a very difficult and consequential year—2020—while also reflecting on the myriad implications of this year for understanding communication as we enter the remainder of the 2020s.

I am indebted to each of the chapter authors for lending their expertise to this project as well as disclosing deeply personal stories and reflections. Their willingness to be vulnerable and confide parts of their journey richly enhances this book. I appreciate the opportunity to work with each and every one of the talented and smart contributors.

Truly, editing this book has been a joy. I am honored for the invitation to serve in this role, and I'm glad that it has been part of my own scholarly journey. I am grateful to Brian Eschrich at Routledge for reaching out to me about this possibility. I would also like to thank Jennifer Scott Mobley for her help in thinking through options for organizing chapters in the collection.

Finally, I am very thankful to my family for indulging my time on this project. To Roger, thank you for your continual support and encouragement! To Brittany, Chelsea, Emmy, and Ellie-Kate, thank you for inspiring me every day! I love all of you, and I am so appreciative to God for the gift of each of you in my life.

1

INTRODUCTION

Christina S. Beck

Five hundred twenty-five thousand six hundred minutes
Five hundred twenty-five thousand moments so dear
Five hundred twenty-five thousand six hundred minutes
How do you measure? Measure a year?
In daylights,
In sunsets,
In midnights,
In cups of coffee,
In inches, in miles, in laughter, in strife
In five hundred twenty-five thousand six hundred minutes
How do you measure a year in a life?

("Seasons of Love" by Jonathan Larson)

We write a family Christmas newsletter every year. In 2019, as always, we invited our readers to pour a cup of hot chocolate, pull up a chair, and enjoy our annual year in review. However, I remember thinking that the 2019 edition had a more bittersweet tone than most. Even though good things certainly happened, it had been a tough year. Grandma P. fell in early February, 2019, breaking her arm and never quite recovering from the trauma before she passed away at age 90 that June. In March, my husband, Roger, caught the flu at an indoor softball tournament (along with our youngest daughter, Ellie-Kate, who was playing with her travel team). Shockingly, in less than 24 hours, his flu symptoms morphed into full-blown pneumonia and then septic shock. He spent days in the ICU, fighting for his life.

As we got ready to welcome 2020, I was eager to get back to our normal lives, filled with the usual blur of work, church, sports, and 4-H. We looked forward to travel with Ellie-Kate's basketball and softball teams and visits to our college

DOI: 10.4324/9781003220466-1

student daughter, Emmy, for Parent Weekends. By the time that we put the 2020 calendar on the wall on January 1, we had already filled many of the blocks with tournament names, hotel reservation numbers, special occasion details, 4-H meetings, and orthodontist appointments.

As 2020 ensued, though, we crossed out most of those calendar notations, and our annual family newsletter described a year that was anything but "usual." No spring softball season or sixth-grade graduation for Ellie-Kate. Emmy came home from college for spring break, finished her courses online, and mourned the cancellation of cherished campus events and traditions. Our second-oldest daughter, Chelsea, a consultant for a Big Four accounting firm in New York City, quarantined with a group of friends in the city, worked from home, and, mercifully, remained safe while in the spring epicenter of the pandemic. Our oldest daughter, Brittany, a fifth-grade teacher, figured out how to teach online while my husband and I did the same for our courses at Ohio University.

Those 525,600 minutes of 2020 proved to be impactful for my family and life-altering for our world. The year 2020 turned out to be overwhelming, exhausting, and frightening (see, e.g., Roberts, 2020). Individuals around the globe experienced life disruptions, isolation, loss, anger, and grief (see, e.g., Von Drehle, 2020; Zacharek, 2020). We witnessed shocking instances of racial injustice, some captured by horrified spectators on their cell phones, that compelled many to raise their voices and march in the streets against systemic racism and police violence (see, e.g., Worland, 2020). Residents scrambled to save their homes and lives from unprecedented, catastrophic wildfires in Australia, California, and Colorado and a record number of hurricanes hitting the U.S. Gulf Coast. Mainstream news outlets chronicled political turmoil and the health risks and economic impacts of a global pandemic while users flooded social media platforms with conspiracy theories and debates over which posts should be treated as "fake news" (see, e.g., Barry, 2020; Faris, 2020; Picheta, 2020). This turbulent year underscored the critical importance of communication for us to work, educate, advocate, celebrate, mourn, connect, inspire, protest, call to action, remain healthy, and save lives.

The year 2020 taught us just how much that we rely upon communication in times of strife. It also reminded us of just how much that communication permeates our daily lives. Through communication, we enact who we are, express our ideas, relate to others, make a difference, and decide what to believe. In this book, we discuss the legacies and lessons of 2020 for understanding communication as we now go through the decade of the 2020s. We hope that our experiences and reflections help our readers to learn more about communication and its centrality to how we construct and present ourselves, navigate relationships, and strive to be part of an ever-changing, dynamic world.

The Centrality of Communication

We have a sign that hangs in our living room: "This Family has a Season Pass for Sports." We love going to the NCAA Women's Basketball Final Four when it's within driving distance, and we get extremely competitive during our annual family NCAA basketball tournament bracket contest. One of the very first words that Ellie-Kate uttered was "ball."

Thus, in early March 2020, when Roger questioned the wisdom of traveling out of state with Ellie-Kate's team to an indoor softball tournament in Indianapolis because of COVID, my jaw dropped. "It's a huge facility," I responded. "It's not like the tiny one that smelled like mold." The one where you caught the flu and almost died last year . . . I didn't say that last part out loud.

For two days, we scoured the internet and watched the news. COVID-19 sounded scary, but was it truly unsafe to go when only a few cases had been reported in Indianapolis? If we did not go, what message would that send about our commitment to the team? Would we just seem paranoid? Alternatively, should we raise our concerns for the greater good?

Watzlawick et al. (1967, p. 49) made the important observation that "one cannot not communicate." We implicitly send messages through our verbal and nonverbal actions (and choices not to speak or act), even if we might not intend (or want) to do so. When we post on social media, text a friend, give a speech, or even ask a question, our message contains content. However, as Watzlawick et al. noted, through that message, we also do the work of informing, persuading, supporting, and constructing our realities, identities, and relationships (see also Gergen, 1991, 1994). Of course, anything that we do or say (or do not do or say) becomes available for interpretation and reaction from others who hear our utterances, read a post, or observe an action or lack thereof. As Sigman (1995, p. 2) emphasized in his book, *The Consequentiality of Communication*, "Communication matters."

Ellie-Kate's softball team decided to drop out of the tournament after a few parents—not just us—expressed concerns. Instead of driving to Indiana on March 13, 2020, we stayed home—where we would remain for nine weeks. The NCAA cancelled March Madness, and the NBA and MLB stopped playing (see, e.g., Wertheim & Apstein, 2020). Our "family season pass for sports" grew dust.

As we learned more about COVID-19 and watched the pandemic sweep through the greater New York area—where Chelsea was sheltering in place—we realized that we had to take it seriously. We heard about hospitals and nursing homes not allowing visitors as patients suffered and died alone, and images from 2019 flashed through our minds. I remembered anxiety-filled days at Roger's bedside in the ICU as he battled septic shock, asking questions, holding his hand, advocating for him. I recalled trying to get Grandma P. to eat just one more bit of food in the nursing home as she recovered from her broken arm. The mere thought of a loved one landing in a medical facility and not being with them fueled my motivation to keep our family out of what we determined to be harm's way from COVID-19.

We did not expect our position to be controversial. However, the behaviors that we adopted (wearing a mask, not gathering inside with others beyond our home, etc.) communicated our orientation to COVID-19 as a legitimate threat, and, through their reactions to us (and posts about their own practices on social media), we soon grasped that some friends and family members envisioned and treated the possible threat of this novel coronavirus far differently. Those revelations came to affect our interactions and relationships.

I am connected on social media with a wide range of people with an equally varied array of perspectives—friends from high school and college, colleagues in the Communication discipline, members of my church family, parents of my daughters' friends and teammates, friends from 4-H, Girl Scouts, and my daughters' schools. As Gergen (1991, 1994) explained, in contemporary life, we juggle a multiplicity of identities and relationships, complicating communication on social media and actions in public (even as simple as wearing a mask).

We navigated what to say, how to say it, and what not to say (see related work on Communication Privacy Management Theory, e.g., Petronio & Child, 2020). We proceeded cautiously, carefully considering what we would do (or not do) in public or share on social media, realizing that posts about the pandemic could (and did) prompt scoffs, praise, anger, support, political debates, and questions about our priorities, commitments, and even our faith.

We balanced assessment of health risk with possible relational ramifications. We permitted Ellie-Kate to re-join her softball team when it resumed practices in May 2020, with the condition that she keep her distance in huddles and remain away from teammates who cheered at the dugout fence. As much as she has always loved to play ball, I have never seen her smile as much as when she ran back on to the field after nine weeks of quarantine.

Our joy in watching Ellie-Kate play again came with twinges of anxiety. Were we putting our family's health in jeopardy? What did her teammates and coaches make of her distancing? In what ways would those implicitly communicative choices be consequential for her relationships and status on the team?

Of course, in the grand scheme of all happening concurrently beyond our home at that same time, a kid playing softball could easily be dismissed as insignificant or trivial—something that simply doesn't merit a second thought. As I recall how we navigated that situation, though, I realize what we communicated to Ellie-Kate by allowing her to play at all, given how we had talked at home about approaching the pandemic. I know that another choice would have sent a different message, with all kinds of relational ripple effects. This example illustrates that even the seemingly less important interactions and decisions involve (and necessitate) complex, interwoven moves that constitute significant and consequential symbolic activity.

Those who lived through 2020 understand that such "minor" moments occurred within the context of a year with far more monumental ones. The year 2020 prompted "new normals" in terms of our family life, as we relied on phone calls instead of holiday visits to support older family members who felt lonely and isolated in their homes out of state. I felt blessed and privileged that, as educators, we could stay safe and work from home. Nearly two years later, I am wondering if our turn to technology has forever changed how we enact university life with Zoom or Teams as a viable option to face-to-face conversations. I experienced deep sadness and anger that some "friends" on Facebook continued to echo former President Trump's racist reference to COVID-19 as the "China virus," even after I argued that using such a label could endanger Ellie-Kate (who was born in China) and other Asian Americans. However, although challenging for our family, even these situations do not at all equate to the trauma, heartache, and life-altering circumstances that many around the world confronted during 2020.

Book Overview

At times, the clock seemed to take forever in clicking through the 525,600 minutes of 2020—minutes that were monumental, mundane, and somewhere in between. According to Bogel-Burroughs (2020), "After prosecutors said that a Minneapolis police officer pressed his knee on George Floyd's neck for eight minutes and 46 seconds, that number became a grim symbol of police brutality."

Record numbers of devastating hurricanes and wildfires amplified the clock ticking on time left to preserve and restore our planet (Thompson, 2020). Photos of body bags in freezer trucks during the pandemic reminded us that for hundreds of thousands in the United States alone, the clock stopped.

The year 2020 overflowed with prominent, highly visible, heart-wrenching situations. It also encompassed personal times as individuals wrestled with the events of the world as they decided what to do next in their own lives, activities, and interactions. Communication comprised a key role in how they grieved, worked, celebrated, played, and remembered.

This pivotal year will surely be measured differently by the billions of people who lived through it and, certainly, by those whose loved ones did not make it through. However, 2020 has left indelible impressions, and, in that context, we write this book.

Drawing from their own personal experiences, contributors throughout this collection of essays considered the implications of 2020 through the lens of a particular area of the Communication discipline. As a book, the chapters spotlight the ubiquity and significance of communication during times of crisis, major life events, or routine exchanges, and they detail how the lessons of 2020 can guide us in this new decade. We hope that this book provides meaningful insights into various sub-areas of the Communication discipline as well as the lingering effects and lasting impacts of 2020 on communicating our identities, building and nurturing relationships, and employing communication to enact positive change.

In the first section, chapters focus on communication as integral to enacting identity and revealing priorities. Chapters in Section I describe work in Postcoloniality and Communication; Gender, Sexuality, and Communication; Race and Communication; Religion and Communication; Disability and Communication, Communication and Ethics, and Risk Communication.

Section II spotlights the implicitly relational dimension of communication by concentrating on how communication enables us to relate to and connect with others and our world. Chapters in this section feature work in the areas of Interpersonal Communication, Group Communication, Family Communication, Instructional Communication, Rhetoric, Political Communication, Social Media, and Sports Communication.

Finally, consistent with events of 2020, Section III highlights the transformative nature of communication. Through communication, we can transform what has been into what can be. Section III includes chapters on Environmental Communication, Health Communication, Communication and Technology, Organizational Communication, Strategic Communication, and Communication and Social Justice.

References

Barry, D. (2020, December 27). Year in review: And we thought other years were awful. *Washington Post.* www.washingtonpost.com/magazine/2020/12/27/dave-barrys-year-review-2020/

Bogel-Burroughs, N. (2020, June 18). 8 minutes, 46 seconds became a symbol in George Floyd's death: The exact time is less clear. *The New York Times.* https://www.nytimes.com/2020/06/18/us/george-floyd-timing.html

Faris, D. (2020, December 23). Baby, it's COVID outside. *The Week.* https://theweek.com/articles/956662/baby-covid-outside

Gergen, K. (1991). *The saturated self: Dilemmas of identity in contemporary life.* Basic Books.

Gergen, K. (1994). *Realities in relationships: Soundings in social construction.* Harvard University Press.

Petronio, S., & Child, J. T. (2020). Conceptualization and operationalization: Utility of communication privacy management theory. *Current Opinion in Psychology*, *31*, 76–82. https://doi.org/10.1016/j.copsyc.2019.08.009

Picheta, R. (2020, December 25). 2020 was a terrible year. But the world's in better shape than you might think. *CNN.* https://www.cnn.com/2020/12/25/europe/2020-improving-world-recap-scli-intl/index.html

Roberts, M. (2020, December 30). 2020 was the worst year, except for all the others. *Washington Post.* https://www.washingtonpost.com/opinions/2020/12/30/2020-was-worst-year-except-all-others/

Sigman, S. (Ed.). (1995). *Consequentiality of communication.* Erlbaum.

Thompson, A. (2020, December 22). A running list of record-breaking natural disasters in 2020. *Scientific American.* https://www.scientificamerican.com/article/a-running-list-of-record-breaking-natural-disasters-in-2020/

Von Drehle, D. (2020, December 31). After a catastrophic 2020, the big story of 2021 could be a hopeful one. *Washington Post.* www.washington post.com/opinions/2020/12/31/after-catrastropic-2020-big-story-2021-could-be-hopeful

Watzlawick, P., Beavin, J., & Jackson, D. (1967). *Pragmatics of human communication.* Norton.

Wertheim, L. J., & Apstein, S. (2020, July). Game, changed. *Sports Illustrated*, *131*(7), 22–29.

Worland, J. (2020, June 11). America's long overdue awakening to systemic racism. *Time.* https://time.com/5851855/systemic-racism-america/

Zacharek, S. (2020, December 5). 2020 tested us beyond measure: Where do we go from here? *Time.* https://time.com/5917394/2020-in-review/

SECTION I

Through Communication, We Enact Identities and Reveal Priorities

2

POSTCOLONIALITY AND COMMUNICATION

Ahmet Atay

Learning Objectives

1. Explain postcolonial turn in communication studies.
2. Illustrate diasporic and transnational experiences.
3. Explain the notion of home, especially during isolating times.

I often wonder where my real home is. I have lived in the U.S. for over two decades now, mostly in college towns. However, I have spent the last 11 years in a small town working at a small liberal arts college. Hence, right now, my home in the U.S. is this small town in Ohio. Yet, I ask myself, is this small town in Ohio really my home? Do I really belong here? Am I simply passing through and stopping for a while until my next destination? Or am I making this place a home where I truly belong?

I welcomed the new decade with these questions. In particular, I spent the first couple of days of 2020 thinking about the abstract concepts of "home" and "belonging." Like me, I am sure other postcolonial subjects often think about home and where they belong, or not belong. I decided to tackle these questions on that very cold January day because I was not able to go home to visit. Instead, I planned to spend the summer of that year away from Ohio, visiting my parents and family. However, as we know, life has different realities in store for us. As I struggled with the notion of home and belonging, their meanings became more complex and complicated as I, along with the rest of the world, had to face brutal realities of the COVID-19 pandemic.

As a postcolonial and transnational body and a scholar, I examine in this essay the notions of "home" and "belonging." These two concepts occupy a paramount role in postcolonial studies, as a colonial past often creates hybrid realities and dislocated lives. Relatedly, I define, perform, and articulate the notions of home and belonging through my own lived experiences.

DOI: 10.4324/9781003220466-3

Postcolonial and Decolonial Studies

As an area of inquiry, postcolonial studies emerged from humanities disciplines, such as literary studies and critical theory, eventually expanding to other disciplines under the humanities and social sciences. According to Communication and cultural studies scholars Rake Shome and Radha Hegde (2002), "Postcolonial studies, broadly described, is an interdisciplinary field of inquiry committed to theorizing the problematics of colonization and decolonization" (p. 250). Several Communication scholars who are trained in cultural studies, critical intercultural communication, performance studies, and media studies, such as Asante (2020), Calafell (2015), Chawla (2013, 2014), Dutta and Basu (2018), Eguchi (2019), Gajjala (2002, 2019), Shome and Hegde (2002), Yep (1998), and myself (2015, 2017, 2018, and 2020) have been using postcolonial and decolonial theories and methodologies to talk about issues of identity, power, oppression, migration, and home. Although our collective work within these areas has gained some visibility and recognition, unfortunately, the scope of postcolonial studies within the field of communication has been quite limited.

Postcolonial studies examine the aftermath of colonization, oppressive political and economic structures, and the hybridization of sociocultural life as outcomes of colonial histories (Shome & Hegde, 2002). The development and expansion of empires, mainly in Europe, let them to occupy lands in different parts of the world for economic and material gains between 1500s and the early 1900s. As these empires, such as British, French, Russian, and others, advanced their political and economic agendas, they also drastically influenced and changed the local cultures, creating hybrid societies. While the mainstream colonial histories glorified these colonial past, local colonial histories articulated the dark and hurtful realities of the colonization. Hence, postcolonial scholars have focused on different aspects of everyday life. Migration, the formation and experiences of diasporic communities, and the notion of home comprise some of these widely examined issues and realities. As a result of their colonial past, some individuals from former colonies chose to leave their homelands and move to the urban spaces of colonial powers to seek economic prosperity and, in some cases, higher education. These movements often result in the formation of diasporic communities.

Cultural studies scholar Stuart Hall (1995) described a diaspora as "the long-term settlement of peoples in 'foreign' places, which follow their scattering or dispersal from their original homeland" (p. 193). Similarly, for Anthias (1998), a diaspora represents and describes "the process of settlement and adaptation relating to a large range of transnational migration movements" (p. 557). Due to these movements and resettlements, postcolonial subjects or diasporic individuals experience the notion of home while living "here" and "there" simultaneously. Hence, for them, the notion of home is a hybrid one, that is, they physically reside in one location but might also be practicing the customs, tradition, religions, and cultures of two different nation-states. In a physical sense, they change geographical locations and create new homes in these locales; however, emotionally, mentally, and culturally, they are often rooted in their respective homelands.

Like so many other postcolonial bodies, I left my homeland to obtain a graduate education in the U.S. As a transnational body, I continue to occupy two different homes and maneuver between two sets of cultures and languages. Hence, in a sense, I belong to multiple places at the same time. As a scholar, I am particularly interested in how diasporic queer bodies create a sense of home through the Internet and other communication technologies in an attempt to maintain links to their home cultures (Atay, 2015, 2018, 2020).

Where Is Home?

When I visit home, Cyprus (a former British colony), people who know me usually ask how my life is, what it is like to live so far away, or when I will permanently return to my home country. In comparison, when I meet new people, they ask me what I do and where I live. When I tell them that I live in the U.S. and work in higher education as a professor, they are often impressed. Some are envious, some are proud, and some have even more questions.

Let us face it. The idea of visiting home is a strange one. How can we visit our homes if we supposedly live in our homes? For diasporic or immigrant individuals, some of us experience being and living in while also visiting different homes. Hence, "home" entails a very convoluted and complex concept for us. One cannot easily define and describe occupying more than one home and belonging to multiple places simultaneously. Those reading this chapter right now may also feel that they belong to more than one home, and that might be true to a certain extent. Students might have rooms on or near campus which become "home," and they likely also have another home with parents, grandparents, other family members, or friends, which could also be considered as home too. Some could be like me, who has moved around in the U.S. between and among college towns or any other town and occupied different spaces that became "home" at certain points, especially if they felt safe in those physical spaces and have fond memories of them.

However, moving around the U.S. or within another county while living in multiple spaces differs from moving between nation-states and maneuvering different cultural experiences. For example, an immigrant must navigate through different laws and regulations, such as immigration laws, between two nation-states, while also translating between and among different languages and cultural practices. Therefore, these transnational border crossings offer complex realities in which one consistently translates between experiences and crosses cultural and linguistic borders. Moreover, these experiences can emotionally affect diasporic bodies and immigrants, often resulting in fear of the unknown, feelings of isolation, or a sense of loss (Anthias, 1998; Hall, 1995).

Since I moved to the U.S., I have been consistently moving between my "homelands." In time, I eventually got used to the idea of belonging everywhere and nowhere simultaneously, as Pico Iyer (2004) put it. However, 2020 brought a new and different meaning to my articulation of home: as I became homebound due to the raging global pandemic, the notion of home gradually became blurred and was redefined drastically.

Diasporic Interruption

As a transnational scholar, I only travel to visit my family during the winter and summer breaks, like so many immigrants, diasporic bodies, and international students. Depending on our schedules, financial situations, and certain regulations, we can only travel between home and home-away-from-home when we have the time and the means. Although improvements in transportation technologies have offered new opportunities enabling people to visit home more frequently, the financial costs of these travels have also increased drastically. Compared to immigrants and diasporic individuals from previous times, we now have more opportunities to visit the homeland. However, for some, the financial costs of traveling, visa processes, and other personal legal and economic concerns have negatively impacted their ability to travel. Except for the privileged few, most immigrants do not have the ability to visit home more frequently. For example, I am only able to visit home once a year or every other year.

As I was unable to go to Cyprus during the winter break of 2019–2020, I was really looking forward to traveling to Europe and visiting my home for a longer stay. As immigrants or diasporic bodies, when we stay too long away from home, reentry becomes much more difficult. As time passes, people back at home continue living their lives, while our memories and ideas of home do not change that much. Thus, as we do not get to move with time and observe and live the everyday events of life, we often feel like immigrants to our home cultures when we reenter. We try to adjust, adopt, and fill the time gap—not an easy process. In reality, we often live in the hybrid space (Bhabha, 1994) where we negotiate our memories of home with the current moment. Once again, as we translate, the process becomes an emotional task that people living in their homelands do not need to endure.

My travel plans were interrupted by the COVID-19 pandemic, which worsened by March 2020. As the virus spread globally and strict lockdowns began, I quickly realized that the summer of 2020 would be different from the other summers of the past. Instead of financial considerations, this time, visiting home for so many diasporic individuals got canceled or delayed because of a pandemic. Hence, the possibility of going back turned into a delayed diasporic desire for millions. I was one of them. March 2020 brought some difficult issues to light, and I began questioning my own transnational belonging of living between homes while also being isolated as I made a small town in Ohio my home.

***

On a cold March evening in 2020, I drove to my friend's house to attend a small social gathering. As we had conversations about the sad realities in China and in different parts of Europe and Seattle, we all agreed that trouble was approaching Ohio and our small town. While we continued to eat delicious food and drink our wine, we knew that it could be our last social gathering for a while. As we were on our spring break, our conversations focused on how our college administration would respond to impending events and what we would do if we needed to be in a lockdown. Obviously, we were worried about the unknown.

Yet, as a transnational scholar in the U.S., I often lived in limbo during most of my adult life. Therefore, I became accustomed to living with uncertainty—not being able to have solid plans while also formulating backup ones if something goes wrong. During my time in the U.S., I witnessed so many uncertainties. The devastation of the September 11 attacks, the aftermath of Hurricane Katrina, and the inland derecho of Illinois, all happened while I was in graduate school, heightening my fear of the unknown and not having any control over my own life. Indeed, fear is part of the diasporic and immigrant experiences.

Back at the gathering, our conversations moved away from how we would teach our courses to how we would survive if we had longer lockdowns. Their fears were real—mine even more so—as I lived alone in our small town in the middle of Ohio. I realized that not only do I need to cope with my fear, but I also needed to find ways to survive alone regardless of what was ahead of us. Once we said our goodbyes, I drove to our local grocery store to buy enough food for myself and my cat to survive for the next several days. In the morning, as the news poured in and the outlook of life looked grim, I knew I needed a better plan to survive the lockdowns. Thus, for the next four nights, I drove to our local store at 9:15 p.m., when not too many people would be in the store, given that it closes at 10 p.m. I guess living alone somehow prepared me well for events like this one. I wanted to make sure that I had enough food items and essentials. Moreover, if I became sick, no one would be able to take care of me, so I needed the recommended painkillers and enough cleaning materials to assure myself of some sense of safety. On the fifth night, as I left the store, I knew that this trip would be my last until I was able to gather more information about the virus and felt safe enough to return to the store.

Making sure that I had enough food was the easier side of my preparation for the pandemic. Even though I spent so many summer and winter breaks by myself on college campuses or in college towns, I was always prepared to be on my own. However, this time, I required a different type of preparation. I needed to internalize the prospect of not physically meeting my friends or colleagues for long periods of time. More importantly, I braced myself mentally for the challenges that lay ahead. Furthermore, until the situation improved, I had no hope of going back home and visiting my family. During those moments, postcolonial realities and transnational loneliness sank in. I was cut out from my community, both here and there. I was caught not only between two places but, to some degree, outside of them as well.

***

Although the early August heat reminded me of home, I was thousands of miles away from the Mediterranean Sea—or any body of water for that matter. Of course, we can count Lake Erie, but the lake never fully felt like home to me. Meanwhile, the summer days had passed in fear as the number of COVID-19 cases increased. The summer of 2020 became all about postcolonial realities, as I realized that living alone in the middle of nowhere with no possibility of visiting home became a new diasporic reality. Instead of maneuvering between and among cultures, I spent most of my summer days walking in the neighborhood, at the local park, or looking at trees in my backyard. For the first time, I paid attention to the sound of nature surrounding me and observed the changing colors of leaves amid the August heat. I tried to create a home space (hooks, 1994) within my home. In the absence of family and the lack of interpersonal communication with local friends, I was introduced to a new type of transnational and diasporic loneliness, and I knew I was still stuck in one, restless and fearful.

Owing to the restrictions brought on by the pandemic, I spent most of 2020 and 2021 being physically absent and digitally present in all my relationships. Thus, while I was teaching courses remotely, I also used the same technologies to talk to my friends and family around the world. In the absence of travel and physically returning home, I lived digitally at home through screens. During those days, my physical home felt a bit lonely and isolated, but at least the Internet and new media technologies offered new possibilities for constructing new homes.

***

At the same time, it dawned on me that, although moving around and maneuvering between and among cultures has been described as a common diasporic and transnational reality—a topic that has been frequently studied (Anthias, 1998; Chawla, 2014; Hall, 1995), transnational isolation and the sense of loss that it produces have been widely disregarded.

It was one of those days. I was in front of my computer screen between 9 a.m. and 7 p.m. Once the October cold wind all but vanquished my remaining hope of stepping outside for a quick walk, I knew that I needed to cook my dinner before 8 p.m. to allow myself some downtime in front of another screen. As my cat purred and I responded to his playfulness in two languages, I was grateful for his companionship. Once I sat down to eat my dinner while watching a British mystery show, I took note of the fact that I had not stepped outside for the past three days, and I had not physically spoken to a single person for days and even weeks. Although I was at home, I also yearned for a different type of home.

Conclusion

As I went through the motions of surviving a global pandemic, I gradually realized that "going home" became less of a reality and more of a diasporic dream. Many times, I thought of others who felt similarly about moving away from their home-lands and traveling thousands of miles away to establish better lives within their postcolonial realities. I thought of others who were less fortunate and did not speak the language of the land to which they were relocating. I thought of others who were stuck here but always dreamed of being there—never able to return and see their homelands again. Although diasporic communities could be more traditional and conservative in their cultural orientations and may sometimes be oppressive to their members who occupy intersectional identity markers (such as diasporic queer individuals), ultimately, they do provide a sense of community and belonging.

At the same time, while some could find comfort in the presence of a cultural community and some connection to their homelands, others preferred to remove themselves from these communities to free themselves from the restraints of the latter. However, in the absence of diasporic communities, transnational bodies who circulate throughout the world, maneuver between cultures, or reside in particular geographical locations. Yet, as they isolated during the pandemic, they found themselves negotiating with the notions of "home" and "belonging" differently. For example, I began seeing cyber platforms or social media as possibilities to connect with family and friends who live in different parts of the world and also use these platforms as community to belong to curb loneliness and cultivate a sense of belonging. As they coped with loneliness, even while enjoying a sense of transnational and diasporic cosmopolitanism, they use other means to recreate a sense of home and belonging.

During the COVID-19 pandemic, I involuntarily found myself in isolating situations in which I negotiated and renegotiated the meaning of "home" and "belonging." As I sat in my living room, I discovered different ways to be here and there simultaneously. Sometimes, certain elements—such as the smell of my homemade dinner, a motif in a song, or a piece of memory—made me feel closer to home and helped me to cope with isolation. Moreover, new media technologies and the screens of my laptop and smartphones have occasionally "brought me home."

In conclusion, I argue that the global COVID-19 pandemic has brought unprecedented challenges for diasporic bodies, who consistently negotiate between here and there as we try to make sense of our postcolonial conditions and identity formations. Moving forward, I contend that communication studies scholars who use postcolonial studies frameworks and approaches should theorize the idea of isolation. Moreover, they should continue to examine the role of new media technologies in the lives of postcolonial subjects, diasporic communities, and immigrants.

References

Anthias, F. (1998). Evaluating 'diaspora:' Beyond ethnicity? *Sociology, 32*(3), 557–580.
Asante, G. (2020). Anti-LGBT violence and the ambivalent (colonial) discourses of Ghanaian Pentecostalist-Charismatic church leaders. *Howard Journal of Communications, 31*(1), 20–34.

Atay, A (2015). *Globalization's impact on cultural identity formation: Queer diasporic males in cyberspace.* Lexington Books.

Atay, A (2017). Theorizing diasporic queer digital homes: Identity, home and new media. *Journalism, Media and Cultural Studies Journal/JOMEC Journal, 11,* 96–110.

Atay, A. (2018). Digital life writing: The failure of a diasporic queer blue Tinker Bell. *Interactions: Studies in Communication and Culture, 9*(2), 183–193.

Atay, A. (2020). Intercultural queer slippages and translations. In S. Eguchi & B. M. Calafell (Eds.), *Queer intercultural communication: The intersectional politics of belonging in and across differences* (pp. 141–156). Rowman & Littlefield.

Bhabha, H. K. (1994). *The location of culture.* Routledge.

Calafell, B. M. (2015). *Monstrosity, performance, and race in contemporary culture.* Peter Lang.

Chawla, D. (2013). Walk, walking, talking, home. In S. H. Jones, T. E. Adams, & C. Ellis (Eds.), *Handbook of autoethnography* (pp. 162–172). Left Coast Press.

Chawla, D. (2014). *Home, uprooted: Oral histories of India's partition.* Fordham University Press.

Dutta, M. J., & Basu, A. (2018). Subalternity, neoliberal seductions, and freedom: Decolonizing the global market of social change. *Cultural Studies ↔ Critical Methodologies, 18*(1), 80–93.

Eguchi, S. (2019). Queerness as strategic whiteness: A queer Asian American critique of Peter Le. In D. M. D. McIntosh, D. G. Moon, & T. K. Nakayama (Eds.), *Interrogating communicative power of whiteness* (pp. 29–44). Routledge.

Gajjala, R. (2002). An interrupted postcolonial/feminist cyberethnography: Complicity and resistance in the "cyberfield." *Feminist Media Studies, 2*(2), 177–193.

Gajjala, R. (2019). *Digital diasporas: Labor and affect in gendered Indian publics.* Rowman and Littlefield.

Hall, S. (1995). New cultures for old. In D. Massey & P. Jess (Eds.), *A place in the world: Places, cultures, and globalization* (pp. 175–213). Oxford University Press.

hooks, b. (1994). Homeplace: A site of resistance. In D. S. Madison (Ed.), *The women that I am: The literature and culture of contemporary women of color* (pp. 448–454). St Martin's.

Iyer, P. (2004). Living in the transit lounge. In F. Eidse & N. Sichel (Eds.), *Unrooted childhoods: Memories of growing up global* (pp. 9–23). Intercultural Press.

Shome, R., & Hegde, R. S. (2002). Postcolonial approaches to communication: Charting the terrain, engaging the intersections. *Communication Theory, 12*(3), 249–270.

Yep, G. A. (1998). My three cultures: Navigating the multicultural identity landscape. In J. N. Martin, T. K. Nakayama, & L. A. Flores (Eds.), *Readings in intercultural communication* (pp. 60–66). Mayfield.

3

COMMUNICATING GENDER AND SEXUALITY

Ashley Noel Mack

Learning Objectives

1. Identify major concepts, methods, models, and theories used to study gender and sexuality in communication processes and practices.
2. Describe the social, political, and ethical consequences of communication about social positionalities, such as gender, sexuality, race, nationality, ability, and class.
3. Describe the complex ways in which social positionalities are impacted by the matrix of domination.
4. Develop an awareness and appreciation of the diversity and plurality of gender and sexual identities in our globalized community.

At the beginning of 2020, 2019 had seemed like a tough year. I was facing an increasing amount of stress at work due to structural inequalities, interpersonal difficulties, a ticking tenure clock, and I had recently come out as nonbinary. In my research and teaching, I examine how communication practices and processes are connected to the production of social inequality and how communication can be wielded by historically marginalized communities to seek social justice. The year 2020 proved to challenge even my basic assumptions about what a bad year might look like. In the United States, we faced the uncertainty of a growing COVID-19 pandemic, overwhelming anger over the unjust murder of George Floyd, and the loneliness of nearly a year of isolation from our communities and loved ones. These social circumstances—and my own personal experiences as a queer, nonbinary faculty member at a research-intensive university who teaches about race, gender, class, and sexuality—served to sediment and expand my own understanding of how communication process and practices constitute and

DOI: 10.4324/9781003220466-4

challenge inequalities in our everyday lives. In this chapter, I explore some key communication concepts, theories, and methods used to examine gender and sexuality. Using the year 2020 as a shared site of social understanding, we can advance our comprehension of communication theories, concepts, and methods as they emerge in our material and lived experiences of contemporary injustices.

Like most researchers and educators, I came to study inequality because of my own lived experiences. I was raised by my mother and grandmother—both white single mothers. We faced abject poverty and housing displacement. I am also a first-generation college student, and, while pursuing my undergraduate degree, I encountered a great deal of uncertainty about what to study and how to maneuver the complex systems of higher education. However, in my sophomore year—by happenstance—I took a Women and Gender Studies class with a friend. The course impacted me greatly. I learned a vocabulary to describe and analyze many of the unjust experiences my family and I had faced. At the same time, the Communication discipline was a core part of my journey. I had competed in speech and debate, and I was heavily involved in Communication Studies. When I graduated college in 2007 from Arizona State University with a BA in Women's and Gender Studies and a BA in Political Science, I decided to pursue a MA and Ph.D. in Communication Studies to research how we communicate about gender, race, sexuality, and class in public life, and what effect that communication has on our material realities.

Studying Gender and Sexuality as a Communication Phenomena

The United States primarily operates using a binary gender system (Butler, 1990, 2004; Lorber & Moore, 2007). This system officially recognizes two **gender markers**, male or female, and uses those gender markers to organize various parts of society (West, 2013). The gender marker **assigned at birth** is used by governmental, financial, and public institutions often based solely on the outer appearance of reproductive genitalia. When a baby is born, a doctor or nurse assigns a particular gender marker of male (referred to as assigned male at birth or AMAB) or female (referred to as assigned female at birth or AFAB) to an individual child. From the birth certificate to driver's license, officials use gender markers institutionally to organize U.S. subjects (Butler, 2004; West, 2013). Such categories serve as the basis for all types of social activities: school, extracurricular activities that segregate based on gender such as sports, bathrooms, job applications, etc. Once a gender marker is assigned at birth, caregivers, social institutions, and others in our communities often reinforce that gender marker by tethering all types of cultural scripts, artifacts, and rituals to that child's assigned gender (Lorber & Moore, 2007; Sloop, 2004). For example, hypothetically, families may paint a child who has been AFAB's bedroom pink, buy them tutus and sign them up for dance classes, call them "princess," and encourage them to play with dolls. U.S.

culture tends to code these actions as "feminine," assuming them to be what little girls want and like—purely based on their assigned gender at birth (Butler, 1990).

Such practices reveal that gender is not just embodied in our "official" gender marker or in our physical presentation of genitalia. In fact, gender constitutes a complex set of **social scripts** that communicate to us what **normative gender** should be and various **performances of self** that we deploy to communicate our gender to those around us (Butler, 1990; Sloop, 2004). Goffman (1959) developed a theory for understanding everyday performances of self in his book *The Presentation of Self in Everyday Life*. For Goffman, individuals present carefully crafted performances of themselves to others, and use these performances to manage their perceptions of self and interactions with others. Butler (1990) further developed an understanding of the presentation of self in relation to gender by arguing that gender is marked by performativity: ongoing, daily, repetitious iterations of gendered performance that communicate, challenge, and solidify gender. Considering these foundational theories, Communication scholars generally conceptualize gender primarily as a **social performance** (Sloop, 2004). Gender comprises a socially constructed set of norms that are communicated to individuals through rituals, toys, films, social media, television, religion, education, and family. **Normative femininity** involves the various social ideals and norms that set expectations of what a real woman is or should be (Butler, 1990). For example, she should be delicate, thin, submissive, attractive but not hypersexual, nice, and good natured (Butler, 1990). Others expect her to be sensitive and emotional. **Normative masculinity,** on the other hand, is the set of expectations and ideals communicated to people about what a man is and what should be expected of him (Butler, 1990). Mainstream U.S. cultural expectations depict men as strong (both physically and mentally), rational (and non-emotional), providers for their families, and virile (Butler, 1990). In many ways, normative masculinity can be understood as rejecting anything that one might consider feminine (Butler, 1990).

Communication, therefore, has a profound impact on how we understand ourselves as gendered subjects in the world. Imagine this: a young boy falls to the ground, scrapes his knee, and begins crying. His father grabs his arm and pulls him up explaining, "Get up off the ground! Stop crying! Boys don't cry!" This message communicates to that young man that he should not feel pain and that, if he does feel pain, he should not cry about it because it is not something that boys or men do. This message marks crying as something only women or girls do—feminine and therefore, bad. This tiny communicative interaction between a parent and a child simultaneously teaches the young man about masculinity, femininity, and the value of each of those concepts in relation to each other. Communication plays a key role in the development, maintenance, and circulation of gender, sexual, racial, and class-based social scripts and norms (Sloop, 2004). Based on our interpretation and internalization of these norms and expectations that are communicated to us, we enact everyday performances that communicate gender to those around us (Butler, 1990).

Gender identity and **gender expression** are vocabulary terms to help us articulate the complexities of gender and its communication in everyday life (Human Rights Campaign, 2021). **Gender identity** is our internal feelings and ideas about our gender. Our gender identity is not flippant, but rather how we understand ourselves at our core. Our gender identity impacts our social and cultural values, how we see the world, how we experience it, how other's communication affects us, and how we communicate with others. **Gender expression** refers to the various processes through which we publicly or outwardly perform and communicate gender to others. We express gender through our clothes, mannerisms, cultural sayings, voice pitch and tone, and social and behavior scripts. Each of these communicative practices work together to make up a performance of gender.

Our gender identity does not always match up with our assigned gender at birth or our gender expression, and this inconsistency often means that individuals experience what is called **gender dysphoria** (Human Rights Campaign, 2021). Gender dysphoria occurs when an individual feels a mismatch between their assigned gender at birth and their gender identity. Gender dysphoria can be traumatizing and clinically distressing. For example, an individual may be a woman but was assigned male at birth, and others perceive them as male because of their physical characteristics and their performances of gender which have been crafted and disciplined throughout their life by their peers, families, and others in positions of power over them. Despite their gender identity, they may face immense social expectation and pressure to continue the gender presentation that socially matches the gender marker they were assigned at birth. This situation can be incredibly stressful and traumatizing and can lead to institutional discrimination and suicidal ideation (Hill & Willoughby, 2005). Once we understand that gender expression, gender identity, and assigned gender at birth do not always match up, and we understand the relationship between the three of them, we can develop a much more rich and thorough vocabulary to describe the nuances of human experiences of gender.

I was assigned female at birth, yet the marker of woman or female never represented how I felt internally. I struggled to socially identify with women, and in women-centered spaces I often felt like an outsider. Beginning in my teens, I was aware of what being transgender was, but I only understood it in relation to binary gender. Even though I did not believe I was a woman, I knew I did not identify as a man either, so I decided that I could not possibly be trans. For many years, especially in my late teens and early 20s, this was incredibly distressing for me. I often felt in social, and especially romantic, situations that I was expected to perform for others according to their perceptions of me, not my own understanding of myself. Yet, when I was 22, I entered a relationship with another queer-identified person who did not expect me to perform and engage through social expectations of womanhood and femininity. For the first time, I felt free.

In early 2015, I stumbled upon some nonbinary (often referred to colloquially as "enby") Instagram accounts that deeply reflected some of the internal feelings that I had about my own gender and relationship to being AFAB. I felt like I had a community that understood me and at least some way to explain to others how I felt. At the end of 2019, I began to publicly transition with my family, friends, and my students and my colleagues at Louisiana State University. I wanted my gender identity to be recognized as nonbinary/genderqueer by these communities, and I was hoping to deal with some of my gender dysphoria. I took this step with great trepidation, as in just the previous year then President Trump had made several policies that indicated I could legally be discriminated against by my employer based on my gender identity. I also was not sure how students or colleagues would respond. I felt incredibly anxious about the possibility of conflicts, and I worried it would produce even more dysphoria. As I went public, I also desperately wanted my gender journey to stay my own—I was still untangling myself from the social scripts and social norms that others always placed on me regarding gender. I was experimenting, trying new things. I cut my hair and tried different styles of clothing that I hoped would also help me feel happier and more aligned with my gender expression. I was concerned that, as I made my gender identity clearer to those around me as "nonbinary," some of the liminality that I had been able to explore about my own gender would be impossible to access.

Then came 2020. By mid-March, we were forced into quarantine and suddenly my classes were entirely online and mostly asynchronous. I no longer interacted with colleagues or students in the flesh. In the context of the digital sphere, certain performances of gender expression mattered far less. My performance of self to others became confined to digital markers and representations. My clothes, gestures, and other performances of gendered suddenly no longer were present to communicate my gender expression. As I sat, mostly in yoga pants and t-shirts, my gender expression became almost exclusively reduced to "Ashley Noel Mack (they/them)" accompanying my talking head in Zoom meetings.

I had never really experienced the gender dysphoria that I did in public places while I was at home. My partner always accepted me as I am. I did not feel an expectation to perform gender at home really—at least I did not feel the need to consciously think about it—I was just me. My understanding of what my gender identity is and what its expression should be, and, most importantly, who that expression was for, became even more muddled in 2020. Who was I performing gender for? Is my gender dysphoria rooted in others' perceptions of me? Why is it that, when I was at home, I felt so completely safe and comfortable? Teaching asynchronously also reduced opportunities for others to validate and understand my gender identity as well. I introduced myself in writing and in video with "they/them" pronouns, but students rarely had to interact with me, and they often defaulted to "she/her" pronouns. Furthermore, I certainly did not believe that my gender could be entirely reduced to my pronouns. While gender identity constitutes an internal phenomenon, gender expression is a communal phenomenon. Our sense of ourselves is bound in how we communicate and perform our gender to others, how they perceive those performances, and how that perception in turn impacts our understanding of ourselves.

Sexuality is also made up of corporeal performances and communicative interactions (Morris, 2007). Our sexuality, or **sexual orientation**, is our desires, sexual feelings and thoughts, actions, and attractions toward others (Human Rights Campaign, 2021). We not only communicate our sexual orientation to others through various performances, but also our expression of attraction and other sexual actions are themselves communicative performances of desire. Just as with gender social scripts, we learn through film, television, social media, our families and friends, and religious communities, what appropriate or **normative sexual and romantic scripts** are (Gagnon & Simon, 1973). Since the early isolation of quarantining for COVID-19, normative sexual and romantic scripts have been disrupted. How do you take a partner on a potential date, for example, when you cannot go out together and you must stand six feet apart? How do you meet people if bars and clubs are closed? How do you express intimacy without touch? While these experiences challenge preconceived social scripts, we gain keen insight into human behavior and structural inequality by examining gender and sexuality as communication phenomenon in 2020.

Gender and Sexuality in the Matrix of Domination

We cannot understand gender and sexuality as singular issues. How we come to understand each as social and communicative phenomena is intimately related to not only the other, but also to other signifying markers of **social positionality**, such as race, ethnicity, nationhood, ability, and class. Signifying markers, such as our perceived skin color and, therefore, race, may communicate our identity and background to those around us, or be used as the basis for **stereotyping** us based on socially ingrained **myths of difference** (Hall et al., 2013). Social positionality is part of deeply rooted social structures that have been embedded in our social and political institutions and lives.

Historically in the U.S., our social structures have relied on **hierarchical ordering** of social positionalities (Hall et al., 2013). A belief that the white race is superior to other races, for example, was not only used as the basis for justifying the trans-Atlantic slave trade, chattel slavery, segregation, Jim Crow laws, but also as the contemporary over policing and mass incarceration of Black people—especially Black men—in the U.S. Those in power used the social-ingrained belief that men are superior to women to justify why women could not vote or be envisioned as full persons in U.S. society at its inception, and such beliefs continue to be used (even if subconsciously) to justify lower pay for women, especially Black women, in American workplaces. In the U.S., **heterosexuality** (attraction solely to those of the opposite gender) has historically and presently been understood as the normative sexual orientation (Rich, 1980). Normalizing and centering heterosexuality has historically led to rationalizing discrimination of lesbian, gay, bisexual, asexual, pansexual, and other queer relationships, including criminalizing gay sex and marriage. Warner (1991) referred to the complex social practices that work to compulsively center heterosexuality as **heteronormativity**.

Such attitudes and beliefs of superiority and inferiority can even be more mundane and experienced in the everyday. For example, I have been an avid gamer for years, and, during 2020, I turned to online gaming communities as a primary source of social engagement and support. I play a multiplayer battle royale game that often involves talking with complete strangers over voice chat. These individuals have no context for who I am, outside of my username (embarrassingly, it is "smash") and my voice. Strangers, especially men, often intrusively ask within the first few minutes in the voice chat: "Are you a girl or a boy?" Such a question is rarely asked to my guy friends with whom I regularly play. My response to the question is always the same, "I am an alien." They usually laugh, sometimes exclaim "You have to be a boy! You are a boy!" Other times, they admit the core of their confusion that my voice sounds not quite feminine, not quite masculine. Several times, my refusal to answer has been met with anger and bullying. I remember one young man telling me "To shut the fuck up until I answer him."

Such questioning illuminates the dominance of the binary gender system, the lack of recognition of gender outside of that binary, and allure of heteronormative and homophobia. They seek to categorize me so that their desire or lack of desire will make sense in their symbolic worlds. In other words, their preference to place a binary gender marker on me also reflects an inclination to place me in their order of things properly. In my interactions, I challenge those binary assumptions and stereotypes through my very existence as a nonbinary, genderqueer "alien" (Butler, 2004; Sloop, 2004). Yet I am still subjected to the misogyny so deeply rooted in the treatment of women in the context of gaming.

As a white, queer, nonbinary person, my experiences at that particular social location are also vexed. I experience my gender and sexuality, both of which are non-normative, simultaneously with my white- and middle-to-upper class positionalities, where I experience and obtain social privileges. To suggest that my experiences as a queer and nonbinary person are the same as others would be to deny the intersectional nature of social positionality. **Intersectionality** comprises a broad concept originating from the work of Black feminists, such as Crenshaw (1991) and Collins (2002), to describe how social positionalities function simultaneously to inform experiences of domination and oppression. In other words, our location at the intersection of multiple social markers simultaneously impacts our experiences of domination and oppression.

Intersectionality is often discussed in popular culture and news media, but it is often misrepresented as just the ways in which different parts of our identity intersect (see Collins, 2002; Collins & Bilge, 2020; Eguchi et al., 2020; Nash, 2019). However, Collins and Bilge insisted that it also pertains to systems of oppression and domains of power. They argued that the **matrix of domination** has an impact on our experiences of oppression and domination as an individual, but these experiences are conditioned by systems and not just rooted in individual identity. Collins and Bilge used the matrix of domination to refer to how power relations are organized in a society through both 1) systems of oppression that intersect including race, sexuality, gender, class, ability, etc. and 2) domains of power (structural, disciplinary, interpersonal, and cultural/hegemonic). The matrix of domination, then, refers to how systems of oppression interlock with each other (and how we experience these at an individual level simultaneously), how domains of power interlock with each other, and how systems of oppression and domains of power also interlock and intersect.

These theories provide us with rich vocabularies not only to describe the experiences of individuals who exist at multiple marginalized positions but also to understand the role that various domains of power play in constituting that experience (see, e.g., Calafell, 2017; Griffin, 2012). For example, social commentary on the wrongful murder of George Floyd by a Minneapolis police officer often focuses on his race, or blackness, as the primary reason for the discrimination that led to his death. However, we must consider Floyd's position as not only Black, but also a man, in our social analysis of this issue. Communication scholar McCann (2017) argued that we encode Black masculinity as criminal and Black men as monstrous "brutes" (see also Jackson, 2006). Some use such social stereotypes and caricatures as the basis for rationalizations of violence against Black men like Floyd from police officers and the U.S. criminal legal system more broadly (McCann, 2017).

The Future of Communication Research about Gender and Sexuality

Communication in 2020 has presented experiences that lay bare inequality in our society. The mediums through which we communicate gender, sexuality, race, class, and inequality have also been transformed. Globalization and the effects of the pandemic, climate change, and global catastrophe are surely going to continue to change how we communicate social differences. We will also experience new insights into how gender and sexuality can be understood through communication, and how we can challenge structural inequality through communication practices and performances. Beyond 2020, research and teaching will hopefully focus on what role communication plays in making a better world. After all, communication helps us connect and reconnect with each other, experience intimacy, and express ourselves. Through communication practices, we constitute our shared humanity and communicate our need for equality.

References

Butler, J. (1990). *Gender trouble: Feminism and the subversion of identity*. Routledge.

Butler, J. (2004). *Undoing gender*. Routledge.

Calafell, B. M. (2017). Brown queer bodies. *Qualitative Inquiry, 23*(7), 511–512. https://doi.org/10.1177/1077800417718290

Collins, P. H. (2002). *Black feminist thought: Knowledge, consciousness, and the politics of empowerment*. Routledge.

Collins, P. H., & Bilge, S. (2020). *Intersectionality: Key concepts*. Polity Press.

Crenshaw, K. W. (1991). Mapping the margins: Intersectionality, identity politics, and violence against women of color. *Stanford Law Review, 43*(6), 1241–1299. https://doi.org/10.2307/1229039

Eguchi, S., Abdi, S., & Calafell, B. M. (2020). *Dewhitening intersectionality: Race, intercultural communication, and politics.* Lexington Books.

Gagnon, J., & Simon, W. (1973). *Sexual conduct: The social sources of human sexuality.* Aldine.

Goffman, E. (1959). *The presentation of self in everyday life.* Anchor Books.

Griffin, R. A. (2012). I am an angry Black woman: Black feminist autoethnography, voice, and resistance. *Women's Studies in Communication, 35*(2), 138–157. https://doi.org/10.1080/07491409.2012.724524

Hall, S., Evans, J., & Nixon, S. (2013). *Representation: Cultural representations and signifying practices.* SAGE.

Hill, D. B., & Willoughby, B. L. B. (2005, October). The development and validation of the genderism and transphobia scale. *Sex Roles, 53*(7–8), 531–544. https://doi.org/10.1007/s11199-005-7140-x

Human Rights Campaign. (2021, October 24). *Sexual orientation and gender identity definitions.* https://www.hrc.org/resources/sexual-orientation-and-gender-identity-terminology-and-definitions

Jackson, R. L., II. (2006). *Scripting the black masculine body: Identity, discourse, and racial politics in popular media.* SUNY Press.

Lorber, J., & Moore, L. J. (2007). *Gendered bodies: Feminist perspectives.* Roxbury.

McCann, B. J. (2017). *The mark of criminality: Rhetoric, race, and gangsta rap in the war-on-crime era.* University of Alabama Press.

Morris III, C. E. (2007). *Queering public address: Sexualities in American historical discourse.* University of South Carolina Press.

Nash, J. C. (2019). *Black feminism reimagined: After intersectionality.* Duke University Press.

Rich, A. (1980). Compulsory heterosexuality and lesbian existence. *Signs, 5*(4), 631–660.

Sloop, J. (2004). *Disciplining gender: Rhetorics of sex identity in contemporary U.S. culture.* University of Massachusetts Press.

Warner, M. (1991). Introduction: Fear of a queer planet. *Social Text, 29,* 3–17.

West, I. (2013). *Transforming citizenships: Transgender articulations of the law.* New York University Press.

4

RACE AND COMMUNICATION

Keep Your Knees Off of Our Necks: Black Girl Video Prowess Bearing Witness against the Grisly Minnesota Police Murder of George Floyd

Elizabeth Desnoyers-Colas

Learning Objectives

1. Explain the importance and significance of "bearing witness."
2. Define the structure and storytelling power of the African American Eulogy.
3. Examine and outline the factors and parameters of "the Talk."
4. Amplify, specify, maintain effective solutions to problematic racial issues that frame the Communication discipline.

> ". . . Police. They stay on us like tattoos . . ."
> Lil Kim, Hip Hop artist, *Lighters Up*
>
> "For the dead and the living, we must bear witness."
> Elie Wiesel, Holocaust Survivor
>
> "Communication, I suggest, remains so white because its experts and leaders continue to ignore its own institutional DNS, deliberately not knowing profoundly raced element of its own intellectual history."
> Roopali Mukherjee, Professor, Media Studies

I am a story teller, a modern-day African Diaspora griot. I am articulate. My voice is strong, sonorous and powerful. Frequently garbed in elegant, colorful Afrocentric garments, I am the quintessential, tall, Nubian exemplar reminiscent of Maya Angelou's *Phenomenal Woman*.

From my earliest days of flaunting the bodacious vigor African American scholars, social media aficionados alike herald as "Black Girl" power, I have been blessed to confidently work, teach, and perform in multiple spheres of illustrative, illuminating, and imaginative careers. Throughout my pedagogic creativity, I have had the unique privilege of bearing witness to the greatness of segments of

DOI: 10.4324/9781003220466-5

the African Diaspora and the vast collective kinship that it represents. An integral part of such Black Girl power splayed into my interdisciplinary scholarly background as performance art. I especially enjoy taking the opportunity to engage in, foster, and cultivate storytelling via aspiring student thespians through established theatrical works of African American playwrights. Since 2007, on the mid-sized property of my three-campus grounds university, I have directed seven works that were either written by African American women or featured them as the primary protagonists. In 2020, I began displaying the theatrical fruit of my seventh play when I served as a co-coordinator of the Patti Pace Performance Festival, a national festival/conference. The festival program celebrated the fourth time that our university had hosted the festival, and 20 years since the festival first convened as the Georgia Performance Festival (renamed in subsequent years for Dr. Patricia Pace, Professor of Theatre and Communication Studies at Georgia Southern). As the play director, my contribution to this festival would be my student cast's frenetic yet excellent 30 minutes of performing Scene Two of Bruce Norris' 2010 Tony Award and Pulitzer Prize winning play, *Clybourne Park*, a production that imagines the events that unfolded in, before, and after Lorraine Hansberry's classic 1959 Broadway play, *A Raisin in the Sun*. *Clybourne Park* adroitly examines how frank and not so politically correct discussions about gentrification, racism, sexism, and classism have not changed over 50 years. I directed *A Raisin in the Sun* on my campus in 2008 to packed theater audiences. I was anxious to see how me directing this play would fare.

Laying the ground work for crafting our work's authentic rendition and delivery in the hearts and minds of our potential audiences, I spent the first month of 2020 in my storytelling role, teaching my cast about Lorraine Hansberry and what her anti-racial ground breaking Broadway play meant to American society in the late 1950s. Especially challenging was training my young white cast members how to believably deliver the play's borderline crude racist lines despite where to them even saying something remotely like the "N" word is Generation Z anathema. I also trained our Black cast members to appear to the audience that they were "taking" and "delivering" some of the insults as good as they got; their rage was palatable but not over the top inedible. However, our time together as an ensemble was not all taxing. That year, collectively, we learned how to converse in American Sign Language for some of the play's Act I dialogue.

Admittedly, prior to the festival, my student ensemble only had three weeks of rehearsal to get ready for their Act II finale performance for the festival, but I felt they were ready to take the challenge. Since our campus sponsored this national event, after our last performance practice together, I pulled out one of my Black Girl Theater braggadocio mantras exhorting them, rhythmically swaying, hand waving, and having them boldly repeat after me: "Whose House! (Our House)! Whose House (Our House!) We gonna show 'em how it's done in our House."

Paraphrasing Black Gospel singer, John P. Kee, the cast "showed up and showed out." Emboldened and pumped up by the time that they performed the memorable ending 30 minutes of Act II via black book fashion—reading yet acting out scripted lines concealed in a black notebook—the festival's overall Coordinator noted that they "understood the racial themes and tensions of the times the scenes portray," and, in doing so, my directorial work with them cultivated greater understanding and awareness in the audience. To my great relief and joy, we received a superlative, positive performance review response from the Chair of the Department of Theater at Louisiana State University and topped it off with a vibrant post-performance discussion between the cast and the audience members. From that day forward especially until we formally performed the play on March 5–8, I felt that I could readily testify and bear witness that African American people like me can cultivate, sustain our voices, and successfully share our memories with disparate sociocultural audiences, especially on the stage. Incredibly, my Black Girl enchanting fashion of sharing and telling such stories recompensed magically when later in 2020, I found out that I was awarded Excellence in Directing from Festival 52 for the Kennedy Center of American College Theater for Region 4 (Southeast Region). Even with smaller than usual audiences—we were just starting to hear about the pandemic in Georgia and schools nationwide were not closed yet—I was ecstatic. Once again, I was, at the end of my director's day, a bona fide storyteller bearing witness.

Two months after the spiritual high of the play's triumphant run ended, I fell into deep despair. I, along with millions of African Americans—in the midst of the raging COVID-19 pandemic—collectively bore witness to a profoundly evil human rights desecration when a Minnesota Black man was brutally murdered by four policemen. On May 25, 2020, the gut-wrenching narrative of this crime was first framed in a graphically raw and intense YouTube, Facebook video filmed by a 17-year-old African American girl. Civil Rights Attorney Jennifer M. Kinsley (2020) asserted that while capturing this riveting, yet gruesome macabre police crime on a simple cell phone, Darnella Frazier became a 21st century anti-racist crusader simply by using her Black Girl video, vocal and social media prowess, ultimately helping people globally bear witness to this felony.

This chapter briefly provides a timeline of how shared African American pain in 2020 unfolded when Darnella's media witnessing bearing of George Floyd murder combined with Reverend Al Sharpton's powerful eulogy admonition and warning to racists to "Keep your knees off our necks" ultimately became the foremost global protest catalyst rallying cry of that summer. This segment also explicitly examines the problematic challenges of race and communication and how we as Communication scholars must confront them in our academic discipline.

BIPOC Bearing Witness and Storytelling: Having the "Talk"

United States history is one marked by racial oppression and a quest for racial justice. Ten years ago, a student gave a powerful informative speech presentation in one of my classes where she noted that, by the time young Black males are 21 years old, 75% of them have had some type of negative encounter with law enforcement simply because they are Black and automatically perceived and treated as suspicious. I remember that while the White students audibly gasped at this statistic, my African American students and other BIPOC (Black, Indigenous and People of Color) students did not appear remotely surprised. They knew. No doubt, they most likely would agree a decade later with Rogers et al.'s (2021) assessment:

> Because of pervasive racism, Black children often become aware of race earlier than White children and typically rate race as more important. . . . These racial identities are also meaningful. Black children refer to racial pride more frequently than White children of the same age (Rogers et al., 2012). Rowley and colleagues (2008) also found that Black children with higher racial centrality and the belief that others held negative views of Black people also expected to experience more racial in cross-racial interactions in school. (p. 89)

Typically, BIPOC adults, especially Black parents, prepare their children for surviving in a racist society by teaching them how to cope with racism, particularly prejudice and racism experienced during police encounters. Even in the 1960s, I remember holidays and family reunions all over the country during which we sat and listened to my parents, grandparents, uncles, and aunts give all of my cousins and siblings "the talk" which consisted of cautionary verbiage that was designed to help us learn how to handle ourselves around the police. The "talk" was usually told in the form of a scary, afro raising "I was stopped by the cops, beaten, and locked up" story by one of the family's best storytellers. Cultural critic Walter Benjamin (1969) best amplified the value of "the talk" stories, stating that "[t]he story teller takes what he tells from experience-his own or that reported by others. And he in turn makes it the experience of those who are listening to his tale" (p. 87, as quoted by Bauman, 1986). Today, as one of the family's more senior storytellers, I now find myself telling the same stories including my own scary encounters with law enforcement and teaching the succeeding generation how to respond when being forced to bear witness to these types of tragedies.

What is bearing witness? Merriam-Webster Dictionary defines bearing witness as an idiom that signifies "to show that something exists or is true; to make a statement saying that one saw or knows something" (https://www.merriamwebster.com/dictionary/bear%20witness). In that light, African American journalism professor Allissa Richardson (2017) asserted that "the notion of bearing witness is woven deeply into the historic narratives about human rights violations against marginalized groups" (p. 674). In the 21st century, several memorable examples of Black Witnessing bearing instances have ended up piquing people's interest from the forefront of social media (e.g., Black Twitter), front page stories of national newspapers, and top stories of local, regional, and national cable television news.

Richardson (2017) explained that:

> Today's Black witnesses can be front line witnesses like Feidin Santana who filmed Michael Slager, a white officer shoot Walter Scott, an unarmed Black man, in South Carolina in 2015. Similarly, Kevin Moore captures the last images of is best friend Freddie Gray alive in Baltimore before his crumpled body was hauled into a Baltimore city police van in 2015. (p. 676)

I'm sure Darnella did not start out that day thinking that she was going to bear witness to such an appalling, visually, and psychologically traumatic crime. After all, she was taking her 9-year-old girl cousin to get a treat at a local convenience store when, unexpectedly, they saw a crowd watching four policemen in the throes of violently arresting George Floyd. No doubt, Darnella had too heard family and friends' stories about deadly encounters with law enforcement. Her one pivotal historical act (brandishing her cell phone and videoing this arrest) demonstrated that she had learned what many BIPOC peoples have discovered over this past decade: using a cell phone and its archival apps to document atrocities against marginalized peoples will help them become citizen journalists since their individual and collective lives can depend upon it. Black feminist scholar Brittany Cooper (2020) asserted:

> here is an extant narrative that helps us understand, even if uncomfortably, why Black men keep getting killed. That narrative also allows for other actors besides Black male victims and cops who kill. The murder of George Floyd merely confirmed what Black people have always known, . . . that plenty of white people know too: that the cops routinely harm Black people for the thinnest of reasons or no reasons at all. (para. 4–5)

Unbeknownst to her, Darnella began an unexpected foray into such witnessing while she and her equally stunned and traumatized little cousin and the growing crowd of secular witnesses heard and saw their collective pleas go unheeded while police callously restrained and immobilized George Floyd's body, forcibly pinning him face down as he struggled to breathe on the cement ground. In her subsequent testimony in 2021 at Derek Chauvin's trial, Darnella tearfully described how Chauvin, the senior officer who had his knees on Floyd's neck for almost nine minutes until he died, threatened to mace the crowd if they did not quiet themselves. For George Floyd, his tortuous death outlined in this YouTube video link was sheer hell to watch: https://www.youtube.com/watch?v=prZ-bYOUuZo, yet Darnella used her Black Girl Citizen Journalist cellphone videoing skills to share this tragedy in digital storytelling format. The day after his death, she went back to the site and spoke to people (who were now building a makeshift memorial) about how much she hurt for George Floyd and how she wished that she could have done something to help him and his family. Meanwhile, her video, even though it was raw and unedited went viral, viewed by millions of people globally. Ironically, since the pandemic kept more people in their homes and on their various electric devices, this video, along with the oral story she told accompanying it, inspired people who wanted to combat police brutalization of BIPOC to also become online activists (see https://www.pulitzer.org/winners/darnella-frazier).

Why is Darnella's video so important? She no doubt sensed that she needed to tell this story, even if presenting it as a credo for the black men in her family or the collective Black community to free herself and others what I would now categorize as "hapless Black people's pain." As one of the thousands of people who watched her video, I am proud that she spoke her own truth to power in her own way.

Eulogizing: The Masterful Art of Black Folk Storytelling, Bearing Witness

Reverend Al Sharpton, CEO of National Action Network, a nonviolent Civil Rights Grass Roots Organization, is a self-described advocate who frequently helps African American families receive national media and legal attention during grave circumstances that usually involve law enforcement killings of BIPOCs. As a communicator who enjoys rhetoric, I wholly appreciate his mastery of delivering "down home" free-flowing African American eulogies. Typically, the storyteller punctuates the eulogy with a colorful timeline complete with family stories as well as pastoral stories including the death of the person, the person's life, and contributions to the respective community. A eulogist might talk about the deceased's love of God, but not mention it if the person was agnostic or atheist. Giving a eulogy is not a walk in the graveyard park. For example, Harris and Hall (2018) charged the one giving the eulogy with this not always easy task:

> to show respect for the finality of death, follow discursive rules that almost prohibit articulating failures, poor choices, and anything that would present the deceased in a negative light charge . . . validate an individual in the face of tragic loss of life becomes greater than death under normal circumstances. (p. 173)

At George Floyd's Minnesota memorial, Reverend Al Sharpton gave the eulogy. During the eulogy, he plaintively bore witness of Floyd's untimely unjust death first by metaphorically unfolding the overall story of how African Americans had become "sick and tired of being sick and tired" of national law enforcement's strategy of indiscriminately brutalizing and murdering them. The sheer mastery of this eulogy was his oft repeated and masterful using the hashtag-worthy phrase: "Get off of our necks." Sharpton recounted going to the site where George Floyd was killed and suggesting how Floyd's death:

> has been the story of black folks because ever for 401 years ago, the reason we could never be who we wanted and dreamed to being is you kept your

knee on our neck. We were smarter than the underfunded schools you put us in, but you had your knee on our neck. We could run corporations and not hustle in the street, but you had your knee on our neck. We had creative skills, we could do whatever anybody else could do, but we couldn't get your knee off our neck. (https://www.rev.com/blog/transcripts/reverend-al-sharpton-eulogy-transcript-at-george-floyd-memorial-service, para. 9)

A good storyteller in the Black community knows that its audience needs an opportunity to reflect on what has just been said before moving on to telling the audience what it means. Sharpton explained what having the White man's knee on a Black person's neck really implied:

What happened to Floyd happens every day in this country, in education, in health services, and in every area of American life, it's time for us to stand up in George's name and say get your knee off our necks. That's the problem no matter who you are. (https://www.rev.com/blog/transcripts/reverend-al-sharpton-eulogy-transcript-at-george-floyd-memorial-service, para. 10)

Sharpton also suggested that all African American people from every socioeconomic stratum walks of life have had racism hold them back, not just poor people like Floyd and his family. He told his audience:

maybe it was just us, but even blacks that broke through, you kept your knee on that neck. Michael Jordan won all of these championships, and you kept digging for mess because you got to put a knee on our neck. White housewives would run home to see a black woman on TV named Oprah Winfrey and you messed with her because you just can't take your knee off our neck. A man comes out of a single parent home, educates himself and rises up and becomes the President of the United States and you ask him for his birth certificate because you can't take your knee off our neck. (https://www.rev.com/blog/transcripts/reverend-al-sharpton-eulogy-transcript-at-george-floyd-memorial-service, para. 10)

Reverend Sharpton is also an absolute master at challenging and calling his audience to action. As I rocked back and forth on my couch wiping the tears streaming from my eyes, I am waiting for him to tell me what to do or not to. As if he could read my thoughts, Sharpton answered me:

Why are we marching all over the world for George? The reason why we are marching all over the world is we were like George, we couldn't breathe, not because there was something wrong with our lungs, but that you wouldn't take your knee off our neck. We don't want no favors, just get up off of us and we can be and do whatever we can be. (https://www.rev.

com/blog/transcripts/reverend-al-sharpton-eulogy-transcript-at-george-floyd-memorial-service, para. 10)

Every story always has a good ending; a eulogy is no exception. Predictably, Sharpton rebounded from a seemingly caustic rebuke and, at times, fiery eulogy, rehumanizing Floyd by speaking softly, almost wistfully:

> I was thinking maybe he was calling his mother because at the point that he was dying, his mother was stretching her hands out saying, "Come on, George, I'll welcome you where the wicked will cease from troubling. Where the weary will be at rest. There's a place where police don't put knees on you George. There's a place that prosecutors don't drag their feet." Maybe mama said, "Come on George." (https://www.rev.com/blog/transcripts/reverend-al-sharpton-eulogy-transcript-at-george-floyd-me-morial-service, para. 19)

On June 9, 2020, Reverend Sharpton delivered an additional eulogy in Houston, Texas, Floyd's home town. As I watched this funeral, I was once again spellbound, captivated, and ready to do the work against police brutality and murder. This time, I felt that the world was truly watching and ready to do the work with me. Harris and Hall (2018) noted the agency and empowerment that eulogies can bring stating "By establishing why the deceased is worthy of honor, more importantly, martyrdom, the deliberative element of the eulogy is a call to action" (p. 183). For the rest of 2020, I joined in protests, donated funds to anti-racism causes, and taught about the importance of bearing witness as BIPOCs.

Tarpley (1995) shared the essence that people like Darnella Frazier and Reverend Al Sharpton exhibit when bearing witness as a storyteller:

> While the stories we tell are important, the act of telling and hearing them sets us free. And it is at this most vulnerable moment, at the meeting of pain, joy, desire, renewed hope, where we gather up the pieces of the stories that have been waiting to be told, and where our voices, although changing, are clear and strong enough for the telling. (p. 2)

Communication So White: Can Our Discipline Heal Itself?

Earlier in this chapter, I outlined my performance acumen and primary reasoning for directing *Clybourne Park*. One of the most striking things I liked about the play is the diverse cast and the frank, often uncomfortable discussions among Communication students and others about race when they see it. In reality, the playwright Bruce Norris could have never known that I, a decade later, would go one step further and still question why BIPOC students and scholars cannot get past *still* having to habitually fail engaging these counterfeit conversations with their White counterparts. Over 60 years since *Raisin in the Sun* debuted on Broadway, I would not be surprised if Loraine Hansberry would not be turning over in her literary grave if she had not died at a young age.

Communication, like so many other academic fields/disciplines, is woefully marginalized and White-race oriented. Critical/Cultural Studies scholar Washington (2020) wryly noted that, for many who have long had a vested interest in the field, Whiteness has become not just *a* way to examine the world around them but *the* way. In our predominantly white classrooms, White and BIPOC students examine White Communication-oriented theories and pedagogies while ignoring or marginalizing academic works that the discipline's paucity of BIPOC scholars have provided. Further elaborating, Mukherjee (2020) contended that the sheer whiteness of our Communication academic world appears to be the absolute standard of rules and:

> is a profoundly raced and gendered formation that polices our work methodologically, theoretically and institutionally. It is a technology of categorization and assessment designed to undervalue the contributions of women of color, people of color, queers of color, people from the Global South and all of us who live in the intersections of these.

In 2020, I did an exercise in some of my basic classes called #*Communication-SoWhite*. During the exercise, I put 5–7 students into groups and asked them to read and discuss peer review journal articles or segments of book chapters written by a BIPOC scholar. I asked each group a series of questions: 1) What did you learn about the topic? 2) What did you learn about the scholar? 3) Have you read this scholar's work before? Why? Why not? When my students annotated bibliography assignments, I encouraged them to read and write about BIPOC scholars' work. For group projects, again, students learned about fantastic BIPOC Communication or interdisciplinary work colleagues are publishing. I gave my students countless opportunities to hear and participate in Zoom lectures with BIPOC Communication colleagues. That summer, my classes even spent quite a bit of time on Zoom discussing "bearing witness," Darnella Frazier, George Floyd, and protests as communication.

Finally, for Communication students and scholars, I pose this philosophical yet pragmatic challenge quoting Communication scholar Lionnell "Badu" Smith (2019), who asserted that "the light of consciousness is not defined by white thought rather consciousness is achieved through holistic thinking. That is, there is light in understanding all voices and experiences, including marginalized voices" (p. 39). Simply put, when it comes to bearing witness and committing oneself to communicative anti-racist nuances in our field, may we all strive to become the brightest part of our discipline's light.

References

Bauman, R. (1986). *Story, performance and event: Contextual studies of oral narrative*. Cambridge University Press

Benjamin, W. (1969). *Illuminations*. Schocket.

Cooper, B. (2020, June). *Why are Black women and girls still an afterthought in our outrage over police violence?* https://time.com/5847970/police-brutality-black-women-girls/

Harris, M., & Hall, A. (2018). My living shall not be in vain:" The rhetorical power of eulogies in the face of civil unrest. *Journal of Contemporary Rhetoric, 8*(3), 173–183.

Kinsley, J. M. (2020). Black speech matters. *University of Louisville Review, 59*(001), 1–20.

Mukherjee, R. (2020). Of experts and tokens: Mapping a critical race archaeology of communication. *Communication, Culture, & Critique, 13*, 152–167. https://doi.org/10.1093/ccc/tcaa009

Richardson, A. (2017). Bearing witness while black: Theorizing African American mobile journalism after Ferguson. *Digital Journalism, 5*(6), 673–698.

Rogers, L., Rosario, R., Padilla, D., & Foo, C. (2021). "[I]t's hard because it's the cops that are killing us for stupid stuff": Racial identity in the sociopolitical context of Black Lives Matter. *Developmental Psychology, 57*(1), 87–101.

Smith, L. (2019, Winter). Can we share the light? De-centering communication whiteness with Communication pedagogy. *Departures in Critical Qualitative Research, 8*(4), 35–40.

Tarpley, N. (Ed.). (1995). *Testimony: Young African Americans on self discovery and Black identity*. Bean Press.

Washington, M. (2020). Woke skin, white masks: Race and communication studies. *Communication and Critical/Cultural Studies, 17*(2), 261–266.

5

THE NOW AND NOT YET

Reclaiming a Ritual View of Communication in Religious Communication Theory and Practice

Jennifer Scott Mobley

Learning Objectives

1. Identify the difference between a ritual view of communication versus a transmission view of communication.
2. Examine how a ritual view of communication illuminates how religious people and communities make sense of the events of the 2020s.
3. Explore the implications of the historic events of 2020 on the future of religious communication scholarship.

I started graduate school in September 2001. I will never forget sitting in my first rhetoric class and hearing the frantic screams of a young woman running through the hallway announcing that the Twin Towers had fallen. In a mass communication theory class a few hours later, I watched the pallid faces of the announcers on CNN in a dark auditorium in complete silence. My evening class was cancelled so we could attend a candlelight vigil instead.

Perhaps my journey as a religious communication scholar began that Sunday after 9/11. I found myself that morning walking into an Episcopal church that I had never been before and sitting in a pew surrounded by strangers. The priest spoke about the "now and not yet" of the kingdom of God at this moment in time and space. In the aftermath of 9/11, she shared, it can feel like too many things are still "not yet." We are not yet at a time or place that is free from sorrow, free from injustice. We are not yet at a time or place where our grief has ceased, our sicknesses healed, and our brokenness made whole.

Yet, sometimes we can forget that there is power for now too. As I looked around the faces of the congregation that morning, I remember this palpable feeling of connectedness as we participated in the Eucharist. This is the body

DOI: 10.4324/9781003220466-6

of Christ broken for you; this is the blood of Christ poured out for you, Jennifer. Over and over, the invitation was given, until everyone received bread and wine, and everyone heard their name aloud.

Rituals stitch us to one another, knit generation to generation, and remind us that we are part of a larger story. Rituals creep up and under the death and the despair, the injustice and the brokenness, weaving the light of healing and shalom into the darkest and emptiest corners.

What is the power of ritual? Maybe the power of ritual is mostly manifested in our "now and not yet" moments because in these moments, we see that ritual is more than mere symbol; it is a concrete act testifying that we are in this together.

Perhaps, the simple fact that imperfect rituals with imperfect people who commit to coming together comprises the point of the story.

****

I write this essay almost 20 years after 9/11, and we are now grappling with the aftermath of a global pandemic. As I reflect upon the momentous events of 2001 and 2020, I hear similar urgent questions being asked by religious communities and congregations: What answers do religious faiths give to the systemic issues of our day? How should we live well together?

The 2020s have cast a stark spotlight on other realities that many have long wished to ignore. The pandemic exposed appalling disparities between rich and poor while also prompting amazing acts of sacrifice and solidarity. Meanwhile, the murder of George Floyd and the international movement that it sparked have raised new painful, persistent questions about race and justice.

While some parallels exist between 2001 and 2020, I also note stark differences. In 2001, the attacks were clearly visible. Two planes flew into the twin towers of the World Trade Center in New York City; a third plane hit the Pentagon just outside Washington, DC, and the fourth plane crashed in a field in Shanksville, Pennsylvania. However, in 2020, while the coronavirus mutated, multiplied, and carried the threat of contagion, its fiercest weapon stemmed from its cloak of invisibility, its ability to do so much unseen by the human eye. Concomitantly, the coronavirus' attack on the lungs was matched by another invisible force that can take away human breath—the use of tear gas on Black Lives Matter activists across the United States.

Seeing is believing, and seeing, or the inability to see something, constitutes a political act (Berger, 1990). Following the outbreak of COVID-19, the conflation of religious and political divides intensified in 2020 as misinformation and conspiracy theories about the virus seeped from our screens into religious communities. The media in the United States highlighted the stories of religious leaders, particularly white evangelical leaders, that resisted the prohibition to congregate, inevitably attracting scorn and condemnation and reinvigorating the religion versus science debate (Cosgrove, 2020; Wilson, 2020). According to a Pew Research Center survey, about 53% of respondents who were Democrats or leaned Democrat said they had a "great deal" of confidence in medical scientists to act in the public interest during the first few months of the pandemic, an increase of 16% compared to the previous year (Funk et al., 2020). Republicans or Republican-leaning respondents' views overlapped closely with those of white evangelical Protestants. Similarly, about 31% of both groups said they had a great deal of confidence in medical scientists to act in the best interests of the public; notably, this figure marked a lower percentage than white nonevangelical Protestants, Catholics, and Black Protestants, a group whose trust of the scientific community has been irrevocably broken by historic inequities (Funk et al., 2020).

Amid this litany of political divisions and the onslaught of grief, stress, and isolation triggered by the pandemic, religious communities and institutions played a crucial role in addressing the mental health of their members and the greater community by providing rituals to bring people together. Rituals present a fruitful area for communication study, especially given the centrality of face-to-face gatherings typically associated with religious holidays and traditions. In particular, the lockdowns during the months of April and May 2020 entailed a period with strong religious resonance since it involved the dates of the major annual holidays celebrated by the world's three major monotheistic religions—the Jewish Passover, the Christian Easter, and the Muslim Ramadan. Amid the uncertainty, death and grief surrounding the pandemic, religious communities faced the unique challenge of altering the expressions of cherished rituals and traditions due to the need for social distancing.

Indeed, the fabric of rituals, the sense of togetherness, and the meaning of congregation changed dramatically across sectarian boundaries in 2020. Offline and online practices became bridged, blended, and blurred. Some rituals went digital—churches live-streamed or broadcasted baptisms on Facebook and YouTube; clergy ministered to the sick and dying via FaceTime and Zoom, and members of various faith communities made pilgrimages via Virtual Reality. Some communities adopted new measures for hygiene and safety which changed their liturgy; for example, Catholics sprinkled ashes or applied them with disposable cotton balls, and Hindus launched home delivery services to share *prasad* on doorsteps rather than hands. Other communities turned to a seemingly old-fashioned way to redefine what it meant to gather together: the drive-in church service (Chow, 2020).

Religious rituals and practices shape human beings' underlying communicative sensibilities as well as their overarching worldviews. The study of rituals is profoundly important to the Communication discipline because it centers on understanding how people navigate the liminal space of life's important transitions by examining how people process and express their emotions with themselves and one another as well as ways for the community to support the bereaved. Moreover, rituals allow people to process and express their emotions and provide a sense of routine and normalcy in the midst of change. The changes to rituals and the associated patterns of social engagement brought about by the events of

2020, particularly the pandemic, offer numerous opportunities for Communication scholars to explore important theoretical and practical questions regarding the power of ritual and the dialectical tensions of sacred and profane, autonomy and connectedness, and stability and change (for related work, please see Baxter & Montgomery, 1996; Eliade, 1987). How religious people, communities, and institutions manage these dialectical tensions as they engage in rituals serve as a strategic location for viewing some of the ongoing changes to the sub-field of religious communication and a path forward. A ritual view of communication provides a helpful way for us to navigate the 2020s, to reflect and re-imagine, releasing things that need to die away and creating space to bring new things into the world.

Reclaiming a Ritual View of Communication

What should we do in the in-between time, when one chapter of our lives has ended, and the next one has not come into being yet?

When the shutdowns happened, I began meeting with a spiritual director for the first time. My interest in finding a spiritual director stemmed from my longing for ritual and support as I navigated this liminal space. As a close friend fought for her life in the ICU, I searched online to find a spiritual director to learn more about the process.

Around this same time, I found myself returning to the work of James W. Carey. In his most widely cited work, "A Cultural Approach to Communication," Carey introduced us to the ritual view of communication. According to Carey, communication constitutes a "symbolic process whereby reality is produced, maintained, repaired, and transformed" (2009, p. 19). Juxtaposing a ritual view of communication with a transmission view of communication, he stated:

> In a ritual definition, communication is linked to terms such as "sharing," "participation," "association," "fellowship," and "the possession of a common faith." This definition exploits the ancient identity and common roots of the terms "commonness," "communion," "community," and "communication." . . . If the archetypal case of communication under a transmission view is the extension of messages across geography for the purpose of control, the archetypal case under a ritual view is the sacred ceremony that draws persons together in fellowship and commonality. . . . [I]t derives from a view of religion that downplays the role of the sermon, the instruction and admonition, in order to highlight the role of prayer, the chant, and the ceremony. (p. 15)

In contrast to the transmission view of communication, Carey's ritual view of communication encompasses essentially a sacramental approach to understanding how meaning is enacted in culture (Schultze, 2007). Carey's words take on particular resonance in light of the historic events of 2020. The ritual view of communication can help explain the unrest people experienced as beloved rituals went virtual or got punted to some unsettled future. Several studies suggest, for instance, that rituals foster social cohesion and help with emotional regulation, particularly during periods of uncertainty, when control over events is not within reach (Whitehouse & Lanman, 2014). When boundaries become blurred and overly porous, rituals help us mark time and space and set boundaries that give coherence, structure, and meaning to an otherwise seemingly chaotic world.

A ritual view of communication provides some insight to my interest in finding a spiritual director in 2020. Nouwen (2006) referred to spiritual direction as "soul friendship" or

> a relationship initiated by a spiritual seeker who finds a mature person of faith willing to pay and respond with wisdom and understanding to his or her questions about how to live spiritually in a world of ambiguity and distraction. (p. vii)

In the ambiguous and distracting days leading up to and after the presidential election, I watched religious communities become enmeshed in the same patterns of politicization across my rural community in western Pennsylvania. As I grew weary from the disagreements of what "going to church" meant during the pandemic and the admonitions of resistance over the vaccine effort, I decided to reach out to a spiritual director to help me create new rituals in an online space, to counteract "the role of the sermon, the instruction and admonition in order to highlight the role of the prayer, the chant, and the ceremony" (Carey, 2009, p. 15). According to Nouwen, a spiritual director does not lecture but creates the space where the seeker can be addressed by God for only God can do the work of spiritual formation. Nouwen (2006) contended:

> Teachers can teach only when there are students who want to learn. Spiritual directors can direct only when there are seekers who come with a question. Without a question, an answer is experienced as manipulation or control. without a struggle, the help offered is considered interference. And without the desire to learn, direction is easily felt as oppression. (p. 8)

A spiritual director listens deeply to the other in this time of transition as she attempts to live her question. Over the course of bi-monthly sessions conducted via Zoom, I began to engage in deep listening and to appreciate the silence between the words as I lit a candle and prayed with my spiritual director. As I shared my story, I felt deeply listened to in a way that made me reflect on the hope for religious communication in the future and how this experience could transform my work as a Communication scholar. Our communication systems are meant, by virtue of our createdness, to be open to the outside, the other. The practice of hospitality can serve as a fruitful metaphor for the vocation of the religious communication scholar because it is predicated on the hope that both host and guest can be changed for good by entering in discourse with one another. Nouwen (1986) reminded us:

> Hospitality means primarily the creation of a free space where the stranger can enter and become a friend instead of an enemy. Hospitality is not to change people but to offer them space where change can take place. It is not to bring men and women over to our side, but to offer freedom not disturbed by dividing lines. . . . The paradox of hospitality is that it wants to create emptiness, not a fearful emptiness, but a friendly emptiness where strangers can enter and discover themselves as created free; free to sing their own songs, speak their own languages, dance their own dances; free also to leave and follow their own vocations. Hospitality is not a subtle invitation to adore the lifestyle of the host, but the gift of a chance for the guest to find his own. (pp. 71–72)

I believe the vocation of the religious communication scholar involves holding space for the other and engaging in the practice of hospitality so that authentic communication and transformative change can take place.

Future Directions for Religious Communication

Taken together, the social, political, spiritual, and technological forces of the 2020s usher in a new liminal space for religious communication scholars—chrysalis time. In-between being a caterpillar and becoming a butterfly, the chrysalis emerges. This stage marks old things giving way—the stage of goopy mess, of being neither caterpillar nor butterfly. This time of being and becoming something in an undefined, transitional state comprises the liminal space. Victor Turner (1967) is perhaps best known for his work on liminality, the quality of ambiguity, fluidity, and disorientation that occurs during times of intense transition. One category of liminal events includes what Turner called "rituals of affliction," which mark times of struggle by an individual (e.g., illness, grief) or by a collective community (e.g., famine, war). It requires a separation from cultural attachments and a fundamental dissolution of the typical mental and social structures that guide and shape us. Liminal periods comprise a process of becoming and unbecoming. Beliefs, habits, and structures dissolve and become reinvented. Extending from Turner, the person or the community who emerges on the other side of a liminal event is not the same as the one who entered it.

How can the study of religious communication help us navigate this liminal space? Where do religious communities go from here? How will all that we have experienced affect future interactions and social situations? Eschewing the either/or thinking that seemed to permeate many of the divisive events of the 2020s, religious communication scholars can offer a unique contribution to the future of our discipline by holding the dialectics of autonomy and connectedness, online and offline, faith and science, stability and change in tension and stepping forward to offer a productive way forward. Paradoxes can inspire those instances in which individual and organizational efforts may actively work on synergizing a "third way" which can allow us to navigate tensions in a dynamic way. Rather than viewing contradiction as negative, the events of 2020 suggest that when we engage dialectical tensions, we are better equipped to discover "both/and" options and imagine a hybrid future for religious communication scholarship.

First, religious communication scholars must now re-examine their "embodiment" and "material" turns and devise new methodologies to study the hybridity of religious phenomena that have appeared after COVID-19 (Hazard, 2013). Ritual innovations might outlive the duration of the pandemic and become the new praxis. Digital sacraments and new remediations of rituals are most probably here to stay. Yet the immutability of rituals—their fixed and often repetitive nature—remains central to their definition, and performing a ritual "the right way" carries deep symbolic meaning and religious significance to people that may matter more than the outcome. Following Campbell and Evolvi (2020), religious communication scholars should engage these tensions and explore the connection between online and offline phenomena and how faith communities modify and transform their respective religious practices. Comparative and interdisciplinary approaches and mixed methodologies could help us more fruitfully engage questions related to identity and community and provide new conceptual and methodological approaches that help us synergize a "third way" between online and offline religious phenomena. This work has already begun in digital religion studies, a growing interdisciplinary area and field of research that "investigates the technological and cultural space that is evoked when we talk about how online and offline religious spheres have become blended and integrated" (Campbell, 2013, pp. 3–4). According to Campbell, digital religion studies have demonstrated great promise to model a "third way" that explores the connection and interrelation between online and offline religious contexts and how these contexts become bridged, blended, and blurred over time, and future research should continue this pursuit.

In addition, we can work together to explore a "third way" that embraces the both/and of dialectic tensions by returning to root questions from the history of communication studies, broadly conceived as the road from rhetoric to social science and cultural studies. Carey (2009) provided several key questions that we can consider:

> We create, express and convey our knowledge of and attitudes toward reality through the construction of a variety of symbol systems: art, science, journalism, religion, common sense, mythology. How do we do this? What are the differences between the forms? What are the historical and comparative variations in them? How do changes in communication technology

influence what we can concretely create and apprehend? How do groups in society struggle over the definitions of what is real? (p. 24)

Following Carey, what would the discipline of Communication Studies look like if we reclaimed this ritual view of communication? What if we took the time to engage in dialogue with scholars of our past to see what we could learn from their traces about the "struggle over the definitions of what is real" (p. 24)? What kinds of follow-up questions would we then ask? What compelling and relevant questions might emerge in our scholarship and teaching?

A ritual view of communication provides a helpful way for us to engage these questions, to reflect and re-imagine, to release things that need to die away so that they can create space to bring new things into the world. It can also help us remember to deeply listen to the other and repair what is broken. According to Carey (2009), a ritual view of communication reminds us that this process of repair and transformation is ongoing:

> Reality must be repaired for it consistently breaks down: people get lost physically and spiritually, experiments fail, evidence counter to the representation is produced, mental derangement sets in—all threats to our models of and for reality that lead to intense repair work. Finally, we must, often with fear and regret, toss away our authoritative representations of reality and begin to build the world anew. (p. 24)

Amid a year fraught with divisiveness and loss, the discipline of Communication in the 2020s should seek to illuminate a broader re-imagining of what binds us together. Just as the circumstances surrounding the pandemic have caused many people to rethink such systemic issues as racial inequality, healthcare provision, and the role of education in a thriving society, the mandated "pause" has allowed religious communication scholars the time and space to develop innovative approaches to understanding how religion continues to shape people's lives in the 21st century. This pause has allowed some time to reflect and re-imagine, repairing what we need to, and creating space to bring new things into the world.

I hope the Communication discipline in the 2020s will be characterized by what we unlearn as much as learn, a time when we revisited our own assumptions and built new bridges across our divides. Carey (2009) reminded us what we stand to gain if we engage in this recovery and reclamation work:

> The object, then, of recasting our studies of communication in terms of a ritual model is not only to more firmly grasp the essence of this "wonderful" process but to give us a way in which to rebuild a model of and for communication of some restorative value in reshaping our common culture. (p. 27)

While we will emerge from this chrysalis transformed into something new, we should also look to the future as an opportunity to discover or rediscover what we have in common on the other side.

References

Baxter, L. A., & Montgomery, B. M. (1996). *Relating: Dialogues and dialectics*. Guilford.

Berger, J. (1990). *Ways of seeing*. British Broadcasting Corporation and Penguin Books. (Original work published 1972).

Campbell, H. (2013). Introduction: The rise of the study of digital religion. In H. A. Campbell (Ed.), *Digital religion: Understanding religious practice in new media worlds* (pp. 1–22). Routledge.

Campbell, H. A., & Evolvi, G. (2020). Contextualizing current digital religion research on emerging technologies. *Human Behavior and Emerging Technologies, 2*, 5–17.

Carey, J. W. (2009). *Communication as culture: Essays on media and society*. Unwin Hyman. (Original work published 1989).

Chow, A. R. (2020, March 28). "Come as you are in the family car": Drive-in church services are taking off during the coronavirus pandemic. *Time*. https://time.com/5811387/drive-in-church-coronavirus/

Cosgrove, J. (2020, November 8). LA megachurch pastor mocks pandemic health orders as members fall ill. *Los Angeles Times*. https://www.latimes.com/california/story/2020-11-08/la-pastor-mocks-covid-19-rules-church-members-ill

Eliade, M. (1987). *The sacred and the profane: The nature of religion*. Harcourt Brace Jovanovich. (Originally published in 1959).

Funk, C., Kennedy, B., & C. Johnson. (2020, May 21). *Trust in medical scientists has grown but mainly among Democrats*. Pew Research Center. https://www.pewresearch.org/science/2020/05/21/trust-in-medical-scientists-has-grown-in-u-s-but-mainly-among-democrats/

Hazard, S. (2013). The material turn in the study of religion. *Religion and Society, 4*(1), 58–78.

Nouwen, H. J. (1986). *Reaching out: The three movements of the spiritual life*. Doubleday.

Nouwen, H. J. (2006). *Spiritual direction: Wisdom for the long walk of faith*. HarperCollins.

Schultze, Q. J. (2007). Communication as religion: In memory of James W. Carey, 1935–2006. *Journal of Media and Religion, 6*(1), 1–15.

Turner, V. (1967). *The forest of symbols*. Cornell University Press.

Whitehouse, H., & Lanman, J. A. (2014). The ties that bind us: Ritual, fusion, and identification. *Current Anthropology, 55*(6), 674–695.

Wilson, J. (2020, April 4). The rightwing Christian preachers in deep denial over Covid-19's danger. *The Guardian*. https://www.theguardian.com/us-news/2020/apr/04/america-rightwing-christian-preachers-virus-hoax

6

DISABILITY AND COMMUNICATION

Julie-Ann Scott-Pollock

Learning Objectives

1. To articulate how compulsory able-bodiedness was both highlighted by and resisted through the pandemic.
2. To articulate the questions and subjects of disability and communication research.
3. To articulate hyper-embodiment as an individual and cultural position that promotes inclusion.
4. To articulate how hyper-embodied cultural positioning is both promoted and resisted by cultural members through the pandemic.

Prologue to a Hyper-Embodied Awakening: But Aren't You High Risk?

I approach the white tent erected in the parking lot outside of my local Pure Barre Studio. I am ready for my first in-person class since before lockdown four months ago. I saw a picture of the outdoor tent on Instagram, so I arrived early to get a spot near a tent pole in case I need help stabilizing during some of the exercises. I unroll my lime green yoga mat and notice a one-inch chunk missing. I know why. Theo, my youngest, toddled over while I was exercising during lockdown and bit my mat. Pure Barre outdoor classes are the only risk that my family is taking during COVID. We discussed this choice with my in-laws that followed us to the North Carolina coast to be hands-on grandparents. We are careful to keep them safe since they are high risk, and we benefit greatly from their help with childcare while under lockdown. An outdoor, socially distanced fitness class is a calculated risk because I need to be able to bend my knees and

DOI: 10.4324/9781003220466-7

ankles without pain, and my boys—who are always home—repeatedly inter-rupted the virtual classes.

I was also struggling and losing mobility without the hands-on correction from the in-person instructors. I adjust the waistband of my purple $120 lululemon leggings that I purchased for $30 on Amazon and a pink Free People tie-dye tank top that I bought on Instagram during my studio's virtual flash sale last month. Pure Barre is as much about fashion and lifestyle as it is about fitness. I am white, approaching 40, and thin, so I manage to blend in with the group through a collec-tion of sale items despite my limping, inflexible body. In my city, Barre participants primarily comprise a group of predominantly white middle-to-upper middle-class, white, fit women in their 30s–60s with an assortment of injuries that make us una-ble to effectively engage in boot camp style workouts or running. When I began Pure Barre, I fit the aesthetic well enough that people assumed I limped because I was recovering from a torn muscle or sprained ankle. As they learned that I have spastic cerebral palsy and four little boys, I became an inspirational presence with my strength and defined muscles from a lifetime of physical therapy. They would say that if I can find the time and energy to do the workouts, then *anyone* can.

I'm used to this sort of response across cultural spaces. I am an "inspiration" to the non-disabled world as a professor in the classroom, a parent at my sons' soc-cer games, and even as a member of my barre studio. Pure Barre has highlighted my journey with barre workouts on the social media for both my local studio and the national chain. A disabled body is uncomfortable in our culture that fears vulnerability and dependence, so when disabled bodies thrive, and are interpreted as aesthetic, and comfortable, we become symbols of hope and admiration, a way to resolve these pervasive cultural fears (Scott, 2012b, 2018).

One of the women who I have not seen since lockdown approaches me and begins to unroll her mat next to mine. Her blond ponytail bounces and around her eyes crinkle with the smile beneath her red satin mask that matches this sea-son's designer shiny leggings.

"Hi Julie-Ann! So good to see you. I didn't think you'd be at the in-person classes once they started up again."

I pause and consider the conversation. I know where it is going, and some-times I cut people off if I do not feel like investing the time to engage. This woman is a kindergarten teacher at one of the neighborhood schools, and I have a children's literature troupe that performs for her class. I like her. She seems open and conversational. It is worth taking a moment to educate.

"Really? Why?" (I know why, but it helps them to articulate their assumptions before I challenge them.)

"Well, I just assumed with your um, disability, you'd be high risk for COVID."

"Cerebral palsy impacts my muscles, not my lungs or immune system. Class is outside with masks. I'll risk it. I take Pure Barre to stay mobile. My knees are not bending well since lockdown. Teaching online is so sedentary. My body gets stiff. I need this to be the parent I want to be. I need it to live life well."

"Oh, of course. I'm sorry. I don't know why I assumed."

"It's fine. Lots of people do."

"I mean, I feel like my body is getting stiff from teaching online, and I don't even have cerebral palsy."

I smile and nod as the instructor turns up the speakers so she can time our workout to the music. We both stand to begin the first socially distanced open-air masked workout of 2020. I am comforted that she realizes how her mortal body is also stiff, vulnerable to change with time and context.

Chapter Preview

In the coming pages, I will map how the COVID-19 pandemic made disability and communication conversations focused on the inescapable vulnerability and inevitable mortality of the human body become mainstream across dominant cultural discourse. I will introduce the concepts of compulsory able-bodiedness and hyper-embodiment and explain how these theoretical positions offer opportunities for a more inclusive and empathetic culture that embraces and values rather than marginalizes and fears the presence of disability across lived experience.

Disability Studies and Communication: Culture Emphasizes the Disabled Body's Mortality

As a disabled person, I am constantly reminded of the susceptibility of bodies to change over time. Disabled bodies know we are mortal. Whether or not disabled are actually dying more quickly than those around us—I am not; my disability is not progressive—in our daily communicative encounters, others remind us that they interpret our bodies as more fragile, vulnerable, and dying more quickly than bodies deemed "normal," unmarked by disability (Scott, 2018). Disability and Communication research maps how we co-create disabled, able, ill, well, normal, and abnormal across our daily interactions, mass media artifacts, live performances, sports culture, and pedagogical design and what steps we can take to be more inclusive. The year 2020 highlighted this map in dominant cultural discourse, drawing attention to our cultural understandings and tensions surrounding our mortal, inescapably vulnerable bodies *and* our personal and cultural responsibility to individually and collectively respond to our *mortal reality*. Suddenly, in 2020, questions that dominate my research as a disability and communication scholar were on everyone's minds.

Pandemic, Protests, and the Reality of Mortality and Social Vulnerability in 2020

COVID-19 forced the inescapable mortality of our bodies into daily conversations. Social distancing and mask mandates reminded us that all people could catch and transmit a deadly disease. These new rules drew our collective attention to the inherent vulnerability of mortal human bodies. Worldwide, people were reminded that bodies are susceptible to illness and that illness can abruptly change and end our lives. To manage the reality of mortality, suddenly we found mechanisms to allow people to work, socialize, exercise, and learn remotely. Grocery delivery became normative. The struggle over whether or not we should manage our own and others' risks of illness as a collective good dominated our public discourse.

In response, a portion of the population grew resistant, angry, and combative, refusing to follow social distancing regulations or wear masks (Koon et al., 2021; Taylor & Asmundson, 2021). Those individuals demanded that everything from schools, to restaurants, to gyms, to sports venues, to hair salons open for their happiness and convenience. Being forced to collectively adapt to our mortal bodies drew rage from those used to being able to ignore their own mortal reality. They expressed anger that their privilege as deemed "healthy" people with social capital that provided them a sense of safety in their daily lives had been momentarily suspended.

In an ordinary, non-pandemic year, the dominant society relegates communication about mortality onto bodies that are deemed disabled and ill (Garland-Thomson, 1997; Scott, 2018; Zola, 1993). Medical professionals tend to diagnosis disabled and ill bodies as "abnormal," "deficient," "fragile," "at-risk," and "terminal" (McRuer, 2006; Scott, 2018). It then becomes the burden of those diagnosed cultural members to navigate their lives seeking accommodations and managing their risks. Through thrusting this failure to meet expectations of "normal" and "healthy" onto these deemed "disabled" and "ill" bodies, the rest of the population can ignore that they are also inescapably growing older and more fragile with time as well as increasingly vulnerable to accidents and illness that could abruptly change their ability and health. Anyone can suddenly join the social category of "disabled." Most people move in and out of that category over the course of their lifetimes, from broken bones causing temporary mobility issues to viruses causing temporary incapacity to participate fully in society. *Any body* that lives long enough will eventually shift into the cultural category of disabled (Zola, 1982).

Social vulnerability and attention to mortality extend beyond disabled bodies, and we were forced to acknowledge this vulnerability along with our own mortalities in 2020. Marginalized bodies across our social identity categories are more at risk for violence and the insecurity that comes with rejection and ostracization. The protests of 2020 over police brutality toward Black bodies further forced white bodies to confront the reality that Black bodies must acknowledge and manage their mortality to a greater degree than white bodies (Johnson, 2015). Lockdown also compelled us, as a society, to acknowledge that many cultural members with low socioeconomic status could not survive as their places of employment shut down. Children without access to quality electronic devices and laptops fell behind in school. The pandemic and protests challenged us to grapple, as a society, with how we are to care for our mortal bodies, both for our own and for others.

This cultural moment provides the opportunity to collectively access the pervasiveness of compulsory able-bodiedness and hyper-embodiment. Disability and Communication research provides the map for this conversation ranging from personal narrative interviews (see Scott, 2019), to ethnographic field interviews (see Lindemann & Cherney, 2008), to mass media (see Haller & Becker, 2014), to staged productions (see Quinlan & Bates, 2008), to medical procedures (see Cyper, 2010), to pedagogy and the classroom (see Fassett & Morella, 2008). These works intersect with gender, sexuality, race, ethnicity, and socioeconomic status as scholars grapple with how the intersections of our identities impact our interactions with others.

Understanding the Goals of Disability and Communication Research

In the remainder of this chapter, I introduce two concepts fundamental to the study of disability and communication. First, I discuss Compulsory Able-Bodiedness which is the cultural expectation that bodies that deviate from social expectations of "normalcy" are socially punished (McRuer, 2006). Second, I explain Hyper-embodiment as a personal and collective perspective that allows us to collectively pursue a state of ease with our inescapably changing mortal bodies that allow us to plan for rather than fear these changes (Scott, 2018). Resisting Compulsory Able-Bodiedness through Hyper-embodiment enables us to work together to create a culture that adapts and flexes around our forever-changing bodies. In doing so, we avoid ostracizing them from society and our dominant cultural interactions once they grow too uncomfortable and disruptive in their reminders of human beings' inevitable susceptibility to perpetually change and eventually die. As the vulnerability of all bodies became salient through the pandemic and the targeting of Black bodies took center cultural stage in the United States, the need for Disability and Communication research that embraces how our bodies are inevitably open to change over time with age, illness, injury, and social interpretation became more tangible to our dominant cultural conversations. Our bodies and how people categorize and respond to them is inescapably vulnerable. As we move beyond 2020, I hope that, through Hyper-embodiment, we can embrace the inescapable susceptibility of our bodies and cultural interpretations of them to change, and in response, build a culture that flexes around our mortal bodies across social locations for as long as they are here. Realizing that our bodies (and cultural understandings of them) remain perpetually open to change helps us not only to realize our vulnerability, but also the hope and possibilities that come with the inevitability to change. This realization begins with the acknowledgment of how compulsory able-bodiedness dominates our cultural interpretations and response.

Compulsory Able-Bodiedness and the Consequences of Disabled Deviance

Unlike some other identity categories (such as race and gender), disability does not have a set of observable, predictable traits; it is just the diagnosed absence of normal embodiment (Garland-Thomson (1997). McRuer (2006) drew upon Rich's (1980) compulsory heterosexuality to create a theory of Compulsory Able-Bodiedness. McRuer revealed how similar to Rich's argument that any deviance from straight, heteronormativity is met with social consequences, any deviation from able-bodiedness leads to a body being less valued and included in society. Compulsory Able-Bodiedness asserts that non-disabled bodies are envisioned as the "natural order of things." Any perceived departure from non-disabled is met with stigma and marginalization. McRuer argued that compulsory able-bodiedness is more pervasive than compulsory heterosexuality. To be able to meet the cultural standards for able-bodiedness, one must be able to "pass" with both aesthetics and independent/self-sufficient or risk social rejection and ostracization. Disability and Communication researchers have explored how compulsory able-bodiedness is managed by disabled bodies with varying responses, interpretations, and perceived levels of success in daily life. These studies include the workplace (see Scott, 2012a), contact sports (see Lindemann, 2008), live performance (see Davies, 2008), parenting (see Scott, 2020), education (see Consenza, 2014), pedagogy (see Scott & Herold, 2018), and relationships (see Scott & Houtzer, 2018). They have also mapped this occurrence in popular culture and mass media (see Haller, 2010) and questions that emerge surrounding disability in the research field (Scott, 2013). Disability and Communication research seeks ways for us to understand how we construct our understandings of disability and health through our cultural encounters with one another and popular culture artifacts, how these understandings enable and constrain us in our daily lives, and how new understandings that resist compulsory able-bodiedness can help us live better together with inclusivity and flexibility that allows us to accept the inevitable change of mortal bodies interacting within a culture without fear or social consequence (Henderson & Ostrander, 2010; Scott, 2018).

In 2020, the resistance to masks and social distancing highlighted the presence of compulsory able-bodiedness. Self-defined healthy bodies' desire to ostracize deemed vulnerable, disruptive bodies from daily life remain pervasive (Savulescu & Cameron, 2020). Some cultural members interpreted mandates to wear masks and social distance as encroaching on their freedoms. They argued that they were "healthy" and would most likely fully recover from COVID. Those individuals wanted to assume the personal risk of infection rather than disrupt their daily lives. Public health officials mounted campaigns to explain that masks stop individuals from spreading rather than contracting the virus (see, e.g., https://www.astho.org/Press-Room/Health-Officials-Launch-Ad-Campaign-to-Encourage-Mask-Use/08-12-20/).

Yet those who disputed that message argued instead that bodies deemed "at risk" remove themselves from society and limit contact beyond their homes, despite how this complicates not only one's quality of life but survival. Those resisting mask and social distancing perpetuated the idea that "normal," "able" bodies should not be inconvenienced, and the burden of survival and consequences of being safe should be relegated to abnormal, disabled bodies. The pervasiveness of compulsory able-bodiedness was suddenly tangible to deemed "normal bodies" as the country struggled over how to collectively move through the 2020 pandemic.

Interlude: Mask Mandates and Compulsory Able-Bodiedness

I just arrived at the Pure Barre Studio. I am 15 minutes early in hopes of getting my favorite spot by the side mirror with people on either side of me to watch in case I forget how to do each move. It is a cardio barre class, and it moves so quickly. The studio classroom normally holds 35 people, but state restrictions for in-door gyms are 30% capacity with masks, so the class consists of 10 students, plus an instructor and desk assistant. I have my son, Theo, in my arms. He is wearing his mask. He has to use the bathroom before I hand him off to my husband to go grocery shopping during my workout. I walk past a woman with long highlighted hair and a deep tan arguing with the 20-year-old desk assistant about wearing a mask to work out. I pretend that I do not hear them. After I walk past for the third time after re-entering the studio from strapping him into my husband's van, the woman calls to me:

"Julie-Ann, don't you think this is just unreasonable? I mean how are we expected to do a cardio barre workout with masks on. This doesn't make any sense. It's not safe to wear masks. I mean we aren't getting enough air."

I reply: "I think it's been okay. Get a disposable mask. They're a bit lighter. Really, if you don't have the lung capacity to be in the studio comfortably with a mask on, you probably should just do the virtual workouts, don't you think? If your breathing is compromised, it may not be worth the risk of catching COVID."

The woman's eyes narrow above her black matte satin mask, and she walks away. I hope the desk attendant can see how my eyes are smiling. Her body language relaxes as the woman walks away.

"I'm so happy you came today, Julie-Ann."

"Thanks. Me too. I need to go get my spot." I turn and head toward the barre and think of how I just used the power of compulsory able-bodiedness to stop that conversation. Instead of trying to argue the importance of wearing a mask for the greater good of society, I positioned her as one of disabled bodies that she wished to ostracize rather than be inconvenienced if she could not make it through a cardio workout with her mask. That idea of being among the "disabled bodies" was unpalatable enough that she stopped arguing.

Embracing Hyper-Embodiment in Post-2020 Communication

Within Disability and Communication Studies to be hyper-embodied is to embrace the inevitable change of one's inescapably mortal body and to plan for these changes rather than ignoring and/or fearing them (Scott, 2012b, 2018, 2019). However, the term hyper-embodied can evoke negative images since the focus on the physical body is often frowned upon in our society (Scott, 2018). For example, some might think of a woman with an eating disorder as obsessed with calories. Doctors so focused on diagnoses could forget the patient is a multifaceted person. A body builder obsessed with perfect symmetry or even a comic book artist fantasizes about unattainable proportions in the bodies of their fictional heroes. For me, as a disabled person, theorist, and methodologist to be hyper-embodied involves awareness that our bodies will inevitably change and that cultural responses to our bodies are equally open to reinterpretation. Moreover, we should embrace inevitable change and diverse interpretations and strive to move with these changes (Scott, 2018). If enough cultural members become hyper-embodied, we can resist compulsory able-bodiedness and instead work together to create a culture that flexes around all bodies to value and include them for as long as we are alive and here, communicating together.

In 2020, a pandemic forced us to confront the reality that all bodies are mortal, each time we were reminded that we could not be as physically close together as we once were or see each other's full faces. When common activities like going to a concert, a restaurant, gym, or work suddenly became high-risk activities, we began to daily attend to the mortality of our human bodies—a realization often ignored. With our mortal bodies at the front of our consciousness, and evidence that how we move through culture is forever vulnerable to change, we can begin the collective path toward hyper-embodiment that changes how we understand what it means to be in our bodies, communicating with others.

Epilogue: But the Virus Isn't Gone

"Mama, are we really going to Disney World this summer." My 7-year-old looks up at me skeptically as I tuck him into bed.

"Of course, honey. I already booked the trip, and we are staying at a beautiful hotel. The Beach Club has a water park attached. You'll love it."

"How do you know we will be able to go? What if another virus comes? Couldn't that happen?"

I stare into his dark eyes and brush his shaggy bangs out of them. In March of 2020, viruses were not a threat of any kind. Now this question looms over him since a virus has defined a year of his short life.

"I don't know, Vinny, but usually viruses like COVID-19 that become pandemics and prevent us from traveling usually aren't that close together. Disney has plans to keep us safe with social distancing and our masks. They won't let the park get too full. They're ready, even if another one did come. They're ready for us even though you aren't able to be vaccinated yet, and they'll be ready if there's another pandemic before we leave."

"Mama, I haven't been sick at all this year. I didn't even get a cold. We know how to keep each other safe now."

"Yes. We now know what to do to stay safe and keep on living."

"Maybe the pandemic isn't only bad."

"Maybe not."

And he rolled over and went to sleep.

In 2020, we were awakened to our bodies' mortality. Caring for our own and others' bodies meant drastic change to daily experiences, policies, and, ultimately, cultural paradigms of individual and collective worth, engagement, and productivity. We also learned that we can adapt to allow people to work, learn, and socially connect remotely with each other. These realities do not have to disappear with a vaccine. We have the capacity to be hyper-embodied, to continue to develop via distance technology, flex policies, and social programs for as long as we are here. Future research by Communication and Disability scholars should map how this momentary shift toward inclusion continues and expands or is resisted across cultural contexts.

References

Consenza, J. (2014). Language matters: A dyslexic methodology. *Qualitative Inquiry, 20*(10), 1191–1201.

Cyper, J. M. (2010). Agency and the dominant face: Facial transplantation and the discourse of normalcy. *American Communication Journal, 12*(1), 1–17.

Davies, T. (2008). Mobility: Axis dancers push the boundaries of access. *Text and Performance Quarterly, 12*(1), 43–63.

Fassett, D., & Morella, D. (2008). Remaking (the discipline: Marking the performative accomplishment of (dis)ability. *Text and Performance Quarterly, 28*, 139–156.

Garland-Thomson, R. (1997). *Extraordinary bodies: Figuring physical disability in American culture and literature.* Columbia University Press.

Haller, B. (2010). *Representing disability in an ableist world: Essays on mass media.* The Avocado Press.

Haller, B., & Becker, A. B. (2014). Stepping backwards with disability humor? The case of the NY Gov. David Paterson's representation of Saturday Night Live. *Disability Studies Quarterly, 34*(1). https://dsq-sds.org/article/view/3459/3527.

Henderson, B., & Ostrander, N. (2010). *Understanding disability studies and performance studies.* Routledge.

Johnson, J. (2015). Blasphemously Black: Reflections on performance and pedagogy. *Liminalities: A Journal of Performance Studies, 11*(4). Online, http://liminalities.net/11-4/blasphemously.pdf.

Koon, A. D., Mendenhall, E., Eich, L., Adams, A., & Borus, D. (2021). A spectrum of (dis)belief: Coronavirus frames in a rural midwestern town in the United States. *Social Science and Medicine, 272*(3). https://www.sciencedirect.com/science/article/pii/S0277953621000757

Lindemann, K. (2008). I can't be standing up out there: (Dis)Ability in wheelchair rugby. *Text and Performance Quarterly, 1*(2), 98–115.

Lindemann, K., & Cherney, J. L. (2008). Communicating in and through "Murderball": Masculinity and disability in wheelchair rugby. *Western Journal of Communication, 72*(2), 107–125.

McRuer, R. (2006). *Crip theory: Cultural signs of Queerness and the body.* New York University Press.

Quinlan, M., & Bates, B. (2008). Dances and discourses of (dis)ability: Heather Mills's embodiment of disability on *Dancing with the Stars. Text and Performance Quarterly, 28*(1–2), 64–80.

Rich, A. (1980). Compulsory heterosexuality and lesbian existence. *Signs, 5*(4), 631–660.

Savulescu, J., & Cameron, J. (2020). Why lockdown of the elderly is not ageist and why levelling down equality is wrong. *Journal of Medical Ethics, 46*, 717–721.

Scott, J. A. (2012a). "Cripped" heroes: An analysis of physically disabled professionals' personal narratives as performance of identity. *Southern Communication Journal, 77*(4), 307–328.

Scott, J. A. (2012b). Performing hyperembodiment: Stories of and through physically disabled bodies. *Text and Performance Quarterly, 32*(2), 100–120.

Scott, J. A. (2013). Problematizing a researcher's performance of 'insider status' in the analysis of physically disabled professionals' personal narratives: An autoethnography of 'designer disabled' identity. *Qualitative Inquiry, 19*(2), 101–115.

Scott, J. A. (2018). *Embodied performance as applied research art and pedagogy.* Palgrave Macmillan.

Scott, J. A. (2019). Performing narratives of self in memory loss: The visceral remains. *Text and Performance Quarterly, 39*(2), 116–134.

Scott, J. A. (2020). Disrupting compulsory performances: Snapshots and stories of masculinity, disability, and parenthood in the currents of daily life. In A. Johnson & B. LeMaster (Eds.), *Dancing with gender in the intersections: Critical autoethnography, intercultural communication, and the case for gender futurity* (pp. 24–36). Routledge.

Scott, J. A., & Herold, K. (2018). Almost passing, using disability disclosure to recalibrate able-bodied bias in the classroom. In M. S. Jeffress (Ed.), *Teaching with a disability: Student and teacher experiences of disability in the classroom* (pp. 1–16). Routledge.

Scott, J. A., & Houtzer, H. (2018). She was here: Narrative research as resistance to the loss of 'culturally uncomfortable' identities. *Qualitative Inquiry, 24*(2), 134–150.

Taylor, S., & Asmundson, G. (2021). Negative attitudes about facemasks during the COVID-19 pandemic: The dual importance of perceived ineffectiveness and psychological reactance. *PLOS 1, 16*(2).

Zola, I. (1982). *Missing pieces: A chronicle of living with a disability.* Temple University Press.

Zola, I. (1993). Self, identity and the naming question: Reflections on the language of disability, *Social Science & Medicine, 36*(2), 167–173.

7

COMMUNICATION AND ETHICS

Considering the Conflicting Messages of COVID-19

Sarah M. DeIuliis and Pat Arneson

Learning Objectives

1. Understand the historical background of the shift from grand narratives to petite narratives as it impacts human communication.
2. Understand the various scholarly approaches to ethics and communication.
3. Evaluate the practical engagement of ethics as we evaluate messages in our current historical moment.

•

The consequences of public events occurring in the United States during 2020 will reverberate in this decade and beyond. Throughout much of the past year, we found ourselves feeling unsettled. When we find ourselves in disquieting situations (e.g., confronting conflicting information about COVID-19 and vaccines, aware of inequities in the justice system, listening to political conversations about candidates with whom we disagree, etc.), we want to "do the right thing." And we find that most other people do, too. The challenge is for a person to determine what that "right thing" may be. We often wonder about what to say and/or how to act that will provide a fitting response allowing us to live at ease with the choices we make. We find ourselves struggling to listen, working far too long to find a scientific fact, trying to determine when and how much to engage with or disengage from the other person. Too often, we find ourselves faced with conspiracies, manufactured explanations, and opinions that people try to pass off as social truths. We struggle especially to reconcile such divergent perspectives when others seemingly express these things intentionally, leaving us to wonder about the communication interaction.

We are interested in how a person can use knowledge about ethics to claim an identity as an ethical communicator. In this chapter, we explain the shift from grand narratives to individual values and discuss various theoretical perspectives

DOI: 10.4324/9781003220466-8

that a person may use to evaluate a message for ethical qualities. Using the COVID-19 pandemic as an example, we indicate how a message may be evaluated from different ethical perspectives yet must uphold universal values (Christians & Traber, 1997). We open with a discussion that provides historical background on the place of self in human communication.

From Narrative to Values

The study of ethics often uses polarities to point toward positions and actions that are considered to be right or wrong, good or bad, fair or unfair. Unfortunately, this phrasing does not take into account that cultures change or that people may support different perspectives on what counts as "right," "good," and "fair." The study of ethics in communication includes negotiation about such meanings and concerns a person's judgments about the quality of a person's communication either as harming or benefitting others.

Prior to the advancement of media technology, rapid transit, and personal digital devices, prominent social narratives shaped different norms in various areas of culture. Lyotard (1984) used the term *grands récits*, meaning "big stories" or grand narratives. White (1987), an American historian, identified four master narratives in the West: Greek fatalism, Christian redemptionism, bourgeois progressivism, and Marxist utopianism. Since that time, as Lyotard wrote, these grand narratives have given way to *petits récits* or "little narratives." According to Lyotard, these shared perspectives are localized with no claim to universal truth status and are based on less widespread views of the world. A petite narrative would include various religions or the political idea of a representative democracy. Now, we find that petite narratives may also be falling away in favor of individualized perspectives or stories rooted in personal values.

Thus, when one person communicates with another person, the decision to act is situated within an increasingly individualized turn toward oneself. While grand narratives and petite narratives continue to inform our behavior, individual goals, emotions, and aspirations overwhelm them. Individuals increasingly foregrounded these goods in messages. Johannesen (1983) suggested that the "study of communication ethics" should include close examination of both "individual ethics and social ethics," insofar as ethics involve both our individual choices and the structures in place from society (p. 15). Moreover, as acknowledged by Arnett and Arneson (2014), "no single communication ethic" exists in the midst of postmodernity, further situating the need to historically, socially, and culturally evaluate ethics in communicative life (p. xi). Because ethics are culturally bound, we have seen a change in how one evaluates ethics in communication.

Evaluating Ethical Qualities in Messages

In the 2020s, we communicate against a common background of difference. A person can no longer assume that two people share predominantly the same values. The disconnect between what people value has important implications for ethics in communication.

When a person communicates, that person prioritizes what they value in their life, which Johannesen (1983) referred to as "a good." These "goods" become a primary influencer of a person's behavior and also offer fundamental criteria for making judgments in a situation. The good that a person promotes in a message informs the receiver about what the sender views as a priority in their life, aiding the receiver in determining how to interpret a message. What a person dubs as good directly invokes a value (personal or otherwise) that theoretically provides an ethical touchstone for communication with others. Yet, what is ethical for one person may not be ethical for another person.

When considering ethics, one can best think in degrees of ethicality. Instead of asking "Is that communication ethical or unethical?" we should instead ask the question, "How ethical is a given communicative behavior?" We do not view ethics as a prescription about what is right or wrong, but rather focus on critical thinking to discern the extent to which a message is ethical or unethical, evaluated against a standard held by the person who is interpreting a message.

A person begins to evaluate a message starting with what one has learned and previously interpreted to be "right" behavior. An understanding of what is "right" is informed by one's culture, family, the law, professional codes, religion, and so forth. Those elements of evaluation are then applied to a message to determine the degree of ethicality in that communication. Following that judgment, a person can decide how to respond in an ethical manner. Reflecting on a message requires active critical thinking: one must consider the communication context, type of relationship that exists between oneself and the other communicator/s, characteristics of each person, and the purpose, form, and content of the message.

Literature in the area of communication ethics includes scholarly investigations into all aspects of an interaction, including the process of communication between people, the tensions between the expression of ideas and interpretations, the sense of otherness of ideas and people, and the discourse used to shape the message (Cheney et al., 2010). Further, an emphasis on a single perspective or multiple perspectives in each area offers a starting point to begin to evaluate messages surrounding the changes ushered into society throughout 2020. An overview of this literature provides a sense of the complexity of issues related to ethics and communication.

Christians and Merrill (2009) identified different stances or perspectives from which one can interpret a message, such as an altruistic stance, egoistic stance, autonomy stance, legalistic stance, and communitarian stance. Johannesen et al. (2008) also offered perspectives for making a judgment about ethics in communication. Evaluation may begin with political, human nature, dialogical, situational, religious, utilitarian, feminist, intercultural, and multicultural perspectives. In addition, they addressed the use of formalized codes as another way to evaluate communication within a context. Each of these perspectives may be utilized to think through messages in interpersonal, small group, organizational, and public contexts. Cheney et al. (2010) reinforced the importance of considering a message from multiple perspectives or different angles respects the complexity of ethical thinking.

Ethical thinking recognizes that all communication messages take place within a cultural context, which cannot be excluded from the message evaluation (Christians & Traber, 1997; Johannesen et al., 2008). While some standards exist for normative behavior in different cultures, a person who evaluates the ethics of a message must consider the numerous forces that shape the social context, interaction, and human actors (Johannesen et al., 2008). In the interaction, a communicator has an opportunity to foreground a single aspect or multiple aspects of one's self or a social context. These reflections inform the evaluative process and also aid one's decision about how to ethically reply to a message. Critical thinking about ethics evaluates the interpreted message and choices about how to respond and the medium that the message is delivered through. We put nearly all of these considerations to work as we make sense of messages related to COVID-19 and the use of vaccines.

Ethics and Communication: Considering COVID-19 Messages

The interplay of ethics and communication is tied to the collapse of grand narratives as guiding frameworks and the rise of individual values as criteria for personal decision-making. The ability to step outside oneself and evaluate messages from multiple perspectives has eroded, and the dissemination of falsehoods are equally present alongside social truths. Messages related to COVID-19 have dramatically changed our lives. In this section, we share personal experiences along with a discussion of how messages may be evaluated for ethics from different perspectives.

In October 2019, an illness spread through a senior apartment building in Minnesota. The residents were very ill, and the disease kept spreading. The mother of one of Pat's friends died from the illness, along with several other people in different apartments in the building. The same month, Pat and her mom looked forward to visiting together over Thanksgiving. After receiving their flu shots to ensure that they could visit with one another, Pat's mom came down with an illness; she could not taste or smell and was very ill, confiding to Pat that she thought she would die. Although at the time undiagnosed, both elderly mothers likely contracted what would later become known as the COVID-19 virus.

More than a year of uncertainty and confusion has passed, and much remains to be discussed related to ethics, communication, and COVID-19. Messages about the virus and mutations of the virus, vaccine testing and inoculations, and returning to "normal" swirl around the news, organizations, and neighborhoods. Beginning with the initial reports of a pneumonia cluster in Wuhan on December 31, 2019 until the official proclamation of a COVID-19 pandemic by the World Health Organization on March 11, 2020 (World Health Organization,

2020), human communication surrounding the pandemic has been polarizing and often characterized by a high degree of fear and uncertainty.

Sarah was the mother of a young child at the onset of COVID-19. For her, the fear and uncertainty in messages around the virus translated into a "shelter-in-place" mentality, particularly as the United States began to issue emergency declarations and impose quarantine guidelines in one state after another. Her child did not leave the home, apart from walking in the park, and was denied the capacity to engage in and learn about human interaction and communication.

Many scholars acknowledge the ethical obligations of people when they communicate with others (Arneson, 2014; Arnett & Arneson, 2014). For instance, the importance of ethics has become increasingly apparent as various stakeholders distributed messages about the COVID-19 vaccine rollout across the United States. People interpreted messages in various ways, and the decision to obtain a vaccination has become a polarizing point of discourse. Thus, most human interaction over conflicting messages related to COVID-19 shifts into two dichotomous positions, resulting in communication patterns that do not unite ethics and communication. Two of the most prominent reasons that people cite for refusing the vaccine include the pausing of the Johnson & Johnson vaccine for links to deadly blood clots and fear and uncertainty regarding long-term effects of the vaccine (Lovelace Jr. & Breuninger, 2021; https://www.hopkinsmedicine.org/health/conditions-and-diseases/coronavirus/covid19-vaccine-hesitancy-12-things-you-need-to-know).

Evaluating Ethics in Communication about Vaccines

Stories abound on television news and digital platforms related to decisions to be inoculated with the COVID-19 vaccine (https://www.hopkinsmedicine.org/coronavirus/patient-stories/). While some people actively promote such a decision, other people offer comments against getting the vaccine. As we try to return to moving between private and public spheres with a sense of ease, organizations are now determining whether employees and members should be inoculated against the virus. Vaccination and virus-mitigation efforts help to inform other issues such as contact tracing, access to Personal Protective Equipment (PPE) for medical workers, and the advocacy of specific medicines that may prevent or minimize illness. We evaluate messages from different approaches.

While some messages advocate the efficacy and safety of the vaccine, other messages emphasize the health risks that may be associated with the vaccine. A person may seek to evaluate messages to determine the answer to a question such as: "*Do I have the right to refuse the vaccine, knowing that I may jeopardize the lives of others that I physically encounter?*"

Johannesen et al. (2008) explained the *utilitarian* approach evaluates messages by asking the question: Does the position being advocated "promote the greatest good for the greatest number with the least harm in the long run?" (pp. 93–94).

Christians (2007) extended this discussion, noting that in today's environment, utility as a principle "requires an assessment of an action's consequences only" (p. 115). According to Christians, from a utilitarian standpoint, utility is also individualized (p. 115). Thus, given the personal alternatives one has available to them, the answer would be that one should not refuse the vaccine.

From a *scientific* perspective, scientists have shared that the single shot J&J vaccine is 72% effective in the United States (Bai, 2021). The Moderna vaccine is 94.1% effective in preventing COVID-19 illness in people who had two inoculations (Center for Disease Control, 2021). The Pfizer vaccine is 95% effective in preventing symptomatic COVID-19 after two inoculations (Branswell, 2021). Importantly, the information provided by scientists "show that they [the vaccines] are safe and effective, and present less risk in comparison to COVID-19 infections" (Zahneis, 2021, April 23). In response to the question about refusing the vaccine, one needs to evaluate the statistics and determine how willing they are to potentially become ill.

A *legal* perspective would follow the culture's laws related to vaccination and what one can and cannot be "made" to do by the government. As Johannesen (1983) stated, a legal perspective essentially makes "legality and ethicality . . . synonymous" (p. 95). Therefore, according to Johannesen, one simply turns to "current laws and regulations" to determine the ethical nature of the communicative action (p. 95). One can legally refuse to take the vaccine. However, what is legal is not the same as what is ethical. Some legal behaviors are morally questionable. Johannesen noted that enforcing a behavior at the public level often comes from pressures outside of legislation—including cultural/social pressure. For example, a growing number of universities and colleges will require students and/or employees to be fully vaccinated prior to returning to on-campus education in the fall semester of 2021 (Zahneis, 2021). Drawing from a legal perspective, the pressures in this critical decision suggest that *communication* over standards should assist in the decision-making.

From a *political* perspective, ethics and communication assume that any political "system"—like a government—has embedded within that structure an "ideology" with "implicit and explicit set of values and procedures" (Johannesen, 1983, p. 23). Arnett et al. (2007) further explicated that a political perspective, or "democratic communication ethics," is driven by public argumentation (p. 156) and noted that "informed choice matters" (p. 157). This position assumes a basic rationality demonstrated by informed publics that debate with public and accurate knowledge. Jovanovic and Wood (2006) asserted that even in situations grounded in political approaches to ethics, ethics is a "communicative activity rooted in interaction, rather than a prescribed set of rules to guide behavior" (p. 387). Today, the divisive political environment in the United States has drawn attention to who wears masks, who has received their vaccine, etc. The growing narratives surrounding these decisions can draw forth labels from opposing political parties (i.e., "you must be a Democrat" or "you must be a Republican").

A *narrative* perspective would consider the various stories that people share. For example, Arnett et al. (2007) described this approach as a direct linkage between communication and the stories that "guide people and offer insights" (p. 162). The authors introduced *culture* as an "implicit story supported by a web of communicative practices that orchestrate communicative behavior by guiding and delimiting communicative possibilities for a people" (p. 162). Walter Fisher (1987) suggested that *stories* guide and offer structure while simultaneously addressing a rationality that guides decision-making. The Johns Hopkins Hospital has dedicated one of their webpages to "Patient Stories" (https://www.hopkins-medicine.org/coronavirus /patient-stories/). Currently, media see both positive and negative personal stories and experiences with vaccination. These stories have shaped individual responses and decision-making. News and media outlets, for example, can take on this call by reorienting itself to the task of encouraging Americans to receive their vaccine and countering other "narratives" that frame the vaccine as ineffective or problematic (Wen, 2021). In the midst of competing goods and unknown factors, American adults have relied upon the framing of all vaccination narratives to defend their decisions. However, when a person's values resonate with one of the stories, a person may gain ethical direction regarding whether or not to be vaccinated. Narratives function as a "public story [that] explains the way the world works and the meaning of human life, including what is good for humans to be and do" (Arnett et al., 2009, p. 27). Narratives, thus, are imbued with value that guide action in public and private lives.

These various perspectives and approaches to communication ethics offer insight into decision-making, critical thinking, and communication patterns that currently characterize the cultural and social landscape within the United States. The discourse around vaccination displays and marks related values and goods in a public context. Stakeholders utilize those values and goods for the purpose of evaluating messages, interactions with others, and narratives that shape the current discourse related to responses toward the pandemic. In the context of these various perspectives and backgrounds, we necessarily emphasize the other person in the interaction. How we choose to interact with that other, however, returns back to the interplay of ethics and communication in our current historical moment.

From Ethical Relativism to an Ethical Protonorm for Human Communication

The norms of each culture inform what counts as ethical within that culture. Herodotus (484–425 BC) initially introduced the idea of ethical relativism, noting that different cultures have different norms which members of the culture developed to identify acceptable and unacceptable forms of behavior (Empiricus, 1990). No culture-neutral standards exist by which we can refer to identify whether one society's ethics are superior to another. However, an unethical message can certainly be twisted to become ethical.

Christians and Traber (1997) identified an ethical protonorm for human communication. A protonorm is an ontological norm found to be present across cultures and rooted in our existence as human beings. Although cultures continually undergo change, Traber (1997) concluded that, to be with others, one must extend them dignity which is "grounded in a universal culture of respect for life, which in turn is based on core values from many different and specific understandings of human dignity" (p. 340). Traber used the term universal from the perspective of anthropology as a philosophical discipline: "We are in search of the ultimate and unconditional characteristics of human life from which the meaning of human actions can be derived" (p. 341). Traber contended that

> certain ethical protonorms—above all, truthtelling, commitment to justice, freedom in solidarity, and respect for human dignity—are validated as core values in communications in different cultures. . . . The universality of these values is beyond culture. It is rooted ontologically in the nature of human beings. (p. 341)

Traber associated ethics with communication that holds life-affirming qualities toward another person, rather than the construction of a message intended to advance oneself.

This situation calls forth the need to understand and respond to the growing number of ways that a communicator searches for and synthesizes information that informs both one's individual perspective and subsequent communication with others. Vaccine-hesitancy provides one example that exacerbated the problems of ethics and communication in an age experiencing high levels of misinformation and incivility. The year 2020 amplified the significant difficulties that many of us encountered in the midst of polarizing discourse, social unrest, and public events that called into question the understanding of the relationship between ethics and communication. In any attempt to justify a decision, however, one must always come back to a profound and necessary respect for the other person.

References

Arneson, P. (2014). *Communicative engagement and social liberation: Justice will be made*. Fairleigh Dickinson University Press.

Arnett, R. C., & Arneson, P. (Eds.). (2014). *Philosophy of communication ethics: Alterity and the other*. Fairleigh Dickinson University Press.

Arnett, R. C., Arneson, P., & Bell, L. M. (2007). Communication ethics: The dialogic turn. In P. Arneson (Ed.), *Explorations in communication ethics: Interviews with influential scholars in the field* (pp. 143–184). Peter Lang.

Arnett, R. C., Fritz, J. M. H., & Bell, L. M. (2009). *Communication ethics literacy: Dialogue and difference*. Sage.

Bai, N. (2021, March 16). *How effective is the Johnson & Johnson COVID-19 vaccine? Here's what you should know*. University of California San Francisco. https://www.ucsf.edu/

news/2021/03/420071/how-effective-johnson-johnson-covid-19-vaccine-heres-what-you-should-know.

Branswell, H. (2021, February 2). Comparing the Covid-19 vaccines developed by Pfizer, Moderna, and Johnson & Johnson. *Stat News*. https://www.statnews.com/2021/02/02/comparing-the-covid-19-vaccines-developed-by-pfizer-moderna-and-johnson-johnson/.

Center for Disease Control. (2021, May 27). *Moderna COVID-19 vaccine and safety*. https://www.cdc.gov/coronavirus/2019-ncov/vaccines/different-vaccines/Moderna.html\

Cheney, G., May, S., & Munshi, D. (Eds.). (2010). *The handbook of communication ethics*. Routledge.

Christians, C. G. (2007). Utilitarianism in media ethics and its discontents. *Journal of Mass Media Ethics, 22*(2&3), 113–131.

Christians, C. G., & Merrill, J. C. (Eds.). (2009). *Ethical communication: Moral stances in human dialogue*. University of Missouri Press.

Christians, C. G., & Traber, M. (Eds.). (1997). *Communication ethics and universal values*. SAGE.

Empiricus, S. (1990/Antiquity). *Outlines of pyrrhonism*. (R. G. Bury, Trans.). Prometheus.

Fisher, W. R. (1987). *Human communication as narration: Toward a philosophy of reason, value, and action*. University of South Carolina Press.

Johannesen, R. L. (1983). *Ethics in human communication*. Waveland Press. (Original work published 1975).

Johannesen, R. L., Valde, K. S., & Whedbee, K. E. (2008). *Ethics in human communication* (6th ed.). Waveland Press.

Jovanovic, S., & Wood, R. V. (2006). Communication ethics and ethical culture: A study of the ethics initiative in Denver City government. *Journal of Communication Research, 34*(4), 386–405.

Lovelace Jr., B., & Breuninger, K. (2021, April 13). Panicked patients call doctors as Covid vaccine hesitancy rises with J&J blood clot issue. *CNBC*. https://www.cnbc.com/2021/04/13/more-people-likely-wont-want-jjs-covid-vaccine-following-latest-issues-with-blood-clots.html

Lyotard, J. F. (1984). *The postmodern condition: A report on knowledge* (G. Bennington & B. Massumi, Trans.). University of Minnesota Press. (Original work published 1979).

Traber, M. (1997). Conclusion: An ethics of communication worthy of human beings. In C. G. Christians & M. Traber (Eds.), *Communication ethics and universal values* (pp. 327–343). SAGE.

Wen, L. S. (2021, April 20). The Covid-19 vaccines are an extraordinary success story. The media should tell it that way. *The Washington Post*. https://www.washingtonpost.com/opinions/2021/04/20/covid-19-vaccines-are-an-extraordinary-success-story-media-should-tell-it-that-way/

White, H. V. (1987). *The content of the form: Narrative discourse and historical representation*. Johns Hopkins University Press.

World Health Organization. (2020, April 27). Archived: WHO timeline—COVID-19. *World Health Organization*. https://www.who.int/news/item/27-04-2020-who-timeline—covid-19

Zahneis, M. (2021, April 23). A tipping point? Dozens of public colleges announce Covid-19 vaccine mandates. *The Chronicle of Higher Education*. https://www.chronicle.com/article/a-tipping-point-dozens-of-public-colleges-announce-covid-19-vaccine-mandates

8

RISK COMMUNICATION

Timothy L. Sellnow

Learning Objectives

Based on the context of COVID-19 and the discussion of risk dialogue provided in this chapter, students will be able to:

1. Distinguish between organized skepticism and unthinking cynicism in a risk communication context.
2. Discern the attributes of a realistic narrative in a risk communication context.

My COVID-19 Personal Narrative

Fourteen years before the first case of COVID-19 was identified in the U.S., I stood in the sprawling lobby of the Centers for Disease Control and Prevention (CDC) conference building in Atlanta, viewing pictures and captions of a display chronicling the devastation of the 1918 Spanish Flu Pandemic. I was between meetings to fulfill my responsibility as a CDC Pandemic Influenza Faculty member. The dozen or so academics involved were asked by Barbara Reynolds, CDC Crisis and Risk Communication Senior Advisor at the time, to collaborate with CDC officials in designing and conducting training sessions to help major cities across the U.S. develop plans for quickly responding to the risk of a rapidly spreading pandemic. I eventually helped to design and lead pandemic planning workshops in cities along the east coast of the U.S.

The CDC's 1918 display inspired memories of how the Spanish Flu had impacted my family. My grandfather served in and survived World War I. He and his family were devastated, however, by the loss of his 12-year-old sister, my great aunt, to Spanish Influenza the same year. For the rest of his life, three things sat

DOI: 10.4324/9781003220466-9

on my grandfather's bedside table—a reading lamp, his watch when he was not wearing it, and a black and white picture of his young sister standing in the photo with her long wavy hair flowing the length of her back. Seeing the picture as a child, I asked only once, who was in the picture? My grandmother said that the girl had died and that my grandfather kept the picture because he still loves her very much. Later, my father would tell me the entire distressing story of how my great aunt died and how many others in my family and community that I will never know had died of Spanish Influenza as well. The CDC's display fostered both sadness at recalling these memories and gratitude that I had been given an opportunity to honor the memory of those who had died by helping my generation prepare for such risks in the future. The training materials that we developed more than a decade ago have been revised frequently and are still available at no cost on the CDC's website (https://emergency.cdc.gov/cerc/resources/index.asp). In the risk communication courses that I taught over that period, we always discussed at length what happened in 1918 and the role risk communication can play in planning for and diminishing the impact of future pandemics.

As the COVID-19 pandemic swept through China, Asia, and Europe, I steadied myself with the realization that its arrival in the U.S. was inevitable. I was not, however, prepared to see officials from CDC, the Food and Drug Administration, and the World Health Organization lampooned by high-ranking government officials and political party leaders for their risk communication warnings about COVID-19. Much of the risk planning that we have taught consistently for decades requires a rapid response where messages advising strategies for self-protection are communicated clearly and consistently to all citizens in the U.S. I felt helpless as responses were delayed, and politicians denied medical science while asserting their own opinions on the likelihood that the crisis itself was an elaborate hoax propagated by those with dissimilar political views. I was equally dismayed by the over-reassurance that the virus was spread by fomites and that handwashing was key rather than masks covering the nose and mouth. Having studied risk communication in this context for so long, I knew that these attempts at denial and advisory miscues would have long-lasting effects. Many of the suggestions that we provided in pandemic planning and the related risk communication were not fully enacted until three months after the first cases of COVID-19 were observed in the U.S.

This chapter provides an overview of how skepticism and cynicism function in risk communication. Next, the role of skepticism and cynicism are applied to risk communication about COVID-19, particularly after vaccines were available. The chapter concludes with considerations of how the COVID 19 pandemic might influence future research in risk communication.

Related Concepts from Risk Communication Theory

Risk Communication, regardless of context, functions best when conducted as dialogue. The National Research Council (NRC), concerned by both the prevalence and ineffectiveness of linear risk communication where content experts set standards for public safety with no input from those at risk, proclaimed that risk communication must involve dialogue. The NRC argued that risk communication, when done properly, is an "interactive process of exchange of information and opinion among individuals, groups, and institutions" (1989, p. 21). Dialogue of this nature engages publics in informed discussion to "enlighten choices" about how to best respond to the most pressing risks they face (Heath, 2018, p. 40). This enlightenment is based, in part, on a healthy skepticism. Publics are encouraged to weigh the evidence and to reason their way to informed decisions about how to best protect themselves and the ones they love.

All forms of skepticism, however, are not necessarily productive. Krimsky (2007) distinguished between organized and disorganized skepticism. Organized skepticism is systematic in nature. Stakeholders apply credible standards to evidence as they strive to determine its merit. For instance, the peer-review process evaluates scientific evidence and authors acknowledge or avoid conflicts of interest. Such transparency in the research process is essential for organized skepticism. The value of organized skepticism is its inclusion of multiple voices, representing multiple perspectives, in the consideration of evidence and the related opportunities and constraints for enhancing personal and public safety.

Conversely, disorganized skepticism lacks such rigor. Because risk communication is often fraught with competing interests, the potential for bias, manipulation, and politicization of the risk messages is always present (Heath & Nathan, 1990). Rather than objective standards, disorganized skepticism employs partiality and fabrication of opposing evidence. Thus, disorganized skeptical claims can be amplified based on "unchecked, false or biased information" appearing unvetted on the Web and in social media networks (Krimsky, 2007, p. 160). Conspiracy theories based on fabricated evidence or information taken out of context comprise a form of disorganized skepticism. At best, according to Krimsky, skepticism can bring a dose of rigor to analyzing the scope and voracity of evidence and related risk recommendations. At worst, skepticism prioritizes prior beliefs and demotivates information processing as the pursuit of knowing "what is real" (de Boer et al., 2016, p. 1614).

Transparent public dialogue entails explaining evidence and its relevance to the risk at hand and welcoming questions as the primary means for overcoming bias and exposing manipulation. Without such transparency and interaction, however, disorganized skepticism can reach the level of what Arnett and Arneson (1999) called unthinking cynicism. Defensiveness, distrust, and resentment of opposing forces can create subgroups of a community that reject recommendations for reducing risk simply because they come from "the other side" or inflict a disruption to the comfort they derive from the routine patterns of the status quo.

Unthinking cynicism is not caused by conflict alone. Arnett and Arneson (1999) explained that risk communicators can foster unthinking cynicism through their own communication failures. Overpromising about the benefits of a risk reduction strategy or understating the potential for negative outcomes, anticipated or completely unanticipated, can diminish trust and inspire unthinking cynicism in disillusioned publics. For example, individuals in a neighborhood near where I once lived were told, before building their homes, their property was out of the major flood plain and highly unlikely to flood. Two decades later, the homes were damaged or destroyed in a devastating flood. Later, when community leaders asked these residents to accept a federal buyout for their property so that the community could build a dike to protect the city, many of these residents were cynical and combative. Several of these residents felt misled or manipulated and resisted the city's efforts to buy their homes for years. Simply put, the communication failures of the past created lasting cynicism in some of these residents.

To avoid communication mistakes that can foster unthinking cynicism, risk communicators should create a realistic narrative (Arnett & Arneson, 1999). Realistic narratives include an open and honest admission of the limitations that the community faces in responding to a high-level risk. Such narratives avoid over-reassuring publics and welcome a dialogue emphasizing organized skepticism. Realistic narratives include four readily identifiable attributes:

1. A realistic narrative passes the highest standards of organized skepticism.
2. The fears and concerns of individuals at risk are recognized and reflected in the narrative on an ongoing basis.
3. Realistic narratives translate evidence so that it is easily comprehended by the publics without specialized scientific training.
4. Realistic narratives include a clear explanation of both the benefits and potential failures of the plan.

When responsible risk communicators commit themselves to a realistic narrative, they simultaneously devote themselves to an ongoing dialogue where they openly and honestly respond to audience concerns by sharing what they know, what they do not know, and what they are doing to learn all they can about the risk.

COVID-19 through the Contrasting Perspectives of Skepticism and Cynicism

As someone who helped to develop a risk communication plan for creating a realistic narrative in response to a pandemic, I was dismayed to watch as high-ranking officials engaging in unthinking cynicism refuted attempts to share such a narrative about COVID-19. This cynicism resulted in repeated denials of the threat that COVID-19 posed for Americans (Baker, 2020). Unfortunately, the most predictable outcome of such cynicism is crisis denial, "defined operationally as claims challenging the authenticity of widely viewed crises by depicting them as hoaxes" (Sellnow et al., 2019, p. 122). Regardless of how much evidence is readily available, those engaged in crisis denial typically insist that what others believe constitutes a risk to their lives is nothing more than deception. Some who embraced this cynical view were so committed to crisis denial that even as they lay dying in intensive care beds, diagnosed with COVID-19, they remained defiant. An intensive care nurse in South Dakota describing some of her patients during a COVID-19 surge said despondently:

> I think the hardest thing to watch is that people are still looking for something else and a magic answer and they do not want to believe covid is real. . . . Their last dying words are, "This can't be happening. It's not real." (Villegas, 2020, para. 5–6)

Conspiracy theories also fortified COVID-19 cynicism about vaccines. As COVID-19 vaccines became widely available, conspiracy theories continued to thrive, despite being debunked by science. Some of these conspiracy theories, though believed, were completely preposterous. For example, some conspiracy theories claimed that the vaccine contains a micro-chip enabling global surveillance of individuals, that the vaccine changes a person's DNA, that a sizable and undisclosed number of people had already died after receiving the vaccine, and that the vaccine itself is the source of COVID-19 variants (McEvoy, 2021). Another popular conspiracy theory suggested that those who were vaccinated spread the virus through shedding, a rare occurrence in which someone receiving a vaccine created through a weakened form of the virus infects someone else with the weakened virus (Centers for Disease Control and Prevention, 2021). In the case of the COVID-19 vaccine, though, shedding could not occur because the ones used in the U.S. were created with a single gene from the virus, not with a weakened form of the live virus (Sweet, 2021). Despite clear and widely distributed evidence that these conspiracy theories were false, many took a cynical view and refused to be dissuaded (Fiore, 2021; Vakil, 2021).

A history of previous failures also stoked cynicism about COVID-19 vaccines. For example, Lewis (2021) reflected on how the CDC's recommendation that a vaccine for Swine Flu be administered broadly in 1976. The CDC feared that this strain of flu could become deadly for Americans. The vaccine was expediently created and administered. Persistent problems arose with the vaccine that were deadly to some individuals with health vulnerabilities. Public dismay was compounded by the fact that the anticipated outbreak did not occur even among those not vaccinated. Lewis (2021) explained that memories of such failures can fuel a lifetime of cynicism for some individuals. Cynicism also arose from those who claimed COVID-19 was not outside the realm of a normal flu season. They claimed doctors were blaming COVID-19 for deaths caused by other illnesses, such as typical flu and pneumonia, simply to exaggerate the reported number of deaths. In reality, the limitation on testing for COVID-19 early in the pandemic and the standard guidelines for determining cause of death meant that, at least early in the pandemic, officials likely underestimated the total number of deaths (Stellino, 2020).

Though cynicism captured many headlines and became a constant adversary to agencies such as WHO and CDC on social media, traditional and new media widely shared a realistic, evidence-based narrative which explained protective actions and offered transparent information about the COVID-19 vaccines. Initial claims that the disease was spread through fomites on surfaces rather than by particulates in the air resulted in confusion and frustration. Yet as more was known about how the disease spread and how masks could reduce this spread, the narrative adapted.

Public health officials acknowledged skepticism about the COVID-19 vaccines. As scientists first developed the vaccines, some expressed skepticism regarding the vaccines by emphasizing their preferred criteria for vaccination. For example, when asked their preferences before vaccines were available, Americans expressed an increased willingness to be vaccinated if the vaccine could be at least 90% effective, have low likelihood of even minor side effects, and be administered in a single dose (Motto, 2021). For skeptics, these conditions were not necessarily "deal-breakers." Rather, a vaccine's failure to meet these expectations required explanation by those advocating vaccinations. This explanation began with, first, listening to and acknowledging the concerns and unmet expectations and then explaining why some of the expectations could not be met. This combination of listening sincerely and generating an explanation addressing key concerns comprised the making of a realistic narrative. Public health officials hoped—both early in the vaccination process and in the later stages—that those skeptical of the vaccine would receive the information that they needed through this realistic narrative so that they could make informed decisions (Chou et al., 2020).

In the end, the number of vaccinations administered and the number of citizens willing to comply with such protective strategies as wearing a mask and remaining socially distanced provide the evidence by which the realistic narrative will be judged. Although little is certain in such risk communication outcomes, we can confidently assume that, had politically and socially influential people expressed less unthinking cynicism in their depiction of COVID-19, the number of people engaging in protective behaviors would have been higher and the number of American who died would have been lower.

How COVID-19 Could Shape the Study of Risk Communication

As a member of the CDC Pandemic Influenza Faculty, I was aware that a pandemic would bring about some degree of unthinking cynicism. I also knew that a pandemic would be economically harmful as businesses were either forced to close or as customers chose to avoid social contact. I further knew that families and children would suffer in many ways when schools were closed. Some children would miss important meals. Others missed out on services addressing their special needs. Many children simply would not learn as well in isolation as they would in a room together with their peers. Additionally, I worried about disruptions in the food supply chain and other essential services. As a nation, we were fortunate that, for at least one critical period during the pandemic, all states complied in limiting social contact. Many could not, however, accept the realistic narrative's explanation that the pandemic would linger for over a year and that one period of isolation would not eliminate or contain it.

Future research in risk communication must address this tendency for citizens to need to see progress or an end to the risk before one can be created. Many complied willingly with the risk narrative during early stages of the crisis but became less inclined to do so over time (Kam, 2020). We lack extensive research for understanding how risk tolerance changes in prolonged, high-risk settings. COVID-19 makes it clear that more work is needed to understand how a risk narrative can remain viable and realistic over an extended period.

As stated earlier, we know that cynicism draws sustaining power from many divisive issues unrelated to risk communication. Still, the ease with which so many Americans denied science in reference to COVID-19 is alarming. Risk communication relies on translating the best science and evidence available into a realistic and compelling narrative. The growing tendency to deny science warrants further study. If science loses its persuasive appeal for many Americans, what alternate form of testimony might be more appealing? If not, how can we rebuild confidence in science? Message design research in risk communication needs to explore these questions.

Finally, although we realized some degree of cynicism was inevitable, we did not fully anticipate the impact of political leaders engaging in crisis denial and helping to circulate conspiracy theories. How does a risk communicator respond to such authoritative challenges? If government agencies are censored, who can credibly fill this void by providing a realistic narrative that is well-documented and sensitive to audience's needs and concerns? Future research should consider this difficult challenge.

Conclusions

As I sat in a chair for my required recovery time having received my second COVID-19 vaccination, I reflected on my grandfather and the struggles that he endured in 1918. He fought in a war where many of his comrades were killed before their adult lives fully began. My grandfather's homecoming only intensified his grief when he lost a young sister, who he adored, to the pandemic. As he and the rest of his family, community, and country waited out the 1918 pandemic, they had no hope for a vaccine. Sitting in my chair, I felt nothing but gratitude for being fully vaccinated. And I hoped silently that my getting vaccinated, in some small but meaningful way, paid tribute to my grandfather and to all those who mourned the loss of loved ones in 1918. I also reflected on the fact that although we saw communication failures and complications that likely intensified cynicism about COVID-19, we also observed scientific collaboration at its best and the fortitude of many public health spokespersons who dedicated themselves to creating and sharing a realistic narrative that likely saved millions of lives.

References

Arnett, R. C., & Arneson, P. (1999). *Dialogic civility in a cynical age: Community, hope, and interpersonal relationships.* SUNY Press.

Baker. (2020, July 24). 'Mugged by reality:' Trump finds denial won't stop the pandemic. *New York Times.* https://www.nytimes.com/2020/07/24/us/politics/coronavirus-trump-denial.html

Centers for Disease Control and Prevention. (2021, June 23). Myths and facts about COVID-19 vaccines. *COVID-19.* https://www.cdc.gov/coronavirus/2019-ncov/vaccines/facts.html

Chou, W. S., Burgdorf, C. E., Gaysynsky, A., & Hunter, C. M. (2020). *COVID-19 vaccination communication: Applying behavioral and social science to address vaccine hesitancy and foster vaccine confidence.* National Institutes of Health. https://obssr.od.nih.gov/sites/obssr/files/inline-files/OBSSR_VaccineWhitePaper_FINAL_508.pdf

de Boer, J., Botzen, W. W., & Terpstra, T. (2016). Flood risk and climate change in the Rotterdam area, The Netherlands: Enhancing citizen's climate risk perceptions and prevention responses despite skepticism. *Regional Environmental Change, 16*(6), 1613–1622.

Fiore, K. (2021, April 29). The latest anti-vax myth: "Virus Shedding". *MedPage Today.* https://www.medpagetoday.com/special-reports/exclusives/92336

Heath, R. L. (2018). How fully functioning is communication engagement if society does not benefit? In K. A. Johnston & M. Taylor (Eds.), *The handbook of communication engagement* (pp. 33–48). Wiley Blackwell.

Heath, R. L., & Nathan, K. (1990). Public relations' role in risk communication: Information, rhetoric and power. *Public Relations Quarterly, 35*(4), 15–22.

Kam, K. (2020, July 21). Crisis fatigue: Are we emotionally overwhelmed? *WebMD.* https://www.webmd.com/lung/news/20200721/crisis-fatigue-are-we-emotionally-overwhelmed

Krimsky, S. (2007). Risk communication in the internet age: The rise of disorganized skepticism. *Environmental Hazards, 7*(2), 157–164.

Lewis, M. (2021). *The premonition: A pandemic story.* Norton.

McEvoy, J. (2021, June 3). Microchips, magnets and shedding: Here are 5 (debunked) Covid conspiracy theories spreading online. *Forbes.* https://www.forbes.com/sites/jemimamcevoy/2021/06/03/microchips-and-shedding-here-are-5-debunked-covid-vaccine-conspiracy-theories-spreading online/?sh=21d80fb726af

Motto, M. (2021, January 13). Americans have unrealistic expectations for a COVID-19 vaccine. *The Conversation.* https://theconversation.com/americans-have-unrealistic-expectations-for-a-covid-19-vaccine-152745

National Research Council. (1989). *Improving risk communication.* National Academy Press.

Sellnow, T. L., Parrish, A., & Semenas, L. (2019). From hoax as crisis to crisis as hoax: Fake news and information disorder as disruptions to the discourse of renewal. *Journal of International Crisis and Risk Communication Research, 2*(1), 122–142.

Stellino, M. (2020, June 28). Fact check: CDC did not add flu and pneumonia cases to its COVID-19 death count. *USA Today*. https://www.usatoday.com/story/news/factcheck/2020/06/28/fact-check-confusion-cdcs-covid-19-death-count/3254404001/

Sweet, J. (2021, May 7). What is "vaccine shedding"? Why there's absolutely zero chance of viral shedding from the COVID-19 vaccine. *Health*. https://www.health.com/condition/infectious-diseases/coronavirus/what-is-vaccine-shedding-covid

Vakil, C. (2021, June 13). Near 30% of Republicans say they won't get vaccinated: Poll. *The Hill*. https://thehill.com/policy/healthcare/558225-nearly-30-percent-of-republicans-say-they-wont-get-vaccinated-poll

Villegas, P. (2020, November 6). South Dakota nurse says many patients deny the coronavirus exists—right up until death. *Washington Post*. https://www.washingtonpost.com/health/2020/11/16/south-dakota-nurse-coronavirus-deniers/

SECTION II

Through Communication, We Relate to and Connect with Others and Our World

9

INTERPERSONAL COMMUNICATION

Kristina M. Scharp

Learning Objectives

After reading this chapter, you will be able to:

1. Identify key interpersonal communication concepts that people experienced during the events of 2020.
2. Apply key interpersonal communication theories to your own experiences during the 2020s and beyond.

Personal Narrative

As a professor, I specialize in Interpersonal Communication (IPC). It is probably not a surprise, then, that the largest class I teach at the University of Washington (UW) is Interpersonal. In fact, during the Winter Quarter 2020, I was teaching a 500-person IPC large lecture. I recognize that sitting in a large lecture class might not always be the most engaging college experience, so I strive to connect course concepts to everyday life and to teach my large lecture like a smaller class. This quarter had me particularly excited because, knowing how isolating the college experience can be and the ways all humans have a fundamental need for affection, I had assigned Dr. Kory Floyd's (2015) *The Loneliness Cure* as the only reading in class instead of a textbook. Little did my students know, Dr. Floyd had also agreed to fly from the University of Arizona to surprise my students and give a talk about the ways in which **affectionate communication** is beneficial for our physical, psychological, and relational health. Little did I know, preparing my students all quarter to combat loneliness might have been even more useful than I had anticipated, given the COVID-19 pandemic. Indeed, the same week that

DOI: 10.4324/9781003220466-11

Dr. Floyd made it to Seattle in the beginning of March, I had to cancel his in-person lecture and move my class online for the remainder of the quarter. Seattle was the first city in the U.S. to document cases of COVID-19, and everyone at UW was unsure of what to do and how COVID-19 would ultimately affect us. In preparing my students for Dr. Floyd's visit, I hope that they became better equipped to respond to the potential isolation and **relational distance** that they would experience in the next year.

As we all became more and more **uncertain** about the nature of the novel coronavirus, how it spreads, and its effects, I also became more uncertain about my own welfare, the safety of my parents, the health of my friends and colleagues, as well as what would happen in the world at large. I knew early on that, if I did not move quickly, I might not have a chance to get back to my parents who live across the country. Thus, in mid-March 2020, I packed up my car and drove with my dog, Holly, from Seattle, WA to New Jersey where I grew up with my parents, Barb and Bill (or as they much prefer to be called, mom and dad). There, I quarantined with my parents until August when I inevitably returned to Seattle to move because my lease was up. Yet, during our quarantine time together, many interpersonal communication concepts informed our interactions, often made more salient by the fact that we all are adults, and none of us could reasonably leave the house for any extended period without potentially endangering the other people living there. In many ways, I was in the same situation as my students who had to or chose to return home to live with their families. Together, we learned to **manage privacy boundaries** and **enact resilience processes** to build a new sense of normal in what felt like the most abnormal time.

While in NJ during the summer of 2020, I watched on television as Seattle and many other communities rose up in response to George Floyd's murder. The Black Lives Matter protest in Seattle led to the abandonment of the East Precinct in the Capitol Hill District, which turned into the Capitol Hill Occupied Protest (CHOP). Protesters and police were at a standoff, and thousands of people showed up to march for Black lives. I felt torn, being so far away from my community but also relieved that I could support my parents. Nevertheless, watching Seattle's response led to **difficult conversations** with friends and family about social justice and safety in the city that I call home. Complicated conversations about IPC scholarship and within the IPC division also arose as my IPC colleagues and I continuously try to (re)consider the generalizability of our research, the research methodology we employ, the populations we engage, and our own positionality as IPC scholars. I think it would be fair to say that we have some opportunities to make meaningful changes in the questions we ask and the goals of our research as it pertains to **marginalized and underrepresented populations and relationships**.

Thinking about the change that I wanted to contribute to in my community and my own scholarship, I returned to Seattle to move and welcome my first doctoral advisees to UW's graduate program. Concerned that my advisees would have a difficult time transitioning to an online graduate program, we all decided to form a bubble and quarantine together. This decision enabled us to conduct research meetings in-person and allowed us to spend time face-to-face. In particular, I hoped that I would be able to provide my advisees the **supportive communication** that they needed to thrive in their new graduate program. In reflecting on the Autumn of 2020, I also recognized the ways in which they supported me as well. In fact, despite being difficult in so many ways, 2020 reminded me of the strong community of friends, family, and colleagues who all did their best to lend a hand when they could despite being exhausted and scared themselves. In many ways, the pandemic reinforced the importance of interpersonal relationships and the opportunities that interpersonal communication scholars have to improve our everyday lives.

Application

Multiple IPC theories and literatures offer insight into my personal narrative and might easily be relatable to our experiences including (a) Affection Exchange Theory, (b) Uncertainty Management Theory, (c) Communication Privacy Management Theory, (d) Communication Theory of Resilience, and (e) Supportive Communication.

Affection Exchange Theory (Floyd, 2015; Floyd et al., 2021)

Affection comprises one of the big three interpersonal needs, in addition to inclusion and control (Schutz, 1996). We can think of affection as feeling warmth and fondness for another person; essentially, affection is liking someone else (Floyd et al., 2021). Even if we do not feel affection, we still can communicate it. Indeed, affectionate communication is any verbal or nonverbal message that conveys support, love, or fondness. As I mentioned earlier, Dr. Kory Floyd (2015) developed Affection Exchange Theory (AET). He argued that AET consists of five important propositions:

- **Proposition 1**: People have inborn need and capacity for affection.
- **Proposition 2**: Affection and affectionate communication are different concepts even though they often co-occur.
- **Proposition 3**: Affectionate communication helps people survive and reproduce.
- **Proposition 4**: People have different needs for affection and affectionate communication.
- **Proposition 5**: When people get too much or little affectionate communication, they experience adverse physiological outcomes and well-being.

As we move forward from the pandemic, affection and affectionate communication might play even more important roles as people learn to readjust from social distancing practices. We might also consider how we create routines and rituals to garner an optimal level of affection even when not face-to-face. For example, Floyd (2015) detailed six strategies for overcoming loneliness, including (a) being open to affection, (b) inviting/modeling the relationship you want, (c) recognizing affection in different forms, (d) nurturing multiple affectionate relationships, (e) avoiding toxic affection, and (f) balancing optimism and realism. As 2020 taught us, asking for and expressing affection can be challenging, but these strategies can be useful in overcoming loneliness and attaining an optimal level of desired affection. As pandemic restrictions are lifting, I am grateful for the recent visit I was able to make to Tucson to see Dr. Floyd.

Uncertainty Management Theory (Brashers, 2001; Hogan & Brashers, 2009)

Uncertainty comprises one of the most common feelings that we experienced during the pandemic. Uncertainty occurs "when details of situations are complex, unpredictable, or probabilistic; when information is unavailable or inconsistent; and when people feel insecure about their own state of knowledge or the state of knowledge in general" (Brashers, 2001, p. 478). When it comes to IPC, uncertainty can pervade our relationships making us question whether we want to be in a relationship, whether the other person wants to be in a relationship, and even the future of our relationships themselves (see relational uncertainty; Knobloch & Solomon, 1999). During 2020, individuals certainly could have felt uncertainty about the safety of friends and family members, how people behaved during the pandemic or protests, and/or deciding whether to get a vaccination. Hogan and Brashers (2009) argued that seven principles guide our management of uncertainty:

- **Principle 1**: Uncertainty has cognitive (i.e., thought) and affective (i.e., feeling) components.
- **Principle 2**: Uncertainty can have multiple sources.
- **Principle 3**: Information can have multiple sources.
- **Principle 4**: The relationship between uncertainty and information is not straightforward.
- **Principle 5**: People appraise uncertainty for its meaning.
- **Principle 6**: People might seek to reduce, maintain, or increase their uncertainty.
- **Principle 7**: When people acquire new information, they reappraise their uncertainty.

Perhaps two of the most useful principles of Uncertainty Management Theory (UMT) are numbers 6 and 7. Principle 6 reminds us that uncertainty is not always bad or unwanted. In some instances, uncertainty helps us retain hope or fosters creativity. For example, even though I was uncertain about whether the FDA would approve emergency vaccines, the possibility provided me with hope that we would eventually be able to reduce social distancing. If I were certain that all vaccine approvals would take multiple years, I might have been more depressed about the prospect of not seeing friends and family in person soon. Furthermore, reducing uncertainty by attaining new information can help with feelings of unease but, as Principle 7 reminds us, can also create new uncertainties. Thus, we should remember that managing uncertainty constitutes an ongoing process. During the last year, for instance, the more information I learned to reduce my uncertainty about how coronavirus affected people's bodies, the more uncertain I became about whether I was taking enough precautions to avoid it or what would happen to my parents if one of them contracted it.

Communication Privacy Management Theory (Petronio, 2013)

During quarantining with my parents, I felt a lot of empathy for my students who suddenly found themselves back at home with their families. When it comes to private information, Petronio (2013) contended that each of us owns our own private information. In this sense, people form personal boundaries around information belonging to them. As Petronio explained, this concept about private information ownership informs the first three tenets of communication privacy management theory (CPM): (a) privacy ownership, (b) privacy control, and (c) privacy turbulence. These three tenets illuminate the eight principles of CPM:

- **Principle 1**: People believe that they are the sole owners of their respective private information and thus, have the right to protect and share it.
- **Principle 2**: When original information owners share their information, recipients become authorized co-owners.
- **Principle 3**: Because people believe that they own their private information, they also believe they have the right to control it.
- **Principle 4**: People control information by creating privacy rules such as, "Don't tell anyone."
- **Principle 5**: Coordinating and negotiating privacy rules help to control post-disclosure.
- **Principle 6**: Coordination leads to a collective boundary shared by multiple people.
- **Principle 7**: People regulate collective boundaries by deciding who knows what and who can share information with others.
- **Principle 8**: Privacy regulation is unpredictable and results in anything from a disruption to a total breakdown.

Although I was not actively trying to keep information from my parents, which would make that information secret, I think it is fair to say that I did not want my parents knowing every detail of the conversations that I was having with my friends and colleagues while I was living in their home for five months. Thus, I kept some information to myself, but I also made my parents co-owners of other information by confiding it to them. As I think about the pandemic, I think about the important role of privacy management. For example, people's vaccination status might create turbulent conditions if someone asks another person to keep their status private but the information recipient thinks keeping the person's status secret could create health risks. In this regard, people should attend closely to privacy rule negotiation and develop clear expectations for information management.

Communication Theory of Resilience (Buzzanell, 2018)

Although scholars have often conceptualized resilience as a trait (Theiss, 2018), Buzzanell (2018) reconceptualized resilience to emphasize the ways in which it is constructed through communication processes that enhance a person's ability to create a new normal. Thus, when we are triggered, we can actively communicatively work on our own behalf to improve our situations. Specifically, as Buzzanell detailed, the Communication Theory of Resilience (CTR) has three components: (a) trigger events, (b) anticipatory and reactive resilience responses, and (c) five core processes:

- **Process 1**: Crafting normalcy
- **Process 2**: Foregrounding productive action while backgrounded negative feelings
- **Process 3**: Affirming identity anchors (i.e., important aspects of the self)
- **Process 4**: Maintaining and using communication networks
- **Process 5**: Putting alternative logics to work

According to Buzzanell (2018), an event or experience that disrupts our everyday life can trigger resilience. In 2020 alone, each of us might have experienced multiple triggers that required resilience. For example, some crafted normalcy by creating new routines and rituals that reflected the need for distancing and wearing a mask. Instead of dwelling on missed opportunities to hang out with friends in person (i.e., backgrounding negative emotions), some developed creative ways to socialize via technology (i.e., foregrounding productive action; Scharp et al., 2022). When it comes to affirming identity anchors, people focus on key aspects of themselves that help them remember what is meaningful. Personally, I sought activities to engage with my students even though I was no longer seeing them face-to-face. By holding "Ask K" forums, I reaffirmed my identity as an engaged teacher. Maintaining and using communication networks is a process whereby people rely on the people in their lives to provide supportive communication (see the next section). Another resilience practice entails putting alternative logics to work, such as trying to reassess a situation to envision it in a new light. From my own experience, crafting normalcy was a particularly useful strategy. To get exercise and establish routine, my parents and I committed to taking Holly to the park every morning and for a walk around the neighborhood in the evening.

Supportive Communication (MacGeorge et al., 2011)

Supportive communication can be any verbal or nonverbal message/behavior enacted to assist others when they are in need (MacGeorge et al., 2011). Six common types of supportive communication include

- **Type 1**: Emotional—offering comfort, concern, affection, intimacy
- **Type 2**: Esteem—reassuring someone of their worth or enhancing their self-esteem
- **Type 3**: Informational—providing advice, sharing information, offering guidance
- **Type 4**: Network—expressing connection, making introductions
- **Type 5**: Tangible—offering financial assistance, material goods, transportation, housing, or other services
- **Type 6**: Social presence—communicating support availability, letting others know that they can count on support

Notably, the extent or quality of social support depends on the perspective of the recipient, not the provider. Because social support takes so many forms, gaps can emerge between what people want and what others offer to them. For example, sometimes while quarantining, I became frustrated that I could not complete my work as fast as normal. Although my dad offered me advice (i.e., informational support) about how to be more efficient, what I really wanted was some tangible support in the form of quiet time to complete my work. Instead of remaining frustrated, however, I remembered that support gaps can be avoided if individuals directly ask for desired support instead of engaging in less-effective strategies such as hinting, crying, or sulking. Once I asked my parents for some quiet work time a couple hours a week, I was much more successful at completing my work. Yet, I also recognize that, with other types of problems, people might have reasons for not requesting help. Indeed, sometimes people feel bad asking for help because they feel like they should be able to solve their own problems. Other times, people are worried what others will think of them (Lim et al., 2013). We call these the intrapersonal and interpersonal costs of seeking supportive communication respectively. When it comes to my advisees, I try to explicitly ask them if there is anything I can do to support them and try to normalize their concerns.

The Direction of Interpersonal Communication

IPC, in general, is essential to helping making sense of what has happened and essential to moving forward. Indeed, IPC is the building block of building relationships, collaborating, and communally coping. Although many fruitful areas merit exploring, my journey through 2020 suggests three areas that might be particularly ripe for interpersonal communication scholars to apply and advance in addition to the theories detailed earlier: (a) relational distancing, (b) difficult conversations, and (c) marginalized and unrepresented experiences.

Turning Attention to Relational Distancing Processes (Scharp & Dorrance Hall, 2019)

IPC scholars tend to value and study "close" relationships (Scharp & Dorrance Hall, 2019). Yet 2020 taught that we cannot always maintain as close a relationship with others as we might like, given possible physical, emotional, and/or relational constraints on closeness. For some, the pandemic might have even given people the excuse to distance themselves from unhealthy relationships. For others, relational distance might have caused negative outcomes we cannot yet anticipate. Relational distance might take multiple forms but includes (a) pulling away from interpersonal relationships, (b) being pushed out of interpersonal relationships, (c) parting mutually, and (d) experiencing distance as a result of third-party interference (Scharp & Dorrance Hall, 2019). As a scholar dedicated to the study of relational distance, I also think about the ways that issues of racism, political differences, religious differences, and general differences in values might contribute to whether people choose to maintain certain relationships while limiting others. In the future, scholars should (re)consider the importance and role of closeness in interpersonal relationships and attend to the importance and role of distance. Better understanding relational distance could help better support people when they must make sense and cope with the inevitable ways they might experience relational distance throughout their lifetime (e.g., termination of an important relationship, homesickness, moving away, death of a loved one, etc.).

Turning Attention to Difficult Conversations

Difficult conversations are typically emotionally charged and foster uncertainty (Dorrance Hall & Scharp, 2020). Regardless of context or relationship type, respondents often rank sex as the number one taboo topic (Baxter & Wilmot, 1985). Yet, 2020 highlighted other topics that are becoming increasingly important to consider. For example, discussions about race can be difficult but essential in understanding racism, privilege, and stopping destructive patterns (Lingras, 2021). Discussing the end of life/death can also be a difficult conversation but have meaningful consequences. The pandemic might have also highlighted the need for people to discuss their finances in ways that they did not feel was important before. In some cases, people might also have to have difficult conversations about substance abuse and addiction. Regardless of the topic, IPC scholars have a tremendous opportunity to better understand how people can have these difficult conversations, what messages are meaningful and memorable, and what outcomes communicating might have on people's well-being, relationships, and communities at large. As such, communication theory and concepts could play an important role in understanding negotiating difficulty and difference.

Turning Attention to Marginalized and Underrepresented Experiences (Afifi & Cornejo, 2020)

Last, but in many ways the most important, IPC scholars need to turn their attention to marginalized populations and underrepresented experiences. Currently, IPC research is dominated by WEIRD populations: populations that are white, educated, industrialized, rich, and democratic (see Afifi & Cornejo, 2020). Attending to only WEIRD samples fails to capture what an experience is like for most people. IPC researchers have a tremendous opportunity to engage with communities, seek underrepresented experiences, and increase the potential about whom we can make claims. To do so, IPC researchers should consider expanding the epistemologies and methodologies they value, employ, and reward. For example, critical scholarship often conducted with qualitative methods necessarily interrogates issues of power, oppression, and emancipation. Interpretive scholarship also lends itself to illuminating experiences of less dominant voices. Post-positive scholars too can benefit from more representative samples to strengthen their claims of generalizability. Indeed, regardless of paradigmatic orientation, IPC scholarship can become more valuable when we include more perspectives.

References

Afifi, W. A., & Cornejo, M. (2020). #CommSoWEIRD: The question of sample representativeness in interpersonal communication research. In M. L. Doerfel & J. L. Gibbs (Eds.), *Organizing inclusion: Moving diversity from demographics to communication processes* (pp. 238–259). Routledge.

Baxter, L. A., & Wilmot, W. W. (1985). Taboo topics in close relationships. *Journal of Social and Personal Relationships, 2*(3), 253–269. https://doi.org/10.1177%2F0265407585023002

Brashers, D. E. (2001). Communication and uncertainty management. *Journal of Communication, 51*(3), 477–497. https://doi.org/10.1111/j.1460-2466.2001.tb02892.x

Buzzanell, P. (2018). Communication theory of resilience: Enacting adaptive-transformative processes when families experience loss and disruption. In D. O. Braithwaite, E. A. Suter, & K. Floyd (Eds.), *Engaging theories in family communication* (2nd ed., pp. 98–109). Routledge.

Dorrance Hall, E., & Scharp, K. M. (2020). *Communication in family contexts: Applying theories and processes to family relationships.* Wiley-Blackwell.

Floyd, K. (2015). *The loneliness cure: Six strategies for finding real connections in your life.* Adams Media.

Floyd, K., Hesse, C., & Generous, M. A. (2021). Affection exchange theory: A bio-evolutionary look at affectionate communication. In D. O. Braithwaite & P. Schrodt (Eds.), *Engaging theories in interpersonal communication* (3rd ed., pp. 27–38). Routledge.

Hogan, T. P., & Brashers, D. E. (2009). The theory of communication and uncertainty management: Implications from the wider realm of information behavior. In W. Afifi & T. Afifi (Eds.), *Handbook of uncertainty and information regulation* (pp. 45–66). Routledge.

Knobloch, L. K., & Solomon, D. H. (1999). Measuring the sources and content of relational uncertainty. *Communication Studies, 50*(4), 261–278. https://doi.org/10.1080/10510979909388499

Lim, V. K. G., Teo, T. S. H., & Zhao, X. (2013). Psychological costs of support seeking and choice of communication channel. *Behaviour & Information Technology, 32*(2), 132–146. https://doi.org/10.1080/0144929X.2010.518248

Lingras, K. A. (2021). Talking with children about racism. *Journal of Health Service Psychology, 47*(1), 9–16. https://doi.org/10.1007/s42843-021-00027-4

MacGeorge, E. L., Feng, B., & Burleson, B. R. (2011). Supportive communication. In M. L. Knapp & J. A. Daly (Eds.), *The SAGE handbook of interpersonal communication* (4th ed., pp. 317–354). Sage.

Petronio, S. (2013). Brief status report on communication privacy management theory. *Journal of Family Communication, 13*(1), 6–14. https://doi.org/10.1080/15267431.2013.743426

Scharp, K. M., & Dorrance Hall, E. (2019). Reconsidering family closeness: A review and call for research on family distancing. *Journal of Family Communication, 19*(1), 1–14. https://doi.org/10.1080/15267431.2018.1544563

Scharp, K. M., Wang, T. R., & Wolfe, B. H. (2022). Communicative resilience of first-generation college students during the COVID-19 pandemic. *Human Communication Research, 48*(1), 1–30. https://doi.org/10.1093/hcr/hqab018

Schutz, W. C. (1996). *The interpersonal underworld.* Science and Behavior Books.

Theiss, J. A. (2018). Family communication and resilience. *Journal of Applied Communication Research, 46*(1), 10–13. https://doi.org/10.1080/00909882.2018.1426706

10

GROUP COMMUNICATION IN THE 2020s

Rethinking Identity, Managing Shifting Boundaries, and Designing Dialogic Conversations

Laura W. Black

Learning Objectives

1. Groups play an important role in our lives, and group membership shapes our identities. Group communication theory highlights that we are members of multiple groups, and those groups relate to each other within a context.
2. Communication between different groups can be difficult and is strongly influenced by power and politics.
3. Groups have norms and typical communication patterns that shape how well members maintain relationships, manage conflicts, make decisions, and accomplish tasks. Disrupting those patterns can be very difficult for groups.
4. Technology, group facilitation, and attention to diversity can help groups engage in ethical and productive intercultural dialogue.

Introduction

Groups comprise a centrally important part of our everyday lives. Our close personal lives involve families and friend groups. For many of us, work involves collaborating in teams. Our social lives involve groups ranging from social clubs, volunteer groups, sport teams, religious groups, or groups associated with activities or causes we believe in. We communicate with these groups face-to-face and through technologies, and some of our groups might exist solely online. We also belong to larger identity groups related to our background and heritage, and our membership in those social and cultural identity groups can provide us with a sense of connection to others (Abrams & Hogg, 2001; Hogg et al., 2004). I believe that we live our lives in relation to others. We build our sense of who we are through the groups with which we affiliate, and we develop ideas about other

DOI: 10.4324/9781003220466-12

people based on their connection to groups. The way we communicate within and between groups is of the utmost importance for our quality of life and the future of our communities, workplaces, and nations (Frantell et al., 2019).

In the year 2020, group life took center stage. As the COVID-19 pandemic grew, we became isolated through quarantine. We lost access to many of the groups that were previously part of our life (school, sports, work, friends, social networks), and those fortunate enough not to be completely alone became sequestered with a select small group, such as our family or roommates. This disruption meant that we may have had the potential for intense interactions with a few people in our "pods," but we lost the meaningful, important larger connections with other groups. We used technology to communicate across groups to both get our work done and try to maintain some of the social cohesion we missed from in-person interaction, and the unfolding political situations related to COVID, racial justice, and a highly contested U.S. Presidential election highlighted our divisions and group identities.

In this chapter, I share some of my experiences in 2020 and highlight some group communication theories and concepts. Rather than presenting the narrative and concepts as separate sections, I have chosen to weave them together to illustrate how different aspects of group scholarship can be useful in understanding the events of 2020 and the likely situations and experiences of the coming years. The chapter concludes with a reflection on how 2020 can shift the directions of group communication scholarship for the future.

Group Communication in the Time of COVID

The year 2020 disrupted our lives and forced us to shift the way we work, attend school, and communicate with each another. Simultaneously, it highlighted how centrally important that groups are to our lives. Below, I share two personal narratives of my own life in 2020 and highlight the connection between these experiences and core concepts from the field of group communication.

Personal Experience 1: Disruption of Work, Family, and Friendship Groups

The bona fide group perspective highlights that groups are embedded in a context, are interconnected with other groups, and have fluid and permeable boundaries (Beck et al., 2016; Putnam & Stohl, 1990, 1996). Thus, it is normal for people to be members of multiple groups, for group membership to shift over time, and for the communication within a group to be impacted by changes in the surrounding context. The COVID-19 pandemic created major changes in our social environment, which impacted the context for our groups, the way we communicated within groups, and our awareness of the boundaries of our group membership. I experienced these challenges in both my work and family domains.

In the spring of 2020, my personal world shifted enormously. Like other college professors and teachers, I completed the academic year with a great deal of scrambling, switching from in-person classes to online learning and meetings. I knew that my students did not all have adequate internet access and that some were going home to unhealthy or unsupportive environments. I worked hard to stay personally connected to my students and help them succeed, and I felt helpless when many of them struggled and stopped responding to class assignments and emails.

At home, we rearranged our living space so we could find good workspaces for two adults and two high schoolers, who were all now at home together all the time. Quarantine meant that we spent a lot of time together as a family, which held potential for both increased closeness and interpersonal conflict. Relational communication is critically important for groups (Keyton & Beck, 2009). Not only does it create and maintain a supportive group climate but it also helps groups accomplish their tasks. So, despite the stresses we experienced with the pandemic, we tried to be open with each other, listen well, and communicate supportively in our family.

As a group scholar, I know how important peer groups are, especially for youth (SunWolf, 2008). Like many other families, we struggled to figure out how the kids could maintain a safe "pod" or small group of friends who they could still see face-to-face. I missed being with my own friends and engaging in the social and community groups that were important to me, and I wondered when, if ever, I would be able to be together with my extended family again. Like many people, we began doing regular Zoom calls with extended family and friend groups, trying to maintain a sense of connection despite all the uncertainty we were experiencing.

Eventually, we came to terms with the lack of meaningful high school rituals for my daughter, who did not have a senior prom, a senior season as a track athlete, or an in-person graduation to mark her completion of high school. The list of activities that my kids did online grew to include summer camps, music lessons, dance classes, game/movie nights with friends, and virtual internships. My oldest had a virtual orientation to college, and she came to understand that her first year of college would likely also be online. It was challenging to adjust to doing so much of our lives online, but, eventually, we became accustomed to it. Like many others, we improved both the task and relational skills in our online groups as the pandemic stretched on (Klonek et al., 2021).

Personal Experience 2: Polarization, Collaboration, and Diversity in Groups

Although my personal experience described earlier was disruptive and unsettling, it actually became a relatively stable background for much more challenging group-related interactions. In 2020, groups dominated our social worlds and shaped how we viewed politics, the pandemic, and each other. Although political divisiveness has been growing in the U.S. for over a decade (Pew Research

Center, 2014), the pandemic exacerbated the divisions between varied ideological groups (Dimmock, 2021). The algorithms undergirding social media sites and search engines meant that people tended to see information online that confirmed their beliefs and created filter bubbles and echo chambers. Liberals and conservatives got distinct news that presented very different information. Online misinformation grew rampant, and people's views on things like mask mandates, vaccine hesitancy, social distancing, school closings, and so on became clearly mitigated by their group membership.

In May 2020, we witnessed the rapid rise of Black Lives Matter movement, instigated by the violent, widely viewed murder of George Floyd, followed by the shooting of Breanna Taylor and violence against many other Black Americans. Around the U.S., thousands of people took to the streets in protest (Buchanan et al., 2020; Oppel et al., 2021; Silverstein, 2021). The movement grew through people organizing on social media and taking to the streets in groups, with teens and young adults organizing many local protests. My own group research focuses on public dialogue, storytelling, and communication across difference (Black, 2008, 2020), and I was deeply moved by these events. As I engaged in professional and community-based work, I spent a lot of time reflecting on how people's participation in these protests was connected to their group memberships and identities.

I have worked with the local Racial Equity Coalition for several years to support local social justice initiatives and bring anti-racism training to our small, rural community (https://athensfoundation.org/racial-equity-coalition-of-athens/). This coalition consists of community members, public officials, and leaders from educational, legal, nonprofit, healthcare, and activist organizations. As a group that includes a diverse range of people committed to inclusion, we work on developing communication processes that are open, respectful, and centered on learning from people with differing experiences, backgrounds, and perspectives. Our work seeks to change political, health, and educational systems that marginalize or disenfranchise people of color in our community.

Over the years, we had held interracial dialogue sessions and diversity trainings for organizations and community groups. Like other organizations that offer intergroup dialogue (Frantell et al., 2019; Norander & Galanes, 2014), we carefully designed the meetings to promote relationship building, listening, and self-reflection about difference and prejudice. Those meetings were both challenging and emotionally rewarding, and, as leaders, we developed skills in designing and facilitating these meaningful in-person groups.

The surging energy around the Black Lives Matter movement galvanized our work, yet we wrestled with the challenges of 2020. We wondered: How do we keep doing our collaborative work in the time of COVID? How should our group work in ways that acknowledge the differential access to healthcare, technology, and social support for people of color in our community? How should our community respond to Black Lives Matter movement? Is it possible to lead meaningful conversations about racism, politics, policing, education, and community in times like this? It has to be—how can we NOT act in times like this? Yet what do we do and how do we do it safely?

I was deeply involved with one of the coalition's projects to offer an in-depth workshop on facilitating conversations about race and racism. Initially, we planned to host a two-day workshop of intense in-person work, both learning about group processes and discussing ideas related to diversity, inclusion, and anti-racism. As it became clear that we need to shift our plans to offer the workshop virtually, we made a few choices that pertain directly to group communication research and practice.

Honoring Diversity through Group Membership and Norms

First, the Racial Equity Coalition remained very mindful about the diversity of group membership, beginning with ensuring that a racially diverse team planned the event. Our workshop planning team was already in place before the pandemic, but I mention it here because we intentionally chose to institute diverse leadership so that our practices mirrored the mission of the workshop. Additionally, we made a commitment that we would only offer the workshop if we could ensure that at least 50% of the participants were non-white. Now, I live in a small college town (Athens, Ohio) that is overwhelmingly white. The 2018 census notes that Athens is 82% Caucasian, with the next largest racial identity groups being Asian (6%), Black (5%), and Multiracial (3%) (Data USA, 2021) The presence of Ohio University influences city demographics, making it more racially diverse than our surrounding county, which is 91% Caucasian (United States Census Bureau, n.d.).

Given this context, committing to having a conversation where white people made up less than 50% of the participants seemed very daunting to me. Yet, we took this stand on diversity because, as the Black members of our planning team noted, the voices of white liberals dominate conversations about race in our community. People of color who regularly participated in these conversations were tired of being in the minority and feeling compelled to "say the same things over and over" to a disbelieving group of white "allies" who would sympathize, but not make any real changes. As a planning team, we wanted to break that pattern. Once we set this 50% goal, it took a great deal of intentional recruiting and organizing work, but we succeeded in meeting that benchmark, and it was very meaningful for the people who participated in the sessions.

These local experiences mirror research findings from group communication and diversity. Research emphasizes that diverse groups can make better decisions, be more creative, and generally outperform homogenous groups, but these outcomes are only possible when group norms honor diversity and embrace inclusion (McLeod et al., 1996; Oetzel, 2002; Zheng & Wei, 2018). Often groups are divided by what group scholars call fault lines, the "hypothetical dividing lines splitting a group into homogenous subgroups based on the distribution of demographic attributes" (Meyer et al., 2011, p. 257). Such subgroups hinder effective group communication, exacerbate conflict, and marginalize minority group members. Groups can avoid being stymied by such fault lines when they have leaders who value diversity (Schölmerich et al., 2016) and norms that encourage learning from mistakes (Rupert et al., 2019). Diverse groups are also more successful when group members develop a deeper understanding of power dynamics (Norander & Galanes, 2014) and good intercultural communication skills (Oetzel, 2002; Xu et al., 2019; Zheng & Wei, 2018).

Group research also emphasizes that dialogue sessions can be designed carefully to help group members develop these abilities (Barge & Andreas, 2013). As we designed the workshops, we carefully structured the activities to amplify the voices of people of color. We explicitly told workshop participants that we were committed to having at least half of the participants be people of color. We shared material with our participants beforehand that described our workshop goals and our proposed guidelines for how we hoped to communicate together. One of the first workshop sessions asked participants to brainstorm ideas about projects to promote racial equity in our community and present them to the group for larger discussion. As a planning team, we made a choice to ensure that the first round of suggestions only came from people of color. This commitment meant introducing a constraint in the group and structuring the interaction such that white participants had to start from a position of listening, rather than providing the first ideas for the group. It also meant that facilitators were patient with long silences (even when some participants seemed uncomfortable waiting) and, at times, allowed Black participants to share lengthy narratives about their frustrating experiences in our community.

We made these strategic decisions because we recognize that *groups follow recognizable communication patterns* and changing how the group is designed can interrupt those patterns (Aakhus, 2007; Barbour et al., 2018). For example, groups tend to latch on to the first few ideas that are presented and can form a quick false consensus or be swayed by the social influence of powerful group members (Janis, 1972). Additionally, even when group members have unique and important information, they tend to repeat things that the group already knows rather than share information that could be seen as contradictory (Wittenbaum et al., 2004). These patterns are well established in group research and highlight challenges to effective and ethical group processes. Group research on decision making (Pilny et al., 2017), deliberation (Gastil, 2008), and dialogue (Barge & Andreas, 2013; Black & Wiederhold, 2014) provides models for communication processes that help groups avoid such pitfalls.

These research findings resonate with our planning team's own experiences in groups. We had seen that even well-intentioned group members tend to discount ideas that vary too much from the group's early agreement, and often those divergent ideas come from minoritized group members such as people of color, women, or members of the LGBTQ community. So, we intentionally created and facilitated communication processes that pushed back against these widely held group norms. Throughout the workshop, the facilitators explicitly articulated about our reasons for these choices, and we provided support (and sometimes constraints) for participants as needed.

Designing Online Processes for Group Dialogue

Although we had initially hoped that our meetings would be held in person, we quickly recognized the benefits of meeting virtually. The online modality enabled us to include participants from a wide range of places in the county who otherwise may not have traveled to Athens for a two-day workshop, and it provided us with the flexibility to break the workshop into four evening sessions, which took place over several weeks. As the planning team designed our workshops, we sought out and embraced aspects of technology that would maximize the feelings of co-presence and community. These workshops were playful, engaging, and creative. As I participated, I chuckled by how different they felt from any online meetings that I had attended at the university.

Before the workshops began, we asked people to send photos of places or activities in the community that were meaningful to them, and we integrated those photos into our opening session. Each session involved music, art, and opportunities for light-hearted social interactions. We incorporated standard elements of video conferencing, such as slide presentations and breakout room discussions, and participants engaged using Zoom features like chat, annotation, reactions, and polls. One of the design team members managed the technology in each session so that we could maintain engagement and collaboration across all of these different modalities. Finally, we made sure that membership in the breakout groups shifted over time, so participants had opportunities to interact with lots of different people during the workshop. As planning team members, we joined different small groups to help facilitate conversations, and we used online forms and collaborative documents to help group members capture aspects of their conversations.

We made all of these design choices to try to maximize the effectiveness of the technology to help our group reach its goals, which in this case involved building community, learning, and planning actions. Group communication research shows that virtual teams and online groups can struggle to maintain community and engagement, especially if they do not have previously established relationships. However, technologies offer affordances and groups can use technological features to promote good communication processes (Handke et al., 2020; Poole & Zhang, 2005). For instance, meetings that use multiple modalities, like the ones we designed, can allow groups to engage in synchronous video-based conversations while also capturing ideas in collaborative documents or via the chat. Technology minimizes the need for travel, which can promote diversity, accessibility, and participation. Finally, online meetings can be designed to foreground interpersonal communication, rather than communication based on identity categories (Wang et al., 2009), which could mitigate some of the challenges faced by diverse groups, such as limited information sharing, tokenization, or minimizing the input of members of marginalized groups.

Conclusion

As I reflect on my experiences in 2020, I remain convinced that group communication is critically important to how we live our lives. Membership in groups shapes our identities, and the way we communicate within and between groups has a meaningful impact on our ability to function as a society (Frantell et al., 2019). I do not think we can go back to the "normal" of pre-2020 life, nor should we. Instead, I believe we should look ahead to acknowledge both the constraints and the possibilities of our current times.

We live in a time of interconnection and fluidity, where people can work, socialize, and organize remotely. Technology offers incredible possibility for connection with others from a wide range of groups around the world. However, we should also be mindful of the constraints—physical isolation can tie us to our most immediate group identities, and, in a polarized political climate, such isolation can fuel divisiveness, stereotyping, and prejudice (Frantell et al., 2019). As people live in an increasingly diverse society, we should acknowledge the fault lines that divide us and hold the potential to polarize groups against one another. Group membership is very powerful, and I urge us to be mindful about how membership shapes the way we see the world and each other. We should be careful not to unreflectively adopt the opinions and beliefs of those in our most immediate surroundings and risk closing our group boundary to dissenting perspectives. We should also be careful not to exclude or trivialize the positions of people whose identities and group memberships are different from our own. Taking a group communication perspective can allow us to see that intergroup dialogue is ethically imperative (Hogg et al., 2004), and the way in which we design those dialogues can make a huge difference in the outcomes (Barge & Andreas, 2013; McLeod et al., 1996).

Group research and practice can also show us that online groups are not inferior to face-to-face groups, but they present different constraints and opportunities. As we do more multi-modal work and engage in distributed, virtual work, we realize that online meetings require some different communication and leadership skills (Newman & Ford, 2021). This distinction is already having a major impact on group practice in organizations and communities as people experiment with different technologies and interaction designs to promote engaging, productive online meetings (Karl et al., 2021; Klonek et al., 2021).

In the 2020s, I believe group scholars need to become more comfortable with ambiguity and foreground the value tensions faced by groups. On the one hand, groups crave stability, collaboration, and some level of agreement or harmony. On the other hand, group life inherently involves conflict, difference, and multivocality. Group research has sometimes been guilty of privileging stability, consensus, and decision quality over messiness, dissensus, and disagreement (Emich et al., 2020; Vásquez & Kuhn, 2019). Now is the time for group scholars to take a more nuanced and multivocal approach to our scholarship. Group research has become increasingly interdisciplinary over the past few decades, as group communication scholars collaborate with psychologists, management scholars, and others who study teams. As we look to the future, I believe that we need to continue to recognize the interconnection between traditional group research and the scholarship in fields like intergroup and intercultural communication.

The complex problems that we confront in the 2020s and beyond require nuanced understandings of the complexity of group membership, group-based identities, communication practices, relationships, power, and structure. To really address social issues like global health inequities, systemic racism, climate change, and other wicked problems, we need to design and facilitate ethical, engaging, and productive group interaction involving a wide range of stakeholders (Carcasson & Sprain, 2016). Group scholars should be part of the solutions, but, to do so effectively, requires a collaborative and interdisciplinary effort.

References

Aakhus, M. (2007). Communication as design. *Communication Monographs, 74,* 112–117. https://doi.org/10.1080/03637750701196383

Abrams, D., & Hogg, M. A. (2001). Collective identity: Group membership and self-conception. In M. A. Hogg & R. S. Tindale (Eds.), *Blackwell handbook of social psychology: Group processes* (pp. 425–460). Blackwell.

Barbour, J. B., Gill, R., & Barge, J. K. (2018). Organizational communication design logics: A theory of communicative intervention and collective communication design. *Communication Theory, 28,* 332–353. https://doi.org/10.1093/ct/qtx005

Barge, J. K., & Andreas, D. (2013). Communication, conflict, and the design of dialogic conversations. In J. Oetzel & S. Ting-Toomey (Eds.), *The SAGE handbook of conflict management* (2nd ed., pp. 609–634). SAGE.

Beck, S. J., Bourdeaux, R., DiTunnariello, N., & Paskewitz, E. A. (2016). A review and technological consideration of the Bona Fide Group Perspective. *Small Group Research, 47,* 655–691. https://doi.org/10.1177/1046496416665703

Black, L. W. (2008). Deliberation, storytelling, and dialogic moments. *Communication Theory, 18,* 93–116. https://doi.org/10.1111/j.1468-2885.2007.00315.x

Black, L. W. (2020). Catalyzing deliberation: How engaged scholarship helped surface community values and transform conflict in local school facilities planning. In P. Kellett, S. Connaughton, & G. Cheney (Eds.), *Transforming conflict and building peace: Community engagement strategies for communication scholarship and practice* (pp. 35–58). Peter Lang Publishers.

Black, L. W., & Wiederhold, A. (2014). Discursive strategies of civil disagreement in public dialogue groups. *Journal of Applied Communication Research, 42,* 285–306. https://doi.org/10.1080/00909882.2014.911938

Buchanan, L., Bui, Q., & Patel, J. K. (2020, July 3). Black Lives Matter may be the largest movement in U.S. history. *New York Times.* https://www.nytimes.com/interactive/2020/07/03/us/george-floyd-protests-crowd-size.html

Carcasson, M., & Sprain, L. (2016). Beyond problem solving: Reconceptualizing the work of public deliberation as deliberative inquiry. *Communication Theory, 26,* 41–63. https://doi.org/10.1111/comt.12055

Data USA. (2021). *Athens, OH: Diversity.* https://datausa.io/profile/geo/athens-oh#demographics

Dimmock, M. (2021, March 29). America is exceptional in its political divide: The pandemic has revealed how pervasive the divide in American politics is relative to other nations. *Pew Trust Magazine.* https://www.pewtrusts.org/en/trust/archive/winter-2021/america-is-exceptional-in-its-political-divide

Emich, K. J., Kumar, S., Lu, L., Norder, K., & Pandey, N. (2020). Mapping 50 years of small group research through Small Group Research. *Small Group Research, 51,* 659–699. https://doi.org/10.1177/1046496420934541

Frantell, K. A., Miles, J. R., & Ruwe, A. M. (2019). Intergroup dialogue: A review of recent empirical research and its implications for research and practice. *Small Group Research, 50,* 654–695. https://doi.org/10.1177/1046496419835923

Gastil, J. (2008). *Political communication and deliberation.* SAGE.

Handke, L., Klonek, F. E., Parker, S. K., & Kauffeld, S. (2020). Interactive effects of team virtuality and work design on team functioning. *Small Group Research, 51,* 3–47. https://doi.org/10.1177/1046496419863490

Hogg, M. A., Abrams, D., Otten, S., & Hinkle, S. (2004). The Social Identity perspective: Intergroup relations, self-conception, and small groups. *Small Group Research, 35,* 246–276. https://doi.org/10.1177/1046496404263424

Janis, I. L. (1972). *Victims of Groupthink: A psychological study of foreign-policy decisions and fiascoes.* Houghton Mifflin.

Karl, K. A., Peluchette, J. V., & Aghakhani, N. (2021). Virtual work meetings during the COVID-19 pandemic: The good, bad, and ugly. *Small Group Research,* OnlineFirst Publication. https://doi.org/10.1177/10464964211015286

Keyton, J., & Beck, S. J. (2009). The influential role of relational messages in group interaction. *Group Dynamics: Theory, Research, and Practice, 13*(1), 14–30. https://doi.org/10.1037/a0013495

Klonek, F. E., Kanse, L., Wee, S., Runneboom, C., & Parker, S. K. (2021). Did the COVID-19 lock-down make us better at working in virtual teams? *Small Group Research.* OnlineFirst Publication. https://doi.org/10.1177/10464964211008991

McLeod, P. L., Lobel, S. A., & Cox, T. H. Jr. (1996). Ethnic diversity and creativity in small groups. *Small Group Research, 27,* 248–264. https://doi.org/10.1177/1046496496272003

Meyer, B., Shemla, M., & Schermuly, C. C. (2011). Social category salience moderates the effect of diversity faultlines on information elaboration. *Small Group Research, 42,* 257–282. https://doi.org/10.1177/1046496411398396

Newman, S. A., & Ford, R. C. (2021). Five steps to leading your team in the virtual COVID-19 workplace. *Organizational Dynamics, 50,* 1–11. https://doi.org/10.1016/j.orgdyn.2020.100802

Norander, S., & Galanes, G. (2014). "Bridging the gap": Difference, dialogue, and community organizing. *Journal of Applied Communication Research, 42,* 345–365. http://dx.doi.org/10.1080/00909882.2014.911939

Oetzel, J. G. (2002). The effects of culture and cultural diversity on communication in work groups. In L. R. Frey (Ed.), *New directions in group communication* (pp. 121–137). SAGE.

Oppel, R. A., Taylor, D. B., & Bogel-Burroughs, N. (2021, April 26). What to know about Breonna Taylor's death. *New York Times.* https://www.nytimes.com/article/breonna-taylor-police.html

Pew Research Center. (2014, June 12). *Political polarization in the American public: How increasing ideological uniformity and partisan antipathy affect politics, compromise, and everyday life.* https://www.pewresearch.org/politics/2014/06/12/political-polarization-in-the-american-public/

Pilny, A., Poole, M. S., Reichelmann, A., & Klein, B. (2017). A structurational group decision-making perspective on the commons dilemma: Results from an online public goods game. *Journal of Applied Communication Research, 45,* 413–428. https://doi.org/10.1080/00909882.2017.1355559

Poole, M. S., & Zhang, H. (2005). Virtual teams. In S. A. Wheelan (Ed.), *The handbook of group research and practice* (pp. 363–384). SAGE.

Putnam, L. L., & Stohl, C. (1990). Bona fide groups: A reconceptualization of groups in context. *Communication Studies, 41,* 248–265. https://doi.org/10.1080/10510979009368307

Putnam, L. L., & Stohl, C. (1996). Bona fide groups: An alternative perspective for communication and small group decision making. In R. Y. Hirokawa & M. S. Poole (Eds.), *Communication and group decision making* (pp. 147–178). SAGE.

Rupert, J., Homan, A. C., Jehn, K. A., & Blomme, R. J. (2019). Diversity composition and team learning: The moderating role of error culture. *Group Decision and Negotiation, 28,* 695–722. https://doi.org/10.1007/s10726-019-09626-5

Schölmerich, F., Schermuly, C. C., & Deller, J. (2016). How leaders' diversity beliefs alter the impact of faultlines on team functioning. *Small Group Research, 47,* 177–206. https://doi.org/10.1177/1046496416630960

Silverstein, J. (2021, June 4). The global impact of George Floyd: How Black Lives Matter protests shaped movements around the world. *CBS News.* https://www.cbsnews.com/news/george-floyd-black-lives-matter-impact/

SunWolf. (2008). *Peer groups: Expanding our study of small group communication.* SAGE.

United States Census Bureau. (n.d.) *Quick facts: Athens county, Ohio.* https://www.census.gov/quickfacts/athenscountyohio

Vásquez, C., & Kuhn, T. (2019). *Dis/organization as communication: Exploring the disordering, disruptive, and chaotic properties of communication.* Routledge.

Wang, Z., Walther, J. B., & Hancock, J. T. (2009). Social identification and interpersonal communication in computer-mediated communication: What you do versus who you are in virtual groups. *Human Communication Research, 35,* 59–85. https://doi.org/10.1111/j.1468-2958.2008.01338.x

Wittenbaum, G. M., Hollingshead, A. B., & Botero, I. (2004). From cooperative to motivated information sharing in groups: Going beyond the hidden profile paradigm. *Communication Monographs, 71,* 286–310. https://doi.org/10.1080/0363452042000299894

Xu, N., Chiu, C., & Treadway, D. C. (2019). Tensions between diversity and shared leadership: The role of team political skill. *Small Group Research, 50,* 507–538. https://doi.org/10.1177/1046496419840432

Zheng, W., & Wei, J. (2018). Linking ethnic composition and performance: Information integration between majority and minority members. *Small Group Research, 49,* 357–387. https://doi.org/10.1177%2F1046496417749727

11

FAMILY COMMUNICATION

Talking Families into Being

Dawn O. Braithwaite

Learning Objectives

1. Explore communication challenges facing families in the 2020s.
2. Understand three aspects of family communication that can foster understanding and family interactions.
3. Highlight the contributions of understanding families as discourse dependent, created, and changed in interaction.

As we moved toward the second decade of the 21st century, nothing could have prepared us for the very real challenges coming for family communication. In the United States, and in many places around the globe, political divisiveness and unrest prevailed, with increased confrontations over racial injustice and economic disparities, and a global COVID-19 pandemic that impacted most aspects of family communication and life, including physical and mental health, isolation and reduction in social ties, and confronting death and bereavement. All of these issues converged at once, changing and reflecting alterations in our understanding of what constitutes family and highlighting what different people believe that family should be. As I write, we hope that we are moving out of the worst of the pandemic. We are trying to anticipate and discover what the "new normal" will be for our lives and families, as we know that the state of families and family communication is always changing (Galvin et al., 2019).

In addition to being a Communication professor and researcher, like most who read this chapter, I am a family member. Along with many scholars, I am drawn to study issues that I have found challenging in my life. When I teach, I design assignments that give students opportunities to undertake projects that help them understand their own life challenges. I am not surprised to see that many students choose issues related to family communication.

DOI: 10.4324/9781003220466-13

In my case, I was adopted as an infant and, after my mother died when I was 12, my father remarried within a few months, and we became an instant stepfamily. In my research, I study how stepfamilies go from being strangers to a family, how they negotiate conflict, and the central role of communication in this process. Truth be told, being a stepfamily was hardly ever easy, especially in the early years. Because most researchers focus on stepfamily problems, in recent years, my research team has been studying how stepfamilies with overall positive relationships communicate and develop their roles and expectations (Braithwaite et al., 2018). Today, I am close to my stepmother, and I am thankful for her in my life. As the second decade in the 21st century dawned, my stepmother and I were discussing how to be most helpful to each other as we both age, work that was turned upside down as COVID-19 hit.

And Then 2020 . . .

The year 2020 started in very normal ways for my family, and perhaps for others too. I was concerned about political divisions that had grown over the previous years in the United States. By February 2020, the seriousness of COVID-19 became clear, after many in political leadership rejected the advice of public health experts. COVID-19 went from rumor to a full-blown health crisis of a magnitude not seen in over 100 years in the United States. Responses to COVID became incredibly politicized over wearing masks, social distancing, closing public spaces, and later over taking the vaccination (see: https://fraser.stlouisfed.org/timeline/covid-19-pandemic).

I walked out of my office on March 12, 2020, and, by the following week, I would soon be working from home for the next 18 months. My husband, Chuck, also a professor, and I both worked from home. In an ironic turn, Chuck is retiring from the university just as everything is opening up here in June 2021. During our time of sheltering at home, we have spent much more time together than at any time in our 37-year marriage, and it has been a good dry run for what retirement might be like. Fortunately, sheltering at home helped us stay healthy, although we missed tremendously seeing friends and visiting family. We were fortunate to have access to social media to stay connected. Substantial challenges and stressors became opportunities to grow keenly aware of the role of communication in our family and how we negotiate change (Galvin et al., 2019).

For millions of others in the United States, the pandemic brought devastating impacts of illness, unemployment, social isolation, young adults moving home, and parents overseeing children's online education while trying to balance their own work (see Schieman et al., 2021). With all these challenges, many families experienced positive impacts of having more time together.

In addition to the pandemic, what might be understood as a perfect storm of other events came to a head around issues of climate change, economic and health disparities, and especially issues of diversity, equity, and inclusion, for example, LGBTQ rights, racial justice, women's health, and national and local political discourse (see Pew Research Center's "20 Striking Findings from 2020" https://www.pewresearch.org/fact-tank/2020/12/11/20-striking-findings-from-2020/). The enormous divide over values and political differences was strident at best and violent at its worst, magnified by incredible media presence running up to, and past the 2020 election. In the United States, 24-hour news channels, blogs, and social media platforms reflecting divergent political positions grew in number and use. While always a problem, misinformation and political polarization exploded, and public discourse became even more negative and strident (see: https://mitsloan.mit.edu/ideas-made-to-matter/mit-sloan-research-about-social-media-misinformation-and-elections). In June, 2020, outcry over cases involving policing and BIPOC, especially for Black people, heightened with the death of George Floyd at the hands of the Minneapolis police and ensuing public protests. I certainly witnessed my own family's divisions over COVID responses, the 2020 election, and issues of diversity and equity play out in very public and ugly ways on different social media platforms.

I believe the events of 2020 and its aftermath have left the United States and families even more divided. As I write this essay, schools, workplaces, restaurants, sporting events, and other aspects of daily life are re-opening. We understand things are not going back "to normal," and we have to look on this time as developing a "new normal." Some of the changes seem positive, and other changes seem more negative (see e.g., https://news.uchicago.edu/story/life-after-covid-19-vaccine-envisioning-new-normal).

This moment seems an opportune time to reflect on some of the most important contributions and changes for family communication in the remainder of this decade and beyond. It is an important opportunity for each of us to reflect on our own family communication as we navigate some of the changes that might normally occur in a family at particular life stages, added to the issues dominating civic life.

To follow, I will highlight three aspects of family communication that I hope will help with framing the events facing us in the 2020s and also foster better understanding and more successful interactions in our respective families: (a) families in communication, (b) families as discourse dependent, and (c) voluntary families.

Families in Communication

What we believe is [and is not] a family and how a family does or should communicate comprises complex questions. People often think about family communication in overly simplistic ways, focusing in how family members transmit or exchange messages, citing "lack of communication," or "communication breakdowns" as reasons families struggle or fail (Baxter, 2014). On a daily basis, much of our awareness of family communication consists of coordinating schedules and negotiating whose turn it is to do the dishes or let out the dog. At the same time, larger issues—such as coping with illness, drug or alcohol abuse in the family, unemployment, divorce, and disagreements over fundamental values regarding religious beliefs, political values, or cultural expectations—may loom in the background until some event propels them to the forefront, and we confront how the family is going to interact and navigate the storm (Galvin et al., 2019). Even positive events—such as finishing college, becoming a parent, or winning the lottery—necessitate communication and recalibrating some aspects of identity and the family system.

In reality, family communication entails much more than sending and receiving messages; rather, communication occupies the central role in family processes and patterns as families are literally talked into (and out of) being (Braithwaite & Suter, in press). From this perspective, via communication, families form, develop, create, maintain, and alter who we are (Baxter, 2014; Braithwaite & Suter, in press). In addition, families regularly interact and are impacted by public institutions such as churches and schools, laws and policies, and the media (Suter, 2016). When we understand communication as the way in which families co-construct and become who we are, we understand that families can be bounded by biological and/or legal ties, and we can also define family more broadly and in ways that communication plays a central role. Thus, we join Galvin and colleagues (2019) who defined a family as:

> Networks of people who share their lives over long periods of time, bound by ties of marriage, blood, law, or commitment, legal or otherwise, who consider themselves as family and who share a significant history and anticipated future of functioning as a family. (p. 8)

This definition takes a more broad and inclusive view of family, stressing that families can encompass more than biological or legal ties and that we communicate to create and continually work out what family is and does.

When thinking about our own families, we can likely recall important events, both positive and negative, that impacted how we understand "family," who is [and is not] included as family, and how members interact to navigate family change and challenge. All of these processes of course differ from family to family at various times over the lifespan. For example, at present, Black parents find themselves needing to interact with their children about racism they will face and how to navigate encounters with the police (Huguley et al., 2019). Lesbian parents may need to navigate negative messages about their family from others in schools, in public, or even from their own family (Koenig Kellas & Suter, 2012) Other families face potential negative effects of keeping secrets in the family over important issues (Afifi & Olson, 2005).

Expectations about the nature of families certainly get contested, especially when a family does not fit dominant cultural models (Baxter, 2014; Floyd et al., 2006). Understanding what counts as family and the role of communication in co-constructing our individual selves and our family are always important, but especially as 2020 dawned, people were faced with cultural challenges to their identity, what it means to be a family, and what a family should do.

Families as Discourse Dependent

Throughout the 1980s and 1990s, some called for a return to "traditional family values" which, for many, represented a longing for depictions in the popular media of White couples in first marriage families and their biological children. In her book, *The Way We Never Were* (1992), family scholar Stephanie Coontz reminded us that this vision of the traditional family did not ever depict all, or most, families in the United States. For example, we have seen a continual increase in families of color, divorce and stepfamilies, single parent families, multi-racial families, adoptive families, LGBTQ families, and families formed outside of marriage (see Pew Research Center's 2121 summary of cultural changes: https://www.pewresearch.org/fact-tank/2021/02/25/in-vice-president-kamala-harris-we-can-see-how-america-has-changed/).

Diverse families do face additional challenges. Family communication scholar Kathleen Galvin (2006) explained that what we might think of as "traditional" families have cultural models to guide what to expect regarding roles and relationships. Families that fall outside of the "traditional" family model find themselves needing to communicatively create what constitutes family, legitimize the family to others, and handle stress and change. Galvin labeled these families as discourse dependent. Notice that I put "traditional" family in quotation marks as I challenge the existence of a "best" or "normal" family model.

In my own case, being adopted and then becoming a stepfamily, marrying and choosing not to have children, I became very aware of being discourse dependent and needing communication to create, enact, and explain my family. For example, my husband and I found that hinting indirectly that we could not have children, rather than coming out and saying that we made this choice, seemed to stifle questions and judgments that people made about us.

When I became part of a stepfamily, we were forced to figure out who we were to each and what was expected of us. For over 25 years, I have studied the major turning points and different developmental patterns to becoming a stepfamily that are negotiated via communication (see Baxter et al., 1999; Braithwaite et al., 2018). It was not easy to be a stepfamily, I can tell you. It was hard for us kids, and, as a grown up, I realized how hard that it must have been for my stepmother and my father too. In my research, I have learned how stepfamily members can find themselves caught in the middle; one stepdaughter described being stuck between her divorced parents as "like a bone between two dogs" (Braithwaite et al., 2008, p. 41).

Discourse dependent family members do not automatically know what to do and say. Galvin (2006) explained how discourse dependent families must develop ways to communicate internally to build shared expectations and roles. Discourse dependent families also find themselves needing explain, legitimize, or defend their family outsiders who do not understand or accept the family. For example, Communication scholar Karla Bergen (2010) studied families in which the wives were a commuting spouse, a role commonly played by men (e.g., soldiers, long-haul truck drivers). Many commuting wives encountered others challenging their choices and identity in ways that their husbands did not (e.g., "Is that safe, is that smart, is that a good idea?" p. 47) and had to figure out how to respond to a contested identity. Challenges to discourse dependent families can also come from members of one's own family as well. For example, I have several close LGBTQ friends who have been rejected and estranged from the family by their parents, siblings, or grandparents.

Thinking of some families as "traditional" or "normal" gives them (Braithwaite & Suter, in press) legitimacy, inscribing them with power. When we conceptualize some family types and identities as "legitimate," we implicitly marginalize or delegitimize others that do not match our perception. Not surprisingly, being accepted and legitimized as a family brings benefits. For example, in 2021, as many people sought to be vaccinated against COVID-19 as early as possible, we quickly learned that married people could request or even just bring their spouse along to the vaccination center, and the spouse was usually vaccinated. This unadvertised benefit was not available to unmarried partners or single people, and it was only an option for spouses who could come together, cutting out those in low-income jobs with little scheduling flexibility, including many BIPOC. One needed to have access to information from others who had secured the benefit, in this case, other married people.

As I have highlighted, family communication plays a central role in shaping, perpetuating, and re-shaping similarities and differences. Family differences in the form of race and ethnicity, sexual orientation, or social class can be, and are contested. The political foment of the early 2020s clarified that many White people do not, if wish not, to understand the history and experiences of BIPOC who, for example, need to socialize their children and prepare them for racism they will face outside the family. These parents need to create "counter-narratives . . . [that] can create new narratives and possibilities for BIPOC" (Cardwell & Minniear, 2022, p. 250).

One important function of critical examinations of race and social injustice is to bring about emancipation and change. For example, after the 2021 death of citizen George Floyd at the hands of police in Minneapolis, significant unrest followed which sparked discussions of race and racism in the United States. While painful, this discourse opened the doors for important forward movement:

> Floyd's tragic death, and the subsequent mass Black Lives Matter protests, also fueled a growing discourse about structural racism in American schools, especially over their racially lopsided teaching force, heavy police presence that overdisciplines Black students, and ethnically non-representative curriculum.

Dissatisfaction with those areas long predates the traumatic events of 2020. . . . the events of last year have helped lend legitimacy and urgency to some of those efforts, social-justice educators say. (Sawchuk, 2021)

While good things can come from bringing difficult issues to light, change is not easy. Reactions to these events brought forward social protest, debates, and deep divides on issues of race and gender from across the spectrum (e.g., see https://www.washingtonpost.com/religion/southern-baptists-head-for-annual-meeting-at-a-crossroads-on-race-and-gender/2021/06/04/4e4f9f1c-c571–11eb-89a4-b7ae22aa193e_story.html). Many state legislatures debated bills to prevent teaching and training relating to Critical Race Theory. Issues surrounding diversity, equity, and inclusion will continue to be important and difficult to face and navigate, as Galvin et al. (2019) explained, "Racial and ethnic backgrounds, as well as other significant in-group memberships, influence choices concerning family beliefs, values, and expectations for behavior, all of which affect the current family experience and future generations, unless they are consciously altered" (p. 5).

This chapter might raise the question, "wait, aren't *all* families discourse dependent?" Of course, all families are, indeed, discourse dependent, a realization that might become more evident at different life stages. For example, young adults may renegotiate roles and expectations with parents as they leave home (and if they must return). Individuals may become acutely aware of the central role of communication as they form their own families in adulthood, for example, negotiating roles and expectations with a partner in the transition to becoming parents (Stamp & Banski, 1992) or with parents and family members as parents age and may need assistance (Pecchioni & Nussbaum, 2001).

However, in the end, we should recognize the systemic marginalization of some family types are marginalized, and, while members need to interact and create their family expectation and roles, they also struggle for legitimacy with those outside the family. Unfortunately, those families tend to experience heightened discourse dependence, making communication even more important. Examples include a lesbian or gay couple having or adopting children or a multi-ethnic family negotiating religious differences.

Voluntary/Chosen Families

As I mentioned earlier, one of my scholarly interests centers on what I have called voluntary kin—"persons perceived to be family, but who are not related by blood or law" (Braithwaite et al., 2010, p. 390). Discourse-dependent family relationships are often called fictive kin (a label I do not like as it connotes these relationships are not real) or chosen kin. Voluntary kin relationships exist across many cultures and within U.S. subcultures. They may form because of geographic distances, estrangement, death in the family, or when the family of origin is unavailable, unaccepting, or cannot meet needs (Allen et al., 2011; Braithwaite et al., 2010; Nelson, 2013).

Voluntary family relationships have been an important part of my life and Chuck's life. As Chuck was on his own at age 18, his young English teacher and husband became his home base and family for him, and they still play this role. For me, following my mother's death and being in a stepfamily that was not close in the early years, I developed several voluntary family relationships that were very important to who I became. For both Chuck and me, voluntary kin remains important sources of social support and resilience (Braithwaite et al., 2010).

Those with voluntary family ties must work these family relationships out in interaction; they co-determine expectations about what to say and do, how to communicate and manage conflicts, and the role of their biological and legal families in the voluntary relationship (Braithwaite et al., 2016). For example, I had to decide if I would I tell my father and stepmother about the very close relationship that I formed with the couple, now in their mid-90s, I describe as "my pretend parents." My colleagues and I have found in our research that some people knit their voluntary family members into their bio-legal families while others keep these sets of people partially or completely separate (Braithwaite et al., 2016).

As the COVID-19 pandemic hit in early 2020, voluntary family relationships became even more important for many people. Given that many socially distanced from family and friends for over a year, people who live alone and are lonely (not everyone is, see DePaulo, 2006), those who are elderly, mobility impaired, or have mental health challenges needed to discover best practices to support their physical and psychological well-being during the pandemic. While socially distancing from family and friends, some developed voluntary families in the forms of "pandemic pods" of people that they trusted to follow health protocols. Members of such small pods could meet face-to-face (see: https://www.inquirer.com/health/coronavirus/pandemic-pod-coronavirus-safety-social-distancing-20200918.html). In some cases, these pods became more than friends and functioned as voluntary families. My research suggests that some of these voluntary families may become less important or even break apart in the "new normal" of post-pandemic life. Others will remain and communicatively negotiate new roles and functions (Braithwaite et al., 2010).

Clearly, events in the early 2020s provide ways for us to understand and highlight the important role of family communication in providing help, emotional and physical support, caregiving, and the need to confront and come to new understandings and actions in light of challenges facing families. In the best of all situations, whether established through biological, legal, or ties of the heart, families have the potential to help us become and understand who we are and, in the best of circumstances, help us create rich satisfying lives. Family communication is central to identity, helping us create our place in the world and enact resilience across our lives.

References

Afifi, T. D., & Olson, L. (2005). The chilling effect in families and the pressure to conceal secrets. *Communication Monographs, 72*(2), 192–216.

Allen, K. R., Blieszner, R., & Roberto, K. A. (2011). Perspective on extended family and fictive kin in the later years: Strategies and meanings of kin reinterpretation. *Journal of Family Issues, 32*, 1156–1177. https://doi.org/10.1177/0192513X11404335

Baxter, L. A. (2014). Theorizing the communicative construction of "family": The three R.'s. In L. A. Baxter (Ed.), *Remaking "family" communicatively* (pp. 33–50). Peter Lang.

Baxter, L. A., Braithwaite, D. O., & Nicholson, J. (1999). Turning points in the development of blended family relationships. *Journal of Social and Personal Relationships, 16*, 291–313.

Bergen, K. M. (2010). Negotiating a "questionable" identity: Commuter wives and social networks. *Southern Communication Journal, 75*, 35–56. https://doi.org/10.1080/10417940902981816

Braithwaite, D. O., Bach, B. W., Baxter, L. A., DiVerniero, R., Hammonds, J., Hosek, A., Willer, E., & Wolf, B. (2010). Constructing family: A typology of voluntary kin. *Journal of Social and Personal Relationships, 27*, 388–407.

Braithwaite, D. O., Stephenson Abetz, J., Moore, J., & Brockhage, K. (2016). Communication structures of supplemental voluntary kin relationships, *Family Relations, 65*, 616–630. https://doi.org/10.1111/fare.12215

Braithwaite, D. O., & Suter, E. (in press). Family communication. In K. Adamsons, A. Few-Demo, C. Proulx, & K. Roy (Eds.), *Sourcebook of family theories and methodologies* (2nd ed.). SAGE.

Braithwaite, D. O., Toller, P., Daas, K., Durham, W., & Jones, A. (2008). Centered, but not caught in the middle: Stepchildren's perceptions of contradictions of communication of co-parents. *Journal of Applied Communication Research, 36*, 33–55.

Braithwaite, D. O., Waldron, V. R., Allen, J., Bergquist, G., Marsh, J., Oliver, B., Storck, K., Swords, N., & Tschampl-Diesing, C. (2018). "Feeling warmth and close to her:" Communication and resilience reflected in turning points in positive adult stepchild-stepparent relationships. *Journal of Family Communication, 18*, 92–109. https://doi.org/10.1080/15267431.2017.1415902

Cardwell, M. E., & Minniear, M. (2022). Critical race theory: Dismantling racial oppression through interpersonal communication. In D. O. Braithwaite & P. Schrodt (Eds.), *Engaging theories in interpersonal communication: Multiple perspectives* (3rd. ed., pp. 246–257). Routledge.

Coontz, S. (1992). *The way we never were: American families and the nostalgia trap.* Basic Books.

DePaulo, B. (2006). *Singled out: How singles are stereotyped, stigmatized, and ignored, and still like happily ever after.* St Martin's Griffin.

Floyd, K., Mikkelson, A. C., & Judd, J. (2006). Defining the family through relationships. In L. H. Turner & R. West (Eds.), *The family communication sourcebook* (pp. 21–42). Sage.

Galvin, K. M. (2006). Diversity's impact on defining the family. In L. H. Turner & R. West (Eds.), *The family communication sourcebook* (pp. 3–19). SAGE.

Galvin, K. M., Braithwaite, D. O., Schrodt, P., & Bylund, C. (2019). *Family communication: Cohesion and change* (10th ed.). Routledge.

Huguley, J. P., Wang, M., Guo, J., & Vasquez, A. C. (2019). Parental ethnic—racial socialization practices and the construction of children of color's ethnic—racial identity: A research synthesis and meta-analysis. *Psychological Bulletin, 145*, 437–458.

Koenig Kellas, J., & Suter, E. (2012). Accounting for lesbian families: Lesbian mothers respond to discursive challenges. *Communication Monographs, 79*, 475–498.

Nelson, M. K. (2013). Fictive kin, families we choose, and voluntary kin: What does the discourse tell us? *Journal of Family Theory & Review, 5,* 259–281.

Pecchioni, L. L., & Nussbaum, J. F. (2001). Mother-adult daughter discussions of caregiving prior to dependency: Exploring conflicts among European-American women. *Journal of Family Communication, 1,* 133–150.

Sawchuk, S. (2021, April 21). 4 ways George Floyd's murder has changed how we talk about race and education. *Education Week.* https://www.edweek.org/leadership/4-ways-george-floyds-murder-has-changed-how-we-talk-about-race-and-education/2021/04

Schieman, S., Badawy, P. J., Milkie, M. A., & Bierman, A. (2021). Work-life conflict during the COVID-19 pandemic. *Socius: Sociological Research for a Dynamic World, 7,* 1–9.

Stamp, G. H., & Banski, M. H. (1992). The communicative management of constrained autonomy during the transition to parenthood. *Western Journal of Communication, 56,* 281–300.

Suter, E. A. (2016). Introduction: Critical approaches to family communication research: Representation, critique, and praxis. *Journal of Family Communication, 16,* 1–8. https://doi.org/10.1080/15267431.2015.1111219

12

INTO THE UNKNOWN

Instructional Communication in the 2020s

Tiffany R. Wang

Learning Objectives

After reading this chapter, you will be able to:

1. Describe faculty and student challenges that occurred during the events of 2020.
2. Identify a response to a challenge that you experienced during the events of 2020.

Introduction

I have always considered myself to be a planner who thrives on routine. As I look back on the events of 2020, not much of the year was routine. In fact, it has felt more like the scene from Disney's *Frozen 2* where the protagonist Elsa sings *Into the Unknown*. Although 2020 did not go as planned, venturing into the unknown offered opportunities to reflect on the challenges students and faculty members faced during the pandemic and consider how faculty members can adapt technology to teaching and foster safety, equity, and access on our campuses. This chapter will overview my 2020 in quarters as I share how the events of this year can be applied to and shape the future direction of Instructional Communication.

Quarter 1: January–March 2020

Each year, in lieu of a New Year's resolution, I select a characteristic to focus on developing in the coming year. On January 1, I decided that *adaptable* was the perfect characteristic to focus on because I was starting my second decade in the

DOI: 10.4324/9781003220466-14

academy and serving in leadership roles that would require me to face new situations regularly. Little did I know how prescient that choice would be in 2020. The following day, I registered for the Central States Communication Association (CSCA) 2020 convention and booked my flight to Chicago. I began to make plans to see several of my friends at the convention. On January 6, the spring semester began at my university. I was excited about the semester ahead.

On February 4, we marked a time of transition as my department announced the retirement of our chair and the appointment of our new chair. On February 15, our seniors released their logo for our primary recruitment event: Exploring Communication Studies Day. Their slogan was "ignite your passion" which signified the spark between them as they decided to overcome their obstacles, which were depicted by mountains. Like the characteristic that I had chosen in January, this slogan proved to be prescient for the events that would unfold in March.

On March 5, the CSCA Executive Committee posted its first COVID-19 update. I serve as part of this leadership team, and we planned to meet weekly to monitor the situation. Five days later, we made the difficult decision to cancel the convention after the state of Illinois declared a state of emergency—our first cancellation of a convention since World War II. Although I knew that we had made the right decision to protect the health and safety of our members, I still felt a great deal of sadness and disappointment as we canceled a sold-out room block, processed refunds, and tried to do our part to flatten the curve. On March 12, my university hosted Exploring Communication Studies Day. Our event proved to be the last large in-person campus event of 2020. On Friday the 13th, as I was getting ready to go to campus, I got a phone call from our university president. He said that I needed to get to campus as soon as possible for an emergency meeting in my role as Faculty Senate President. At that meeting, we decided to begin spring break early and extend it by one week. Following spring break, we would transition online for what we thought would be a couple weeks before returning to campus to close out the semester.

During my extended spring break, I sent out a survey of course access and redesigned my course calendars to accommodate the loss of one week of instruction and movement online. To cope with the stress of the pandemic, I spent time catching up on shows on my DVR, snuggling with my dog, London, and cooking from scratch. Midway through the extended spring break, my university decided to move the remainder of the semester online which required me to make additional modifications to my courses. As I read responses to my survey of course access, I learned that my students did not have equal access to what they would need to complete the semester successfully. Some students had left their textbooks on campus thinking that we would be returning to campus before the end of the semester while other students lacked the reliable internet access that would be needed to attend synchronous online classes. I shared links to electronic textbooks that publishers had made free during the pandemic and decided to move all my classes to an asynchronous online format to ensure that students could complete their classes.

Reflections on Quarter 1

During Quarter 1, students and faculty members experienced challenges as we pivoted from in-person to online. On my campus, many of my students were front-line essential workers who were at the highest risk for work-related COVID-19 exposure (CDC, 2021, para. 4). Some of my students worked 30–40 hours a week at grocery stores, warehouse clubs, and super centers for minimum wage as Americans grocery shopped and cooked more (PRNewswire, 2021), while others struggled to find work as restaurants and bars transitioned to carry-out or curbside dining and universities transitioned from in-person to online instruction. As a faculty member, I found myself trying to help my students find the food, housing, technology, and internet access that they needed to be successful. In response to the survey of course access that I sent out in March, I directed students to the Falcon Food Pantry, Housing & Residence Life, the COVID-19 Student Relief Fund, and campus computer labs and parking lots that had free Wi-Fi. Although students had access to some campus resources, achieving food and housing security often took priority over academic goals.

As a faculty member at a teaching institution, shifting to online instruction following our extended Spring Break was challenging. Some courses, such as Family Communication, required modest tweaks. I eliminated the group presentation component of a combined group paper/presentation assignment and recorded and posted my remaining lectures. Other courses, such as Foundations of Oral Communication, needed more creativity. Because this course fulfills a General Education requirement, I needed to find a way for students to deliver their scheduled persuasive speeches. I decided to have students record and upload their speeches to Canvas due to concerns with student access. Initially, I thought recording and uploading a speech would be a straightforward task for my students who frequently upload Instagram reels, YouTube videos, and TikTok videos. However, this assignment proved to be more challenging than expected as students struggled to find a quiet place to film, screenshare their visual aid, and find the bandwidth needed to upload their speeches. Although I was relieved to have found a plan that would get us to the end of the semester, I recognized that I would need to develop more comfort with instructional technology in Quarter 2 if we did not return to pre-pandemic instruction in fall.

Quarter 2: April–June 2020

As April began, I struggled to adjust to my new normal. I attempted to work from home in a one-bedroom apartment with no dedicated office space. I drove to campus to pick up an office chair and monitor that I could use in my modified kitchen turned office/virtual classroom. In mid-April, I mourned the loss of our canceled conference. I disliked deleting my scheduled flights from my calendar and thinking about the missed opportunities to see my friends at CSCA. However, one bright spot during this challenging time involved serving as a remote advisor for my program. I enjoyed getting to meet intelligent, engaged, and dynamic new majors who were excited to start our program in the fall. In late April, I finished my last Faculty Senate meeting as Faculty Senate President and passed the virtual gavel to my successor at our Zoom meeting. I also enjoyed getting to make good news calls to my colleagues regarding tenure and promotion, promotion, and emeritus decisions. On the last day of April, I posted my last final grade for what had been an interesting spring 2020 semester.

As May began, my university started making plans to resume in-person instruction in the fall. May was a relatively quiet month as I wrote and submitted our General Education assessment report, did more remote advising, began working with our CSCA 2021 program planner, and started several new Netflix shows. I was disappointed to cancel three planned summer trips including a trip to Vancouver, Canada to celebrate my grandmother's 90th birthday, but I tried to stay busy by writing an article about what it was like to be a faculty member during the COVID-19 pandemic, attending virtual professional conferences, and planning staycations that I could enjoy from the comfort of my apartment patio.

In early June, my department, university, and CSCA released statements in opposition to racism and injustice in response to the death of George Floyd. My university also named a group of university representatives to study campus building names. Concurrently, I served on a university taskforce that met weekly to plan our return to campus as the data suggested that we would not be able to return to pre-pandemic instruction during the fall semester as we had hoped.

Reflections on Quarter 2

As cases continued to rise with no end to the pandemic in sight, faculty on campus including myself continued to struggle with the new normal. Many of us felt "(a) (dis)connection, (b) the need to settle for surface-level instruction, (c) the conditions of unfamiliarity and uncertainty, and (d) the interruption to cultural inquiry" (Berry, 2020, pp. 486–487). As a faculty member who works at a small public liberal arts institution, I have thrived on being able to build and maintain interpersonal relationships with my students and colleagues. As the pandemic continued, I found myself missing the normal I had known (and perhaps taken for granted) pre-pandemic. To prepare myself for what I would face later that summer and fall, I found myself reinventing myself as a teacher by adapting my teaching to my technology. In hindsight, I wish I had been more focused on adapting my technology to my teaching.

The year 2020 felt like a blur as faculty members filmed and posted lectures on our learning management systems; delivered synchronous lectures online via platforms like Zoom, Microsoft Teams, and WebEx; and converted in-person activities, assignments, and assessments to online, hyflex, and hybrid formats (Moore & Hodges, 2020; Swerzenski, 2021). As we move forward from pandemic pedagogy to post-pandemic pedagogy, we need to make sure that our technology tools align with our educational goals (Swerzenski, 2021). Looking back on this challenging time, I wish I had been more focused on considering how I could adapt technology tools to my pedagogy so that these tools better promoted student engagement and student connection. Focusing on this overarching goal would have better allowed my colleagues and I to be the teachers that we dreamed about being when we chose teaching as our profession (Berry, 2020) as we moved into Quarter 3.

Quarter 3: July–September 2020

A quiet June gave way to an eventful July. On July 1, I started my term as CSCA Executive Director as we opened submissions for the CSCA 2021 convention. We were still hopeful that we would be able to meet in person in Cincinnati in March 2021. Decisions for the 2020 National Communication Association convention arrived in my inbox, and I booked my hotel in Indianapolis, the convention location that year.

Two days later, a normal socially distanced trip to the mall took a turn for the worse when a shootout occurred near the mall food court, killing a young boy and injuring three others. On July 8, my family celebrated my grandmother's 90th birthday with a socially distanced outdoor birthday luncheon. Unfortunately, many of us had to join via Zoom due to the rising COVID-19 cases. In late July, I attended our virtual state association town hall meeting clad in what was quickly becoming a new Zoom uniform: a dressy top, soft pants, and fuzzy slippers.

In early August, our university taskforce began to finalize the return to campus plan. My university offered students the option to take any class fully remote which meant that all my classes became hyflex classes. With the need to socially distance, we also moved to rotating in-person schedules to ensure that students were safely spaced. In late August, as we entered the semester, I found myself more worried than excited about the coming semester. The new normal that we were entering felt equal parts uncertain and unknown. Would we be able to retain our students? Would we need to return to fully online operations? Would everyone follow mask and social distance requirements? Would I be able to teach effectively in a hyflex format mask to mask? As the first week of classes and the month of August ended, we were still left with a lot of unanswered questions.

As September progressed, I realized that being *adaptable* was key to making it through the semester. As a person who thrives on routine, I found myself needing to innovate and find new ways to achieve student learning outcomes in circumstances that were continuously changing. In mid-September, I submitted my sabbatical application. As September ended, we made the final push to the submission deadline for the CSCA 2021 convention and started working on our COMS Senior Showcase which was my program's first major virtual event.

Reflections on Quarter 3

Although universities across the country did their best to mitigate the spread of COVID-19, students continued to face challenges as they learned online and in-person. Students experienced precarity (Bahrainwala, 2020), continual wage insecurity, as they continued to struggle with food insecurity (AAC&U News, 2019; Wright et al., 2020), rising student loan debt (Dynarski, 2015), long work hours (Deruy & National Journal, 2015), and homelessness (Wright et al., 2020). As the pandemic continued, many students shouldered additional family and employment demands that made it more challenging to succeed in the classroom.

Coupled with these stressors, students also struggled with health concerns, "including but not limited to sleep deprivation, lack of proper nutrition and exercise, psychological distress, acute illness, and the social pressures to engage in substance and alcohol abuse" (LaBelle, 2020, pp. 267–268). For my students, these health-related issues often negatively impacted their academic performance as students withdrew from courses, failed courses, and earned lower grades than they had in past semesters as they struggled with loneliness, depression, and anxiety.

As a faculty member, I took on several communicative roles in conversations with students about their mental health, including being an empathic listener, referral source, and first responder (White & LaBelle, 2019). These conversations often arose during virtual office hours. As an empathic listener, I tried to provide emotional support for my students as they disclosed mental health challenges. As a referral source, I redirected students to professional resources like our Grainger Family Center for Personal Development. As a first responder, I filed reports that alerted administration and other offices on campus that could help students in distress.

Like our students, many faculty members experienced a difficult 2020. Faculty members experienced precarity as they continued to struggle to find tenure-track opportunities (Harris, 2019), meet rising research expectations (Kafka, 2018), and work contingent positions (Murray, 2019). As the pandemic unfolded, faculty members often had their labor stretched across multiple campuses and multiple modalities as they took on additional family and employment responsibilities. These increasing demands occurred as the profession we knew and loved was paused, interrupted, and disrupted during the COVID-19 pandemic. As the circumstances changed, it became difficult to "encourage, help, affirm and challenge students" (p. 486) and engage in the "heightened attention to engagement, connection with students, dialogue, vulnerability, and safe risk taking" (p. 485) that characterize what it means to be a teacher (Berry, 2020).

In August 2020, we added three new department faculty. One new colleague who had relocated from out of state served as the primary caregiver for her mother who was in and out of the hospital. Another new colleague had a kindergartener who was learning from home half the week when her family's school district moved to a hyflex format. She juggled teaching four new course preps while writing her dissertation. Another new colleague who had transitioned from a staff position to a faculty position was teaching four production classes while pursuing a graduate degree. With students having the option to learn fully remotely, he had to find ways to help students learn what they would have learned in the studio at home. New and experienced colleagues alike remarked that they missed in class discussions and seeing their students and colleagues regularly. We wondered what our postpandemic jobs would look like.

What aspects of our job would return to the prepandemic normal? What aspects of our job would change? As we moved into Quarter 4, I hoped some of those questions would be answered.

Quarter 4: October–December 2020

In early October, I was selected as University Scholar, the highest research award at my university. As with most events in 2020, our annual campus-wide event became a virtual event with prerecorded award speeches streamed on YouTube. My chair suggested organizing a Zoom watch party on October 8 so that we could gather to celebrate. My parents were able to join the Zoom call from Vancouver, and my grandmothers enjoyed watching the YouTube recording several times. In mid-October, I completed remote advising for the Spring 2021 semester. I have a tradition of taking last advising appointment selfies with my graduating seniors each semester. We improvised and took last advising appointment screen captures. As our COMS Senior Showcase event grew closer, we realized we might need to make some modifications as Hurricane Zeta passed over central Alabama. Unfortunately, we experienced heavy rains and high winds on the day of the scheduled event that knocked out power throughout the state. My university closed for a couple days while students, faculty, and staff regained power. The following week, we hosted an abbreviated makeup event.

On November 3, I voted in the 2020 election in a socially distanced line at my city parks and recreation center. This voter turnout marked the highest that I have seen in nearly a decade of living in my county. The following day, I received word that I had been awarded a sabbatical for Spring 2022. In mid-November, I attended the virtual NCA convention. Although the virtual convention led to some Zoom fatigue, I enjoyed seeing colleagues and friends virtually. Virtual meetings continued Thanksgiving week as my family met for a Zoom virtual Thanksgiving.

As December began, a friend shared a *New York Times* article with me about planning for the unknown (Braverman, 2020). December felt like more of the same unknown we had experienced throughout 2020 as COVID-19 case numbers continued to climb with no end in sight. I spent most of December doing Zoom exit interviews with my colleagues for our 24 seniors. On December 10, I finished up what had been the most challenging semester of my academic career with hopes for a less stressful spring semester. On December 13, a friend posted a video of trucks heading to the airport with the Pfizer COVID-19 vaccine. Watching the video, I began to feel a small glimmer of hope that a difficult 2020 would give way to a better 2021.

Reflections on Quarter 4

Although I had opportunities to connect with students in online synchronous classes, virtual office hours, and remote advising throughout Quarter 4, I often felt disconnected as the sea of black boxes with names rose, and the number of masked students in my classroom fell. With the flexible attendance policy that we had been asked to implement in our courses, some students opted to not attend class on Zoom or in-person often choosing to watch the on-demand recordings that I posted after each class period. On November 3, the day I voted in the presidential election, I hit the lowest point of the fall semester as I taught to an empty classroom in-person and three students on Zoom in my Social Media and Public Relations class. I felt disheartened, burned out, and struggled to get through the class period. In fact, I re-recorded my lecture in my office later that afternoon because I felt like I had let my students down.

Although Quarter 4 was a discouraging time as I felt more and more disconnected from my students and colleagues, it also provided an opportunity to consider how I could take a more active role going forward in ensuring a safe, equitable, and accessible classroom and campus for all. As instructional communication scholars, we need to answer Rudick and Dannels' (2020) call to push education beyond what it is toward what it can be and Waymer's (2021) encouragement for us to embrace diversity more fully. As teachers, we need to find individual and collective actions we can take to demonstrate to our students that we care about safety, equity, and access.

Wright et al. (2020) provided helpful suggestions for demonstrating care including adding a section on a syllabus with resources that destigmatize help-seeking, revising course requirements to reduce time and finance costs for students, offering flexible office hours, using open educational resources, and creating student opportunities that pay a living wage. As faculty members, they suggested that we have opportunities to know our students and know our campus better so we can make appropriate and helpful referrals and conduct research that will help us address student challenges like food and housing insecurity.

As scholars, we also need to be willing to address diversity matters and racial justice through our research and our research mentorship. Waymer (2021) recommended studying the factors that lead to underrepresented student success and engaging in pipeline initiatives like collaborating with regional high schools to recruit students from underrepresented groups, providing quality mentorship for these students, and encouraging them to pursue graduate study.

Of course, systemic change takes time. We will not be able to achieve safe, equitable, and accessible spaces for all overnight. However, we can each do our part as teachers and scholars to draw closer toward what instructional communication can be as we adapt to the challenges we will continue to face. As we pivot out of the pandemic, the events of 2020 will continue to shape the direction of instructional communication. We can do our part to be an active agent of positive systemic change.

References

AAC&U News. (2019). Facts & figures: Majority of college students experience food insecurity, housing insecurity, or homelessness. *American Association of Colleges & Universities*. https://www.aacu.org/aacu-news/newsletter/majority-college-students-experience-foodinsecurity-housing-insecurity-or

Bahrainwala, L. (2020). Precarity, citizenship, and the "traditional" student. *Communication Education, 69*(2), 250–260. https://doi.org/10.1080/03634523.2020.1723805

Berry, K. (2020). Anchors away: Reconciling the dream of teaching in COVID-19. *Communication Education, 69*(4), 483–490. https://doi.org/10.1080/03634523.2020.1803383

Braverman, B. (2020, September 23). What my sled dogs taught me about planning for the unknown. *The New York Times.* https://www.nytimes.com/2020/09/23/sports/sled-dogs-mushing-unknowns-planning.html

CDC. (2021, March 29). Interim list of categories of essential workers mapped to standardized industry codes and titles. *Centers for Disease Control and Prevention.* https://www.cdc.gov/vaccines/covid-19/categories-essential-workers.html

Deruy, E., & National Journal. (2015, October 28). At universities, more students are working full-time. *The Atlantic.* https://www.theatlantic.com/politics/archive/2015/10/at-universities-more-students-are-working-full-time/433245/

Dynarski, S. (2015). New data gives clearer picture of student debt. *The New York Times.* https://www.nytimes.com/2015/09/11/upshot/new-data-gives-clearer-picture-of-studentdebt.html

Harris, M. S. (2019, February 7). The zero-sum game of faculty productivity. *Inside Higher Ed.* https://www.insidehighered.com/advice/2019/02/07/academics-should-maketradeoffs-faculty-work-more-explicit-opinion

Kafka, A. C. (2018, May 30). Another sign of a tough job market: Grad students feel bigger push to publish. *Chronicle of Higher Education.* https://www.chronicle.com/article/Another-Sign-of-a-Tough-Job/243536

LaBelle, S. (2020). Addressing student precarities in higher education: Our responsibility as teachers and scholars. *Communication Education, 69*(2), 267–276. https://doi.org/10.1080/03634523.2020.1724311

Moore, S., & Hodges, C. (2020, March 11). So you want to temporarily teach online? *Inside Higher Ed.* https://www.insidehighered.com/advice/2020/03/11/practical-advice-instructors-facedabrupt-move-online-teaching-opinion

Murray, D. S. (2019). The precarious new faculty majority: Communication and instruction research and contingent labor in higher education. *Communication Education, 68*(2), 235–245. https://doi.org/10.1080/03634523.2019.1568512

PRNewswire. (2021, March 15). American food and grocery shopping patterns have changed one year into the COVID pandemic according to latest NC Solutions consumer survey and consumer purchase data. *Cision PR Newswire.* https://prn.to/3yRa4B7

Rudick, C. K., & Dannels, D. P. (2020). "Yes, and . . ." continuing the scholarly conversation about pandemic pedagogy. *Communication Education, 69*(4), 540–544. https://doi.org/10.1080/03634523.2020.1809167

Swerzenski, J. D. (2021). Why teaching technology must adapt to our teaching. *Communication Education, 70*(2), 211–213. https://doi.org/10.1080/03634523.2020.1857414

Waymer, D. (2021). Addressing disciplinary whiteness and racial justice advocacy in communication education. *Communication Education, 70*(1), 114–116. https://doi.org/10.1080/03634523.2020.1811362

White, A., & LaBelle, S. (2019). A qualitative investigation of instructors' perceived communicative roles in students' mental health management. *Communication Education, 68*(2), 133–155. https://doi.org/10.1080/03634523.2019.1571620

Wright, S., Haskett, M. E., & Anderson, J. (2020). When your students are hungry and homeless: The crucial role of faculty. *Communication Education, 69*(2), 260–267. https://doi.org/10.1080/03634523.2020.1724310

13

THE RHETORICAL SITUATION AND ITS PROBLEMS

Expanding the Discursive Elements of Educational Contexts, Disability, and Social Movements

Diana Isabel Martínez

Learning Objectives

By the end of this chapter, students will be able to do the following:

1. Assess the relationship between how rhetorical situations, discursive terms, and social conditions led to specific educational contexts in 2020.
2. Explore ways in which rhetorical terms highlight particular elements of discourse and leave out other equally important elements.
3. Consider generative possibilities of adding terminology to center the 2020 context and how these may equip publics for future rhetorical situations.

Introduction: Rites of Passage in the Context of 2020

Like many other "typical" years, 2020 included milestones for my family, big moments that cause parents to both celebrate their children's accomplishments and lament how quickly they grow. The rite of passage between kindergarten and first grade provides the precursor, visualization, and simulation to a high school or college graduation. These rituals, along with others, such as simulating voting during a presidential election or investing in the stock market, comprise some educational activities that train students in activities that comprise desirable forms of citizenship. Students may see their pictures as young kindergarten graduates with cap and gowns before beginning on the 12-year journey toward a possible high school graduation. Regardless of how families choose to mark the occasion, it serves as a performative rehearsal for what is to come.

Unlike many other years, the year 2020 would result in drastically different-looking graduations, that is, if they took place at all. The closing of schools due

DOI: 10.4324/9781003220466-15

to the COVID-19 pandemic represented one of the myriad circumstances that encompassed the year, including issues over racial injustice, police brutality, family separations at the Southern border, natural disasters, and political and societal divides, to name a few. Some parents of color, such as myself, would grieve the loss of loved ones due to the pandemic and wrestle with the harsh truths regarding how society perceives our existence. My family's intersectional identities also meant adding layers—of medical complexities, neurodiversity, and genetic differences—to the learning environment. Additionally, my working experience added responsibilities of full-time teaching, research, service, and mentoring students, who, like my own daughter, found themselves in an ever-shifting set of norms that would further exacerbate the material and discursive conditions of a prior time.

Unsurprisingly, my daughter's kindergarten graduation did not occur in its usual form, but the new context for this event indulged her pre-existing preferences. Her desire against being the center of attention and amazing effort on the part of educators brought joy to her face from our side of the zoom ceremony. She wore a graduation cap, watched the slideshow of the previous year, and smiled when pictures of her appeared on the screen. The format for this celebration may have been unexpected as school was no longer in session in the face-to-face form. However, watching the graduation video amid her friends' zoom boxes made my daughter feel comfortable. The accommodations forced on us by the unusual constraints in this rhetorical situation meant that I would sit by her side. I recalled that she hated sitting on the stage at her Pre-K graduation, not understanding why she sat far away from her family. At the end of the kindergarten graduation, her teacher and aides told all of us that they look forward to the following year when things would "return to normal."

Unfortunately, online schooling did not end with my daughter's kindergarten graduation in May 2020 when schools operated under survival mode. Educational accommodations were put on hold at this time, such as IEP plans,[1] speech therapy, occupational therapy, music classes, and more. Upon the start of the new school year, in August 2020, however, the "new norm" of online education encapsulated the agreed-upon accommodations legally granted to the children requiring educational supports. As a parent, I had the choice over how to support my daughter during online education. Having a full-time faculty job and college students to teach of my own, I decided to attend the first grade with my daughter, teach my classes in the afternoon, and catch up on administrative work in the evenings.

This chapter encapsulates my experiences as a mother of a student who attended a "special day" class on zoom with my daughter and considers how my training in rhetoric helped me make sense of the situation along with the "equipment for living" (Burke, 1973) that these moments offered.[2] The essay will make use of my experiences in supporting my daughter navigate online education to highlight the consequential nature of theories of rhetoric and communication, particularly how they are crucial for understanding and navigating the complexity of 2020.

Rhetorical Concepts, Their Discontents, and Centering Marginalized Experiences

To gain an understanding of how both my daughter and I found ourselves amid this year—within the context of our status as a neuro- and genetically divergent family, a global pandemic, police brutality, and families separated at the border—key rhetorical concepts help to explore the nuances of the moment. Using the Lloyd Bitzer's rhetorical situation as a starting point, and focusing on spaces in which the terms are not flexible enough to encompass marginalized experiences, this chapter explores discursive concepts in the context of 2020.

Rhetorical Situation and "Fitting" Responses

The rhetorical situation explores "the nature of those contexts in which speakers or writers create rhetorical discourse" (Bitzer, 1968, p. 1). Bitzer provided examples of how discourse may indicate the presence of a rhetorical situation when he mentioned, among several instances, the Declaration of Independence and Lincoln's Gettysburg Address (p. 2). The rhetorical situation of the pandemic resulted in former President Barack Obama delivering a graduation speech to the entire class of 2020—a most atypical practice given the usually more localized, traditional commencement ceremony. Alternatively, the rhetorical situation surrounding my daughter's elementary school involved a kindergarten graduation that occurred on a smaller scale, yet it exemplified a type of event taking place across classes all over the nation. The rhetorical situation can be a starting point to discuss public speeches; this tool also helps to explore other forms of publicly available discourse, such as online interactions on social media platforms, town hall meetings, and advertisements.

When public discourse focuses on the contents of a speech, the context emphasizes the relationship between the rhetor or speaker, audience, and constraints. The theory suggests that the speaker, writer, or rhetor appreciate all aspects of the rhetorical situation to deliver an effective address. Additionally, as we evaluate discourse, we should consider what a communicator passed over, ignored, or highlighted about the situation to determine the nature of public discourse in relation to discourse produced by other publics. Three components of the rhetorical situation exist before the "creation and presentation of discourse," beginning with the "exigence," which is a "defect, an obstacle, something waiting to be done, a thing which is other than it should be" (Bitzer, 1968, p. 6).

An exigence is rhetorical, according to Bitzer (1968), when it can be modified by discourse. Bitzer stated that a natural disaster does not have this quality. As a corollary, pockets of rhetorical opportunities exist in those situations, such as how to send aid in the context of a natural disaster, how that aid gets distributed, and to whom. Communication students should identify the portions of the context which lend themselves to rhetorical intervention. According to Bitzer, "In any rhetorical situation there will be at least one controlling exigence which functions as the organizing principle: it specifies the audience to be addressed and the change to be effected" (p. 7). He asserted that a "right answer" exists for how to respond to events; however, my daughter's identity and my own identity in the context of K–12 education are such that we did not respond in the desired way to messages meant for a general audience. The instructions for accessing zoom and the classroom are based on the general education curriculum which presupposes that students will be with their class for major components of the day and that they have the necessary social skills to interact with classmates when the teacher provides instruction to the entire class, in small groups, and during transitional periods. However, in the context of special education, several factors impact the range of possible responses which differ from conceptualizing zoom instruction in the general education environment.

For example, part of my daughter's schooling requires her leaving class to receive speech therapy, and this space also involves learning socialization techniques to help prevent bullying. Upon a superficial read of the context, it may appear that providing speech services and anti-bullying socialization would not be anything but beneficial. However, upon closer examination, my rhetorical training helped me see the consequences of these generally established practices.

First, I realized that administrators removed my daughter from class during the morning reading lesson. Given that the special day class aims to help students meet grade level standards with additional support, leaving the class put her at an academic disadvantage as she missed the lesson and, on a social level, a major component of the day. This timing puts children in a situation in which they must do three times the work: the reading lesson, the speech exercise, and the social lesson.

Second, I learned that the speech and social training works against the naturally occurring communication patterns of neurodiversity[3] in favor of training students to pass as neurotypical. For example, upon sitting with my daughter on zoom, she was excited to have a session with her friend upon discovering toys in their respective rooms that lit up and made sounds. However, the therapist explained that playing with her friend would not be considered as appropriate behavior; instead, she directed the kids to ask each other questions and practice turn-taking. In watching this interaction, the students followed instructions and produced the desired response to the rhetorical situation; however, the glimmer in their eyes went away. The therapist informed the kids what comprised appropriate communication regardless of how that communication felt to them.

Further, the students were taught to determine when someone was making comments to them that were appropriate and when they were not supportive. In other words, the students learned how to tell if someone was making fun of them. Relatedly, I discovered that children in this school only integrate with their neurotypical peers during recess and music time and that lessons on socialization do not occur beyond the special education classroom. Neurotypical students do not learn these same lessons, which may be beneficial to them in their social world regardless of their brain chemistry; however, they never learn how to adjust *their* communication style to accommodate neurodivergent peers.

In other words, when thinking of the rhetorical situation and its accompanying desired response, we should ask why that response is desired and who that response benefits. Is the desired response of a rhetorical situation creating a more supportive environment for everyone or fostering conditions for exclusion? We should understand what the desired response means to a rhetorical situation and then consider the consequences therein.

Rhetorical Audiences and the Role of Agency

The audience comprises the next component of the rhetorical situation. Bitzer (1968, p. 8) asserted that

> [i]t is clear also that a rhetorical audience must be distinguished from a body of mere hearers or readers: properly speaking, a rhetorical audience consists only of those persons who are capable of being influenced by discourse and of being mediators of change.

An essential element of rhetorical discourse, according to Bitzer, presents itself here: not all "hearers" of a message have rhetorical significance. Although, for Bitzer, people outside of the definition of audience members may be mere "hearers," nuances deserve further attention. What does it mean not to be included in rhetorical discourse or seen as a mediator of change?

This definition holds several consequences for the educational context. While students learn and benefit from the rules and principles used to educate them, they, along with their families, do not fit Bitzer's definition as mediators of change. In other words, in the context of 2020, students followed rules and mandates as they entered online educational environments; however, how administrators ran those contexts, how they received accommodations for adapting to this alternate form of education, or how they determined synchronous versus asynchronous elements of their day was out of their hands. The students had, as a consequence, no defined rhetorical significance. What are the effects of this realization?

Educators assumed that students are digital natives and that the duty of the school district encompasses providing a working laptop for the online educational environment; however, in reality, the digital divide created difficulties for students. Schwartzman (2020) cited a study stating that "approximately one in seven K-12 age children, most with household incomes below $50,000, have no Internet access at home. One-fourth of teens whose household income falls below $30,000 have access to a computer at home" (p. 508). Schwartzman also noted another study that concluded "[b]roadband access limitations prevent more than one-sixth of teens from completing their homework" (p. 508). In practice, students tried to complete their assignments from parking lots or other places with Internet hot spots. Others with connection to the Internet had the option of joining their online classes in their homes; however, bad connections meant that some students' participation was choppy at best. Popular articles surfaced regarding how the digital divide continues to manifest itself, and how it had a particularly detrimental impact on people of color (Population Reference Bureau, 2020; McDonald, 2020, December 8). I witnessed some of this lack of connectivity both by attending my daughter's class and from teaching classes of my own.

In an effort to make sense of my rhetorical options as a mother, I joined online mommy groups in digital platforms. While I hoped to enter spaces of connection and joint collaboration, the space seemed increasingly polarizing. I read heated debates regarding what we should or should not be doing on Halloween and the "secret spots" for trick-or-treating. Regarding the educational context, I noticed the monetization of educational resources. For example, desks were all sold out and highly over-priced. In my home, we opted for a loaner from the school to create a learning space from which to attend zoom classes. While I did have the resources to purchase a desk, the monetization of this good based on supply and demand meant that it was suddenly no longer affordable, especially to those with more limited resources.

Relatedly, pandemic "bubbles" or study buddies quickly formed. Parents, mostly moms, discussed where to find and hire good tutors who would take a "pod" of students and make sure that the students would not fall behind. In order to form this type of group, the assumption seemed to be that families would connect with one another, based on their ability to be on social media, and join one or two families who would be part of their pandemic bubble. Based on my reading of these discussion posts, the students would meet with a few others face-to-face with a hired tutor to ensure that they continued their education with the maximum support.

On the flip side, some of my daughter's classmates did not have such options, particularly children of essential personnel or working parents who sent their children to a district location or private daycare. While this format may have seemed like an alternative to the pod system formed in the mommy circles, these daycare facilities were not equipped for zoom instruction. Some of the other students in my daughter's classroom left unexpectedly, experienced technical difficulties, and/or lacked the tools to communicate with aides who were not able to understand that the child was muted or not speaking loud enough to be heard while wearing a mask. Students also juggled various times for their speech therapy sessions and occupational therapy work that conflicted with math, music, or art. Additionally, when teachers placed students in breakout rooms for their "centers" time, many of them got disconnected or confronted other kinds of technical difficulties. Taken together, these experiences underscored the need to examine all audiences, those with power and those who are affected by policies.

Rhetorical Constraints as Social Factors

The third element of the rhetorical situation, the constraints, are "made up of persons, events, objects, and relations which are parts of the situation because they have the power to constrain decision and action needed to modify the exigence" (Bitzer, 1968, p. 8). This chapter has alluded to constraints in each section preceding this one when exploring the extraordinary context of 2020. This section expands the discussion on constraints to explore how people may experience these moments differently and, thus, lead to a variety of experiences of this moment. Bitzer explained that "[t]here are two main classes of constraints: (1) those originated or managed by the rhetor and his method . . . and (2) those other constraints in the situation which may be operative" (p. 8).

In the context of my daughter's school, several officials communicated with parents and students during this time, such as school district personnel, via e-mail and social media, moms in geographically-based social media platforms, and public health officials via town halls as well as mediated and digital platforms. My daughter interacted with direct figures of authority—including her teacher, classroom aides, and various therapists—who provided supports throughout the day. My interactions with all of these players and my daughter's attendance in class meant that we encountered a myriad of messages to process the evolving rules and environment. In other words, the rhetor (in this case, the school district) "not only harnesses constraints given by situation but provides additional important constraints—for example . . . personal character, . . . logical proofs, and . . . style" (Bitzer, 1968, p. 8).

In the context of a public speaking situation, we might identify a rhetor or speaker, but a single speech may be written by the speaker, a team of speech writers, communication coaches and rarely represent a single idea or respond to a single constraint. In the example of official communication received by a student, multiple actors, divisions, and e-mail lists resulted in receiving messages from multiple sources. Acknowledging the potential of multiple stakeholders involved in messaging, I argue, provides a more holistic perspective of the communication process.

At my daughter's school, each actor operated under the general constraint of being on survival mode and constantly shifting, based on guidelines, expectations, and largely exploratory methods. For example, for the first few weeks of zoom instruction, my daughter had to use a district platform to turn in work; over time, the teacher suggested turning in work over e-mail. The amount of work that was sent home to be completed transitioned from being "mandatory" to "suggested and more than what a student would be able to complete on a given day." Some weeks included strict schedules while others featured "choice boards" which were designed to give students flexibility and agency in deciding what work to complete. The classroom aides were not always fully trained on the technology to ensure that the students were able to see a book or demonstration. Students who had their parents or grandparents with them received more positive attention and praise for completing tasks, while teachers often reprimanded students who were alone for speaking out of turn, failing to mute their microphones, or not understanding how to join breakout rooms.

Additionally, our interactions were shaped by the constraint of neurodiversity, genetic difference, and gender. Neurodiverse girls face a whole other set of constraints than boys, a consequence of the medical model of neurodiversity that uses boys as the prototype for labeling neurodivergent traits (Young et al., 2018). Hyperactivity in the form of misbehavior, for example, requires educators to intervene, informed by corresponding categories of testing required for the IEPs.[4] Educators deem emotional disturbances as educational barriers for neurodivergent children. However, according to Young et al., studies on neurodiverse girls suggest that gendered socialization may result in girls' needs going unnoticed. While girls may "hold it together" in some contexts, they also have needs for accommodations, and they confront the added violence of ignoring or erasing the ways in which they experience and communicate neurodiversity.

For the first time in my daughter's educational journey, I had the opportunity to sit next to her and see how she processes information and learns while attending school. I noticed that the slightest shifts in the classroom, such as the sound of my attempting to type an e-mail while sitting next to her, took her out of the space required for focus. On other occasions, she attempted to answer a question posed to her, and the teacher did not hear her or see her work. Sometimes, the teacher or aide counted items on a sheet of paper that were too close together. We did our best with the help of number lines, visual schedules, and other visual cues to help us complete these tasks—usually items that I devised up during the short breaks, tools to be more independent in these spaces. These moments caused a level of understandable frustration that was difficult to shake off. Eventually, we developed quick phrases that my daughter could use to signal to her teachers that she needed support, such as "It is too loud;" "I need more time," or "This is distracting me." I realized that no one had taught her how to communicate these needs, but, now that she is back in-person at school, her teachers consistently attest that they are better able to support her when she uses these phrases.

The rhetorical situation proves to be a helpful tool for identifying how the context affects communicators at the intersection of the COVID-19 pandemic, K-12 schools, and beyond. Naming each part of the rhetorical situation helps to make sense of this complex web of information, brings to light the assumptions associated with each component, and aids in uncovering where people have opportunities for agency. In other words, using this rhetorical model for analyzing the experiences discussed in this chapter helps students understand how communication responds to significant constraints; however, it also highlights how people who are glossed over can adapt in meaningful ways. Understanding the rhetorical situation enables us to consider the individual actions of rhetors, audience, and "hearers" within a larger context in which those actors are placed.

Additionally, the plethora of social factors—police brutality, the hearing for the murder of George Floyd, protests that I attended, and the continued erasure of separated families enduring cruel and inhumane conditions at the Southern border—also greatly affected the educational context as we entered the 2020s. During President Biden's inauguration day, my daughter and I watched Amanda Gorman—the youngest inaugural poet—deliver her piece, Jennifer Lopez's performance which included some words in Spanish, and Supreme Court Associate Justice Sonia Sotomayor swear in Kamala Harris, the first Black and South Asian woman to hold the office of vice president of the United States. During walks, we stopped at lawn signs that read "Black Lives Matter" and talked about what that meant to us, our family, and our country. These moments were not external to the 2020 context; instead, these integral moments affected our daily conversations, the books we read, the causes we supported, and how we envisioned ourselves. Bitzer (1968) argued that "[s]ituations may become weakened in structure due to complexity or disconnectedness" (p. 12). However, we choose to embrace these conflicting moments of interconnectedness, isolation, and experiences as a family.

The rhetorical situation highlights the already present circumstances coupled with the unique elements presented in 2020, and these concepts help to reveal strategies that were readily available and those that formed out of the existing conditions. The educational context does not center neurodiversity or other differences; however, my daughter was able to find a voice, learn how to make requests that would help her meet her educational goals, and respond with agency when other actors may not have seen her as an agent. The rhetorical situation not only exposes the elements of the situation that solicit a response, but also opens up space to discuss which actors are summoned to respond, under what circumstances, and what tools are available for people who are systematically excluded from these situations. In other words, the concepts offer "equipment for living" and underscore the importance of understanding rhetoric for navigating our everyday lives.

Notes

1. An IEP refers to an Individual Education Plan, which is a legal document that is available to students in the United States taking part in special education services. It includes accommodations and supports to be implemented during the school year by a team of education specialists including the child's teacher, school psychologist, and other specialists as needed such as speech, occupational, and physical therapists. This list of specialists is not exhaustive, but it provides a glimpse into the team of professionals who assess and work with the special education student.
2. Kenneth Burke explains that literature can function as equipment for living by offering its readers with tools for handling experiences in their everyday lives.
3. Neurodiversity considers that neurological makeup will include natural variations, all of which are part of the human experience (Jaarsma & Welin, 2012). When considering how to discuss autism identities for example, a medical model focuses on diagnosis and tends to use terms such as "disorder"; on the other hand, social models and/or paradigms such as that of neurodiversity focus on differences as identities outside of medical models (Angulo-Jiménez & DeThorne, 2019).

4. After the passage of the 2004 Individuals with Disabilities Education Improvement Act (IDEA), functional behavior assessments, which included "various methods used to identify environmental variables that evoke and maintain problem behavior" went from occurring in clinical settings to more educational ones (Anderson et al., 2015, p. 338). This form of assessment is used to come up with behavioral goals and supports in the IEP (Iowa IDEA Information, n.d.).

References

Anderson, C. M., Rodriguez, B. J., & Campbell, A. (2015). Functional behavior assessment in schools: Current status and future directions. *Journal of Behavioral Education, 24,* 338–371.

Angulo-Jiménez, H., & DeThorne, L. (2019). Narratives about autism: An analysis of YouTube videos by individuals who self-identify as autistic. *American Journal of Speech-Language Pathology, 28,* 569–590.

Bitzer, L. F. (1968). The rhetorical situation. *Philosophy and Rhetoric, 1*(1), 1–18.

Burke, K. (1973). *Philosophy of literary form: Studies in symbolic action* (3rd ed.). University of California Press.

Iowa IDEA Information (n.d.). *Behavior in an IEP.* https://iowaideainformation.org/special-education/individualized-education-programs/behavior-in-an-iep/

Jaarsma, P., & Welin, S. (2012). Autism as a natural human variation: Reflections on the claims of the neurodiversity movement. *Health Care Analysis, 20,* 20–30.

McDonald, John. (2020, December 8). Despite improved access, digital divide persists for minority, low-income students. *UCLA Newsroom.* https://newsroom.ucla.edu/releases/digital-divide-persists-for-minority-low-income-students

Population Reference Bureau. (2020, September 2). *Children, Coronavirus, and the digital divide: Native American, Black, and Hispanic Students at greater educational risk during pandemic.* https://www.prb.org/resources/children-coronavirus-and-the-digital-divide-native-american-black-and-hispanic-students-at-greater-educational-risk-during-pandemic/

Schwartzman, R. (2020). Performing pandemic pedagogy. *Communication Education, 69*(4), 502–517.

Young, H., Oreve, M.-J., & Speranza, M. (2018). Clinical characteristics and problems diagnosing autism spectrum disorder in girls. *Archives de Pédiatrie, 25*(6), 399–403.

14

POLITICAL COMMUNICATION

Trevor Parry-Giles

Learning Objectives

Upon completing this chapter, the reader will:

1. Appreciate and understand the ubiquity of political communication in the 2020s.
2. Understand the range of theories to explain how people communicate politically.

Introduction

To fully understand my 2020 political communication experiences, let us go back in time, all the way to 1984; that is when my love of politics and political communication really began. I really do love politics—I am a bona fide political nerd—presidential elections are my Olympics, my Super Bowl. I look forward to presidential elections like a college basketball fan looks forward to March Madness, and all that began in 1984 and the Wisconsin Democratic caucuses.

A few things about 1984: the number one song in the land was *When Doves Cry* by Prince; the highest grossing film that year was *Beverly Hills Cop* (the first one, not the regrettable sequels); not surprisingly, the number one bestselling book was George Orwell's *1984*; on television, viewers by the millions were watching *Dynasty* and *Dallas* every week, and I was a college junior at Ripon College in Ripon, Wisconsin majoring in Communication and Politics and Government. It was my first presidential election—I was too young to vote in 1980, and, even though I had been interested in politics and presidents for a very long time (since at least fifth-grade social studies!), the prospect of voting was very exciting; I was actually going to be a full-fledged citizen.

DOI: 10.4324/9781003220466-16

I should probably say, at this point, that I am a Democrat, and I was a Democrat in 1984. My partisan affiliation is only relevant because, like so many elections to come, the 1984 presidential election involved an active and contested Democratic primary process to select the party's presidential nominee. So not only was I going to get to vote for president of the United States—but I was also going to play a part in the selection of my party's nominee. Even more than that, I was going to be part of history—for the first time in its history, the state of Wisconsin was holding a presidential caucus. All in all, 1984 was pretty exciting and an important moment in my political development.

I remember, very clearly, going to the Ripon municipal center on that Saturday in April for the first-ever caucuses. I remember caucusing for former Vice President Walter Mondale and being dispatched by my companion Mondale caucus-goers to the supporters of another candidate to entice them over to the Mondale camp. I remember the excitement when my candidate prevailed, the excitement when my candidate won the nomination, the excitement when my candidate made history by selecting a woman (the first woman in this role) to serve as his running mate, and I remember the profound disappointment when my candidate lost, and lost big, in the general election in November. I allowed myself the feeble hope that Mondale might actually win, even well into election night, only to have that hope dashed by the landslide re-election victory of President Ronald Reagan.

I recall the events of 1984 every four years and especially when there is an open primary for the Democratic nomination. Indeed, the parallels between 1984 and 2020 were especially notable—the contest for the Democratic nomination featured a former vice-president challenged by candidates more progressive in their outlook. In 2020, as in 1984, a significant challenge in the nomination contest came from a candidate of color (civil rights leader Jesse Jackson), and, in 2020, as in 1984, the nominee of the Democratic Party selected a woman to be his running mate. However, that's where the similarities end, and this chapter begins.

I have specifically recalled the events of 1984 to indicate just how political communication in the United States has changed in 36 years and, conversely, how much of how we communicate politically has stayed the same. In one sense, political communication was, in 1984, the same kind of conversation that it was in 2020—a three-way interaction between voters/citizens, candidates/campaigns, and media/news. By the late 20th century, this conversational dynamic comprised a clear way of understanding political communication, especially at the presidential level. Every two or four years, a whole lot of messages emanate from political parties and candidates, trying to get voters/citizens to contribute time and money and, ultimately, to vote. Yet, political campaigns are never entirely dialogic—for the entirety of American political history, a third party has joined this conversation. Though it has changed considerably in terms of both content and form, some type of news media has functioned as a conduit, a channel for political communication. Understanding political communication in the 2020s and beyond, thus, requires reflection about this specific conversation and how it has developed over time. Only then can we ponder how this conversation will seem in the future and whether it will continue to occur at all.

Voters/Citizens

Not every 20-year-old was as excited as I was in 1984 to finally get the chance to vote. After all, voter turnout in the United States continues to be anemically low, especially when compared to other democracies around the world. According to the Pew Research Center (2020), the percentage of U.S. voting age population that actually voted in 2016 was 55.72%—compare that to the 62.32% voter turnout in the United Kingdom, the 69.11% turnout in Germany, or the 80.79% in Australia. Americans just generally do not get too excited about voting.

Perhaps worse, these figures illustrate just how Americans sometimes seem to take voting for granted. For most of American history, voting has been a very restricted right—women have only been able to vote in federal elections for 101 years; African American men received the right to vote by virtue of the 15th Amendment in 1870 only to endure decades of voter suppression (Keyssar, 2000). Indeed, except for the 15th, 19th, and 26th amendments, the U.S. Constitution is silent as to the right to vote, and states and localities across the country have sought to limit, restrict, control, and/or remove voting rights from large numbers of Americans (Berman, 2015). By taking voting for granted, non-voting Americans validate this history and dishonor the many brave Americans who have fought, protested, even died, to protect and secure voting rights.

Voting constitutes just one marker of citizenship in the American democratic republic. It has changed considerably over the span of American history—Schudson (1998) argued that Americans have progressed through four different stages of citizenship, often defined by approaches and perspectives toward voting. During the founding period in the late 18th and early 19th centuries, a politics of assent and deference defined civic life, with extremely restricted voting, and voters reaffirmed (assented) to the highly stratified social hierarchies in place at the time. By the mid-19th century, civic life came to be defined by growing and powerful political parties; voting was still restricted, and citizens voted mostly on the basis of party affiliation. Voting reforms developed and emerged in the early 20th century, and the party affiliated voter of the 19th century gave way to the informed, educated voter of the 20th century. Civic life changed again, according to Schudson, in the post-World War II period, when the informed voter became the rights-bearing voter who voted mostly to protect newly secured civil rights. When I first voted in 1984, I was a rights-bearing voter as per Schudson's categories. However, a lot has changed in the 20 years since Schudson categorized civic life in the United States—how would we define voting and civic life in the 2020s?

We could answer that voting and civic life in the 2020s is more polarized than ever before—at least that's what journalists and pundits say all the time in the age of Donald Trump. Of course, that claim is entirely de-historicized because

Americans have always been polarized politically (Klein, 2020). The extremes of American polarization were awfully stark during the Civil War, in the lead-up to World War II, and during the Civil Rights era, among other times. While it is true that Americans are polarized in the 2020s, they are not more or less polarized than at other times—the more important questions seek to understand the source(s) of political polarization. Where does such polarization come from? What aspects of contemporary political communication (social media, political ads, cable news coverage) encourage and magnify political polarization? Scholars of political communication spend considerable time trying to answer these questions and come to some clearer understanding of the polarization of American voters and citizens (e.g., Warner, 2018; Warner & McKinney, 2013).

Thinking back to 1984, Americans were less polarized even as they were still clearly divided along partisan and ideological grounds. The ongoing Cold War provided a possible reason for the lesser polarized politics of the 1980s—the United States had an external "enemy" in the Soviet Union, and the Cold War opposition to the Soviets minimized internal divisions. When that conflict ended, in the late 1980s and early 1990s, the political attitudes and communications in the American public sphere fractured along a variety of levels, continuing the fracturing from the 1960s and 1970s along racial and gendered grounds (Rodgers, 2011). It is probably no accident that the 1984 presidential election marked the last one to result in a real landslide. Since then, presidential elections have been close, often very close (Leip, 2019).

In 1984, Americans also protested, petitioned, redressed their government, and performed citizenship in a variety of ways. Citizenship in the United States is, and always has been, about more than just voting, and the 2020 Americans who protested the murder of George Floyd or the presidency of Donald Trump or the worsening of the climate crisis followed in the footsteps of so many before them who had protested and marched and petitioned (see Holbein & Hillygus, 2020). In the end, voters and citizens in the United States bolster and support a robust, polarized, and often complicated political culture; they do so via an array of different, highly charged political communications that enrich and enhance democratic life in the United States.

Candidates/Campaigns

Back in 1984, millions of Americans responded well to the messages and campaign entreaties of the Reagan re-election effort. The Reagan campaign worked successfully to convince voters that it was "morning again in America" and that President Reagan's leadership was good for the United States and had helped the country to recover from the excesses and scandals of the 1970s. As a Democrat, I was not among those persuaded by Reagan's rhetoric even as I was impressed by its effectiveness; I also lamented the ineffectiveness of my candidate's campaign even as I was persuaded that Walter Mondale would be a better president.

Nearly 40 years later, the candidates have changed, and their campaigns have expanded and extended, but the essential dynamics remain the same—candidates and their campaigns strive to demonstrate their viability and possibility as elected leaders to a wide range of voters and citizens. Campaign messages are ubiquitous, and they dominate the airwaves, cable news channels, voter mailboxes, for months on end. For political nerds like me, all these campaign messages are wonderful; for political communication scholars and teachers, they are a treasure trove of teachable moments and research projects.

These campaign messages ask voters and citizens to reach a political judgment, what Beiner (1983) defined as a comprehensive faculty whereby citizens process and comprehend political phenomena. For most citizens, that judgment they are asked to reach is rooted in significant cognitive processes about matters of public policy and political character. In other words, countless campaigns and candidates' messages ask citizens to come to a considered judgment about a lot of information—What do the candidates believe? What will they do if elected? Do I agree with their stated policy positions? Will they be an effective leader? And that is just the beginning. It is no wonder that voters and citizens find all of this communication exhausting, and they regularly report high levels of apathy and disdain for campaigns and political talk (Cappella & Jamieson, 1997).

A lot of the campaign messaging and candidate communication that voters experience is pretty mundane—many of the stump speeches that candidates present are recycled platitudes; many of the political ads on television and radio sound pretty similar (Trent et al., 2011). Every now and then, a campaign speech will move beyond the mundane and the repetitive, and we remember those moments as important rhetorical touchstones in our national story. For example, when Barack Obama spoke about race during the 2008 campaign, he transcended routine campaign oratory and hit more important, significant rhetorical themes for the larger culture (Hernández, 2013; Rowland & Jones, 2011). Some campaign moments of significance occur in debates, or at conventions, or at special speech occasions; sometimes, political commercials can capture the collective zeitgeist in ways that both help the campaign and say something of larger importance to the broader political culture. One instance occurred prominently in 1964 when the campaign of President Lyndon B. Johnson ran an ad about the dangerous prospect of nuclear war—the "Daisy" ad featured a young girl plucking flower pedals while counting them and then morphing into a countdown to a nuclear explosion complete with dramatic mushroom cloud (Jamieson, 1996). Though the spot only ran once, it was re-broadcast repeatedly in news media reports. It became one of the most notorious political commercials of all time (Mann, 2011).

Media/News

When I was an excited, blossoming politico in 1984, my media menu was pretty limited in ways that today's political communication consumer would hardly recognize. Imagine a small diner—it has a restricted menu of just a few items—some hamburgers, perhaps, and a few breakfast items, maybe a steak or some fried chicken. Now imagine the menu at The Cheesecake Factory—pages and pages of different dining options that is almost overwhelming. The small diner menu is what the political media looked like in 1984. The internet was a figment of the Defense Department's imagination then, and not much existed in the way of cable news either. Most citizens got their news from the three main broadcast networks (ABC, CBS, NBC) or from their local newspaper, and all newspapers were local in 1984—*USA Today* was the only national newspaper in circulation in 1984, and it had only been around for two years (Pew Research, 2021). News was cyclical and episodic, not ubiquitous and constant.

In the 2020s, we live in a Cheesecake Factory menu of political news. Every social media feed is filled with political news, ranging from entirely bogus and made up to very credible and fact-based. A burgeoning number of cable news networks fill 24 hours of airtime with nearly endless chatter about all things political. Citizens and voters can find their political news at any time, day or night, from any source, about anything and anyone. Voters in the 2020s have access to more political news from more sources than ever before in American history.

As a result of the proliferating, ubiquitous media, political messaging and communication has changed dramatically. Speechmaking has shifted and changed as the audiences for those speeches have become increasingly remote and distant (Jamieson, 1988). All sorts of political communication have become more intimate and more personal (Meyrowitz, 1985); gone are the days of the big, booming platform speech, replaced now with the closely shot political "video announcement" that voters find in their Facebook feeds or on YouTube. That intimacy via television and other visual media is charming and seductive, changing the nature of the relationship between political leaders and citizens (Hart, 1998).

Candidates and citizen groups now have websites and Twitter feeds, Facebook pages and YouTube channels. The rise of social media and its growing popularity have preoccupied scholars and teachers of political communication; more than any other factor, social media's growth has generated the ubiquity of political communication and resulted in the prolific spread of all types of political messages, both true and false, good and bad (Davis & Owen, 1998; Farrar-Myers & Vaughn, 2015; Hall & Sinclair, 2019; Martin, 2017; Sunstein, 2017). The changes in the mediation of political communication over the past few decades have challenged and provoked (and even alienated) voters and citizens like few other developments in the political history of the United States.

Conclusion

On April 19, 2021, Walter Mondale died at the age of 92. When I heard about his passing, I remembered those heady days in 1984 when I trudged down to the civic center in Ripon, Wisconsin to vote for him; I remembered his legacy, his record, his good nature, and his commitment to public service. It may seem a bit maudlin to the jaded political consumer of the 2020s, but Mondale's passing recalled a time when good people ran for public office and continued to do good work after they had left office, a time when Americans to a more significant degree trusted their leaders and their government.

Therein lie the lessons of the last 36 years. For while political communication has changed and spread and is faster than ever before, it also poses a range of questions for the political communication scholar and student. As voters and citizens, how do we process the increasing volume of political messages coming at us all the time? How can we sort out the false from the true? How do we train our young citizens to be critical consumers of political communication? And most importantly, how do we engage in meaningful and informative conversations with candidates and political leaders?

From another angle, how can our candidates and their campaigns communicate better and more substantially with voters and citizens? How can the political culture encourage good people to seek public office and to pursue public service? How can campaigns and candidates ask for the most considered political judgment from voters and citizens? In terms of that ongoing political conversation, we must also ask about the role of the media. How do we want social media to participate and organize America's political conversations? How do we encourage news media away from the sensational and the clickbait toward the substantive and meaningful? How can our political reporters ask better questions, write better stories, investigate scandals and mendacity in a fair and balanced way that contributes meaningfully to our political conversation?

In the end, it is all about the conversation, the communication. If the political culture and political campaigns in the United States can improve in the 2020s, and beyond, all parties in the ongoing political conversation must strive to be better, must work on renewing our civic faith and our civic duty as Americans to, as the late Arizona senator John McCain often said, a cause that is bigger than ourselves, a purpose that uplifts and upholds.

References

Beiner, R. (1983). *Political judgment*. University of Chicago Press.

Berman, A. (2015). *Give us the ballot: The modern struggle for voting rights in America*. Farrar, Straus and Giroux.

Cappella, J. N., & Jamieson, K. H. (1997). *Spirals of cynicism: The press and the public good*. Oxford University Press.

Davis, R., & Owen, D. (1998). *New media and American politics*. Oxford University Press.

Farrar-Myers, V. A., & Vaughn, J. S. (Eds.). (2015). *Controlling the message: New media in American political campaigns*. New York University Press.

Hall, T., & Sinclair, B. (2019). *A connected America: Politics in the era of social media*. Oxford University Press.

Hart, R. P. (1998). *Seducing America: How television charms the modern voter*. SAGE.

Hernández, C. A. P. (2013). The constitutive role of emotions in the discursive construction of the 'people': A look into Obama's 2008 'race speech.' *Signs and Society, 1*(2), 273–296.

Holbein, J. B., & Hillygus, D. S. (2020). *Making young voters: Converting civic attitudes into civic action.* Cambridge University Press.

Jamieson, K. H. (1988). *Eloquence in an electronic age: The transformation of political speechmaking.* Oxford University Press.

Jamieson, K. H. (1996). *Packaging the presidency: A history and criticism of presidential campaign advertising* (3rd ed.). Oxford University Press.

Keyssar, A. (2000). *The right to vote: The contested history of democracy in the United States.* Basic Books.

Klein, E. (2020). *Why we're polarized.* Avid Reader Press/Simon & Schuster.

Leip, D. (2019). *Dave Leip's atlas of U.S. presidential elections.* https://uselectionatlas.org/.

Mann, R. (2011). *Daisy, petals, and mushroom clouds: LBJ, Barry Goldwater, and the ad that changed American politics.* Louisiana State University Press.

Martin, S. A. (Ed.). (2017). *Columns to characters: The presidency and the press enter the digital age.* Texas A&M University Press.

Meyrowitz, J. (1985). *No sense of place: The impact of electronic media on social behavior.* Oxford University Press.

Pew Research Center. (2020). https://www.pewresearch.org/fact-tank/2020/11/03/in-past-elections-u-s-trailed-most-developed-countries-in-voter-turnout/

Pew Research Center. (2021). *Newspapers fact sheet.* https://www.pewresearch.org/journalism/fact-sheet/newspapers/

Rodgers, D. T. (2011). *Age of fracture.* Belknap.

Rowland, R. C., & Jones, J. M. (2011). One dream: Barack Obama, race, and the American dream. *Rhetoric & Public Affairs, 14*(1), 125–154.

Schudson, M. (1998). *The good citizen: A history of American civic life.* Free Press.

Sunstein, C. R. (2017). *#republic: Divided democracy in the age of social media.* Princeton University Press.

Trent, J. S., Friedenberg, R. V., & Denton, R. E. (2011). *Political campaign communication: Principles and practices* (7th ed.). Rowman & Littlefield.

Warner, B. R. (2018). Modeling partisan media effects in the 2014 U.S. midterm elections. *Journalism & Mass Communication Quarterly, 95*(3), 647–669.

Warner, B. R., & McKinney, M. S. (2013). To unite and divide: The polarizing effect of presidential debates. *Communication Studies, 64*(5), 508–527.

15

MEDIA SELECTION IN THE 2020s

An Unintentional Experiment

Stephanie A. Tikkanen

Learning Objectives

1. Readers will be able to differentiate between various early media selection theories discussing the motivations individuals have in choosing a medium—mediated or face-to-face—for interpersonal communication.
2. Readers will be encouraged to critically reflect on how media selection behaviors may change after users have been deprived of the option for FtF communication.

The year 2020 was supposed to be a year bringing my little family all sorts of happy changes. Less than a week after I received word of my tenure approval, my husband accepted a new role at a large company in California's Bay Area after working from home for six years. The move brought us back to our home state; we had just welcomed a son, in addition to our daughter. We were excited to be closer to our families—only 30 minutes away from my husband's family and a six-hour drive to my own. My husband left for his new role in early January, and, because I was on maternity leave for the semester, the kids and I were able to join him in mid-February as soon as the baby was ready to fly. While I felt very sad to leave my university, I was optimistic about my job prospects in Silicon Valley; as a scholar of technologically mediated communication (TMC), I was excited about bringing my expertise into the "real world." We were about to start an adventurous new chapter filled with a robust social life, exciting new careers, and lots of time spent outside!

2020, however, had other plans for us.

About a week after I arrived in California, reports of a new virus hitting American shores began to spread. Two weeks in, we started to casually stockpile

DOI: 10.4324/9781003220466-17

canned goods, thinking we might need to hunker down for a bit. We remained hopeful and began to unpack our things in the new house. Having a new baby and functioning on a delicate balance of broken sleep and raging hormones, I opted to delay my attempts at exploring the area and making friends until I could form coherent sentences. I knew the only way that I could feel truly settled in our new home was when I had met my neighbors and done things like finding a new favorite local restaurant—but we thought that we would have plenty of time for socializing soon. Then, a little over a month after we arrived, we suddenly received word of a shelter-in-place edict, and, like most of America, our plans came to a screeching halt.

As this abstract threat of COVID-19 became our reality, the typical loneliness that accompanies new motherhood (Lee et al., 2019) became compounded with a lack of a local support network and the claustrophobia of never leaving our new house. As days turned into weeks, and weeks turned to months, I grew increasingly depressed. Political and social tensions were high, and disagreements with my closest relations over politics and risk perception added psychological distance alongside the physical. I did not receive any responses for any jobs to which I applied, and my self-efficacy plummeted: Was it the job market, or was I simply not qualified for industry work? I recognized my incredible privilege: I was healthy, had savings, could stay home, and did not live in a state of constant fear of violence due to the immutable color of my skin. This realization only made things worse: my guilt weighed heavily on my already tenuous mental health, and I—like many others—nearly reached my breaking point.

However, throughout the emotional obstacle course of uncertainty that was 2020, one thing remained constant: the ability to connect with others via technology. As a Communication scholar, I knew that mediated communication often had a bad reputation within the lay public. Other generations tend to ridicule millennials' known preference for texting, and some communicate an implied hierarchy of which media constitute "professional" and "social" communication forms (Myers & Sadaghiani, 2010). However, most of these prejudices developed in a time when we had options, but what happens when our choice is removed? During COVID-19 lockdowns, computer mediated communication (CMC) became many people's only connection to the outside world. I found a strange solace in seeing the research that I had done on interpersonal communication in online spaces coming to life in new ways, and it made me reflect on how we might use CMC theories to better understand how we might select media more thoughtfully in the future—and perhaps change the reputation of technology.

In this chapter, I will briefly outline some of the early broad history of CMC research, and then expand upon several early media selection theories which describe how and why people choose particular media to communicate. Finally, I will relate those theories to my own 2020 experiences and discuss how communication theory may give us some different ways to think about CMC in the future.

"The New Normal": Face-to-Face versus Computer-Mediated Communication

For most of human history, people communicated entirely without the aid of technology. Mediated forms of communication certainly existed, such as letters, but the majority of communication occurred in real time and with access to all nonverbal cue channels. Even as inventors introduce new technologies, such as the telephone or computers (LaFrance, 2015), users remained skeptical, often preferring the more "real" experience of face-to-face (FtF) communication. In short, FtF became the standard by which we judged mediated communication, and scholars generally presumed that CMC would inevitably fall short (see Bordia, 1997 for review).

However, 2020 presented us with the kind of quasi-experiment that would never pass an ethics review for research at colleges and universities; it largely removed the option to engage in FtF communication and made CMC the "new normal." Rather than being free to choose between modalities, pandemic restrictions forced people to communicate solely through mediated environments. We conducted business meetings and classes through large-capacity videoconferencing software like Zoom or Microsoft Teams and "hung out" with friends and family through coordinated video calls or shared-screen videogames. We texted, snapped, and tweeted. Early on, Americans praised technology for its ability to connect us when we were bound to our homes by either law or fear (Auxier, 2020). As time passed, however, and "Zoom fatigue" set in (Bailenson, 2021), even the staunchest supporters of technology grew wistful for physical human contact.

Early Theorizing about Mediated Communication

When the Internet first became widely available to consumers in the mid-1990s, many users feared the unknown (LaFrance, 2015; Stoll, 1995). This new technology sparked myriad new concerns, chiefly the safety of its users; in a space relatively devoid of nonverbal cues, how could we trust anyone? Early approaches to studying computer-mediated communication (CMC) focused primarily on this relative lack of nonverbal cues; things like vocal (e.g., tone, pitch, volume), oculesics (e.g., eye gaze), or proxemic (e.g., interpersonal distance, lean) cues varied in their ability to be displayed across different media. Early researchers assumed that this "cues-filtered-out" (Culnan & Markus, 1987) approach would have detrimental effects on communication outcomes. Initial research confirmed this speculation—individuals using CMC displayed greater amounts of uninhibited behavior known as flaming, such as swearing, name calling, general hostility, and insulting others (Kielser et al., 1984; Sproull & Kiesler, 1986).

However, several studies that demonized CMC were subject to methodological scrutiny (Walther et al., 1994) and a disconnect from real-world findings. At the same time that CMC researchers and the lay public expressed skepticism, mediated interactions outside of the laboratory actually encompassed great amounts of intimacy and trust. Postmes et al. (1998) found that deindividuating experimental conditions did not lead to antinormative behavior, instead finding increased self-awareness and, in fact, *greater* adherence to situational norms. Similarly, Coleman and colleagues (1999) concluded that CMC participants did not demonstrate significantly more negative behaviors than FtF participants; instead, participants reported having more focused and disclosive conversations, long recognized as a stepping stone to relational development and intimacy (Altman & Taylor, 1973). Chan and Cheng (2004) discovered that, over time, positive relational qualities existed equally in both online and offline friendships. Taken together, these early findings suggested that mediated communication could potentially function as an effective tool to form and maintain close interpersonal relationships.

Even in a media landscape far more primitive than what we know today, these findings offered hope that individuals could, indeed, form and sustain meaningful relationships through media. However, now that we had the power to choose how to form and maintain relationships, how would we choose? And how did that change when we lost the choice again—but this time, being left only with CMC?

Reflecting on Channel Selection in 2020

In 2020, a number of experiences prompted me to reflect on how I selected my own communication channels—and how that affected my communication outcomes. I witnessed firsthand how being forced to utilize CMC impacted the difficulty of connecting emotionally with others. On the other hand, I also learned quite a bit about some of the benefits of mediated communication that could reframe how we, as a society, envision and value CMC—and gave me hope for how humans might more carefully consider channel capabilities to interact more effectively. In this section, I will relate a handful of my own experiences in 2020 to some of the more foundational media selection theories in the Communication discipline, reflecting on how my own experiences supported or refuted these theories.

The Importance of Social Presence

Early CMC research focused on media choice: How do users select which channel is the most appropriate to convey their message? In a perfect world, users would weigh their options rationally and select the medium best suited for their interpersonal needs (see, e.g., Walther, 2011). Theorists offered a variety of explanations for motives, moving from an original assumption of rationality to the recognition of personal preference and situational needs.

Short and colleagues (1976) developed Social Presence Theory (SPT) based on the assumption that nonverbal communication constitutes the primary channel for delivering emotional content and immediacy—driving forces behind relational development. SPT proposes that successful interpersonal outcomes result from social presence, the "degree of salience of the other person in the interactions and the consequent salience of the interpersonal relationships" (p. 65). While this notion of presence is not an objectively measured criterion (Biocca et al., 2003), it depends on technological affordances, user perceptions, and contextual characteristics (Culnan & Markus, 1987). The theory assumes that users rationally choose media which they believe will most effectively fulfill their interpersonal and emotional needs. For example, SPT argues that communicators will more often utilize electronic media for messages low in affective content because electronic media transmits fewer nonverbal cues than FtF communication.

While I missed my friends and family, I took a strange comfort in knowing that, even if I had remained in my old home back in Ohio or lived closer to family, I likely would not be able to see them anyway. I enjoyed finding new ways to connect with people. My sister and I watched a movie together remotely using a plugin which allowed us to text chat as the film played. I relied upon online support groups to share my burdens, get advice for entertaining two small children stuck inside all day due to apocalyptic air quality from the wildfires, and even to network for a more permanent job. I appreciated the ability to feel connected with others, sharing emotional connections.

However, when a close family member ended up in the hospital from complications from COVID-19, I felt devastated that technology was essentially my only option. I craved physical touch, and I ached every time that I had to rely on FaceTime to check on them. The speed of group text messages afforded me immediate information, but the lack of "presence" felt devastating. This experience proved to be perhaps the most pivotal for me. I had long believed in the promise of CMC in communicating emotional content, and I observed this promise in so many spaces—but, in the end, I realized that no digital replacement exists for hug. I appreciated technology's efficiency, but when I feared the worst, no amount of emojis could replace human contact.

Media Richness and Equivocality

Like SPT, Information Richness Theory (IRT; previously Media Richness Theory; Daft & Lengel, 1984, 1986; Daft et al., 1987) argues that the lack of social cues held important implications for communication. Daft and colleagues posited that a reduction in the number of cues available ("richness") decreases the medium's capacity for immediate feedback, personalization, and language variety, thus reducing the sender's ability to effectively convey potentially equivocal messages (Daft & Lengel, 1986). Consequently, just as SPT maintains that individuals chose media based on emotional content, IRT claims that individuals objectively match a medium's potential for misunderstanding to the complexity of their message.

Through a connection from a friend online, I took on a role as an adjunct professor during the 2020–2021 academic year. Teaching in a mediated environment was new for me; I had never taught online before, and I was nervous. In line with MRT/IRT, I have always consciously relied upon nonverbal feedback from my students to know if the content was clear enough. Recognizing that lack of feedback in asynchronous learning (or the mural of black rectangles that is a Zoom class) meant that I needed to adjust my style to account for the potential for equivocality. The ability to answer questions in real time was essential for my teaching. Consequently, I not only structured my courses to be primarily asynchronous but also included a weekly synchronous component in which I took the most difficult material and brought it to life through class discussions and activities.

Personal Experience and Perceptions of Richness

SPT and IRT comprise rational choice models based on particular assumptions: (1) media have immutable properties, (2) individuals make media selection choices independently of others in their social environment, and (3) these choices are cognitive and goal-based, efficiency-motivated, and objectively rational (Fulk et al., 1990; Webster & Trevino, 1995). In other words, rational choice models imply that humans possess the cognitive capability to make smart decisions about media influenced only by their needs, and not by their surroundings (e.g., availability of the medium, accessibility of the medium by the intended recipient). Several studies, however, have demonstrated that individuals do not always choose the most objectively appropriate medium (for review, see Fulk et al., 1990). Consequently, numerous other theories have been proposed that make different predictions about media selection.

Carlson and Zmud (1999) offered an alternative to IRT, again emphasizing the importance of individuals' subjective perceptions of media richness, rather than a researcher-determined level based on number of available cue systems. Their Channel Expansion Theory (CET) suggests that perceptions of media richness can change over time when individuals gain more experience with the channel, the messaging topic, the organizational context, and the communication co-participants. Though situated within an organizational setting, Carlson and Zmud's findings may pertain to communication in close relationships as well. Intimate relationships usually involve knowledge of the other person; as such, a more intimate knowledge of the other may lead to a decrease in the need for a wide range of cue channels, resulting in a more effective mediated communication despite leaner channels.

Over the course of each quarter that I taught online, I got to know my students better, and we found ways to make the technology work for us. Shy students felt more comfortable coming to mediated office hours, and recorded videos of myself reading quiz questions aloud helped more audio-focused learners to better understand the questions. Just as CET suggested, as I became more familiar with my students, we began to see the "richness" of the medium in a more subjective way.

Managing Impressions through Technology

Finally, the Impression Management Model suggests that humans recognize the inherent costs and rewards to impression management strategies in both lean and rich media (O'Sullivan, 2000). For example, lean media limit negative nonverbal feedback, while rich media can facilitate "damage control" by making communicators aware of the effects of their messages. O'Sullivan argued that users strategically choose a medium based on its ability to help them achieve specific relational goals.

During 2020 and early 2021, I had job interviews with three organizations, all conducted via videoconferencing platforms. While maintaining eye contact with my interviewers proved challenging at times, I could surreptitiously reference notes up on a second screen, giving me confidence to answer questions. I reveled in the fact that I could wear shorts and no shoes, a stark contrast to the uncomfortable suits and heels of past job interviews. It felt liberating to be able to focus my cognitive energy on what I was saying, rather than how I looked, and I strongly believe that part of my eventual success in these interviews can be attributed to this focus. During this time, I thought of IMM and how, if given the choice, I might choose to interview virtually forever; I appreciated the ways in which I could harness the leanness of the medium in a strategic way to meet my impression management goals.

However, on social media, the change in impression management went in an almost totally opposite direction. The subtle shift in the tone of posts over time proved illuminating; the Instagram pages that I followed became far less about showing off one's best self and more about finding a shared humanity among our suffering from various causes. The disinhibition feared by early scholars became a source of truth and comfort rather than flaming. Many in my network opted instead toward expressing the vulnerability that was normally reserved for FtF spaces, despite technology's ability to present only the most positive version of ourselves.

Media Selection as a Way to Process 2020—and to Move Forward

As 2020 progressed, we, as a global community, needed support more than ever. Deprived of the opportunity to meet FtF—at least any closer than six feet—meant that we had to rely upon technology to maintain our relationships and fulfill our desire for social connection. These constraints stood in stark contrast to what we previously grown to perceive as "normal." In just the past few decades, we have had enormous shifts in the number of channels available to us, and the option to choose often left us biased. After experiencing a world in which our only available communication occurred through technology, so opposite to our sense of "normalcy," I believe that we will encounter a shift in the way that we envision technology. Just as the introduction of any new technological innovation inevitably causes some trepidation, returning back to "normal" will take some adjustment. As many have become accustomed to CMC, the return to FtF communication will likely increase social anxieties and require some behavioral shifts (such as not being able to attend job interviews barefoot!). At the extremes, some users will likely overcompensate by eschewing all technology while others will be hesitant to return to the world of synchronous and uneditable communication. Most, however, will begin to find a balance between media channels, relying on a clearer understanding of the benefits and affordances of each. Now, the biggest change will be finding ways to match our own communicative needs to those of others.

Though researchers have argued that the dichotomy between rational and social models is unnecessary (Rice et al., 1994; Webster & Trevino, 1995), interpersonal scholars must recognize that, regardless of the ways in which individuals choose to communicate a message, perceptions of the medium will shape reactions to the message (Carlson & Zmud, 1999; O'Sullivan, 2000). Some people may believe that a text message is not "personal" enough, or may feel threatened by a FtF confrontation. Rational models presume that certain structural features of the medium are accountable for these perceptions, while social models claim that group norms and values shape media use (Fulk et al., 1990). Both objective and subjective processes likely remain at play when an individual selects a medium. I believe that our perceptions of CMC will have irrevocably changed now that it has been our only option for so long. Future media selection theorizing will need to account for not only our own personal preferences, but also how we account for those of others: What message does the medium communicate? Does the other person prefer one over the other? What does this medium afford to me that can make this interaction better: less equivocal, more personal, or more comfortable for all involved? As we all begin to move past the collective chaos of 2020, media selection theories can help us to understand how we can make more informed and mindful choices about our media selection, moving beyond what is "rational" or our own personal preference to reflect the needs of everyone involved. This may take the form of more thoughtfully choosing ways to support our friends in distress or carefully reflecting on the efficiency of a text message versus the clarity afforded by a phone call. Ultimately, I believe we will become more mindful in these choices and perhaps change the way that we view CMC for the better.

References

Altman, I., & Taylor, D. A. (1973). *Social penetration: The development of interpersonal relationships*. Holt, Rinehart and Winston.

Auxier, B. (2020). What we've learned about Americans' views of technology during the time of COVID-19. *Pew Research*. https://www.pewresearch.org/fact-tank/2020/12/18/what-weve-learned-about-americans-views-of-technology-during-the-time-of-covid-19/

Bailenson, J. N. (2021). Nonverbal overload: A theoretical argument for the causes of Zoom fatigue. *Technology, Mind, and Behavior, 2*(1). https://doi.org/10.1037/tmb0000030

Biocca, F., Harms, C., & Burgoon, J. K. (2003). Toward a more robust theory and measure of social presence: Review and suggested criteria. *Presence: Teleoperators, and Virtual Environments, 12,* 456–480. https://doi.org/10.1162/105474603322761270

Bordia, P. (1997). Face-to-face versus computer-mediated communication: A synthesis of the experimental literature. *The Journal of Business Communication, 34,* 99–118. https://doi.org/10.1177/002194369703400106

Carlson, J. R., & Zmud, R. W. (1999). Channel expansion theory and the experiential nature of media richness perceptions. *Academy of Management Journal, 42,* 153–170. https://doi.org/10.2307/257090

Chan, D. K. S., & Cheng, G. H. L. (2004). A comparison of offline and online friendship qualities at different stages of relationship development. *Journal of Social and Personal Relationships, 21*(3), 305–320. https://doi.org/10.1177/0265407504042834

Coleman, L. H., Paternite, C. E., & Sherman, R. C. (1999). A reexamination of deindividuation in synchronous computer-mediated communication. *Computers in Human Behavior, 15,* 51–65. https://doi.org/10.1016/S0747-5632(98)00032-6

Culnan, M. J., & Markus, M. L. (1987). Information technologies. In F. M. Jablin, L. L. Putnam, K. H. Roberts, & L. W. Porter (Eds.), *Handbook of organizational communication: An interdisciplinary perspective* (pp. 420–440). SAGE.

Daft, R. L., & Lengel, R. H. (1984). Information richness: A new approach to managerial behavior and organization design. In B. M. Staw & L. L. Cummings (Eds.), *Research in organizational behavior* (Vol. 6, pp. 191–233). Jai Press.

Daft, R. L., & Lengel, R. H. (1986). Organizational information requirements, media richness and structural design. *Management Science, 32,* 554–571. https://doi.org/10.1287/mnsc.32.5.554

Daft, R. L., Lengel, R. H., & Trevino, L. K. (1987). Message equivocality, media selection, and manager performance: Implications for information systems. *MIS Quarterly, 11,* 355–368. https://doi.org/10.2307/248682

Fulk, J., Schmitz, J., & Steinfield, C. W. (1990). A social influence model of technology use. In J. Fulk & C. W. Steinfield (Eds.), *Organizations and communication technology* (pp. 117–140). SAGE.

Kielser, S., Siegel, J., & McGuire, T. W. (1984). Social psychological aspects of computer-mediated communication. *American Psychologist, 39,* 1123–1134. https://doi.org/10.1037/0003-066X.39.10.1123

LaFrance, A. (2015). When people feared computers. *The Atlantic.* https://www.theatlantic.com/technology/archive/2015/03/when-people-feared-computers/388919/

Lee, K., Vasileiou, K., & Barnett, J. (2019). 'Lonely within the mother:' An exploratory study of first-time mothers' experiences of loneliness. *Journal of Health Psychology, 24*(10), 1334–1344. https://doi.org/10.1177/1359105317723451

Myers, K. K., & Sadaghiani, K. (2010). Millennials in the workplace: A communication perspective on millennials' organizational relationships and performance. *Journal of Business and Psychology, 25,* 225–238. https://doi.org/10.1007/s10869-010-9172-7

O'Sullivan, P. B. (2000). What you don't know won't hurt me: Impression management functions of communication channels in relationships. *Human Communication Research, 26,* 403–431. https://doi.org/10.1111/j.1468-2958.2000.tb00763.x

Postmes, T., Spears, R., & Lea, M. (1998). Breaching or building social boundaries? SIDE-effects of computer-mediated communication. *Communication Research, 25,* 689–715. https://doi.org/10.1177/009365098025006006

Rice, R. E., Kraut, R. E., Cool, C., & Fish, R. S. (1994). Individual, structural and social influences on use of a new communication medium. *Academy of Management Best Papers Proceedings,* 285–289.

Short, J. L., Williams, E., & Christie, B. (1976). *The social psychology of telecommunications.* Wiley.

Sproull, L., & Kiesler, S. (1986). Reducing social context cues: Electronic mail in organizational communication. *Management Science, 32,* 1492–1512. https://doi.org/10.1287/mnsc.32.11.1492

Stoll, C. (1995). Why the Web won't be nirvana. *Newsweek.* https://www.newsweek.com/clifford-stoll-why-web-wont-be-nirvana-185306

Walther, J. B. (2011). Theories of computer-mediated communication and interpersonal relations. In M. L. Knapp & J. A. Daly (Eds.), *The handbook of interpersonal communication* (pp. 443–479). SAGE.

Walther, J. B., Anderson, J. F., & Park, D. W. (1994). Interpersonal effects in computer-mediated interaction: A meta-analysis of social and antisocial communication. *Communication Research, 21,* 460–487. https://doi.org/ 10.1177/009365094021004002

Webster, J., & Trevino, L. K. (1995). Rational and social theories as complementary explanations of communication media choices: Two policy-capturing studies. *The Academy of Management Journal, 38,* 1544–1572. https://doi.org/10.2307/256843

16

SPORTS COMMUNICATION

Michael L. Butterworth

Sports Communication in the United States after COVID

On May 4, 2020, as Americans were still coming to terms with the gravity of the coronavirus pandemic, sportswriter Jane McManus responded to the chorus of voices insisting that professional sports teams return to the courts and fields of play. "Sports are the result of a functioning society, not the precursor," she tweeted. "If you like sports so much, you should be pushing for a better response to the virus, not the de facto ritual sacrifice of some number of pro athletes and their kin" (McManus, 2020). McManus directed her sentiments primarily toward those who either dismissed the seriousness of COVID-19 or argued that the benefits of preserving the sports calendar outweighed the risks of doing so in uncertain conditions. Her comments took on added significance later in the spring, as George Floyd's death in Minneapolis reignited the Black Lives Matter movement and spotlighted the nation's ongoing problems of racial discrimination and violence. Building on increased activism over the past decade and enabled by the absence of sports competition, athletes were among the most visible and eloquent voices to advocate for racial justice. Responses to both the pandemic and systemic racism then factored heavily into the 2020 presidential election, a contest where the communicative choices of President Donald Trump centered sports once again.

It is possible, of course, to tell the story of 2020 by featuring COVID-19, racial activism, and presidential politics while omitting sports. However, such a narrative would be incomplete, and *Sports Communication* scholars would quickly note that few institutions are more representative of our identities, relationships, and organizations. In short, the symbolic capital assigned to sport, its role in our communities, and its influence in and through media make it one of the most compelling sites to evaluate communication in the 2020s. The Communication discipline has seen

DOI: 10.4324/9781003220466-17

impressive growth in "Sports Communication" scholarship (also often referred to as "communication and sport") since the turn of the 21st century (Billings, 2016; Butterworth, 2021).[1] This growth intersects with many of the discipline's sub-fields, incorporating studies of media, interpersonal relationships, organizational communication, and rhetoric, among others. This chapter, then, surveys a range of approaches to communication in order to center sport as uniquely constitutive of symbolic practices. In doing so, I focus on three learning objectives:

1. To recognize that sport may be a "microcosm" of society but it is also much more; sport *shapes* cultural, political, and social dynamics as much as it *reflects* them.
2. To appreciate that sport affects various levels of society, even for those who view it only as a "distraction" or for those who do not consider themselves to be fans.
3. To acknowledge that it is not possible to "stick to sports"; rather, sport has tremendous symbolic capital and is vital to political identification.

I will attend to these objectives first through an account of my own experiences with sport in the midst of multiple political crises. I then turn to two additional contexts through which we can assess sport's communicative influence. I conclude with some reflections on sport in 2020 and beyond, including commentary on the ways the decade's first year may set the agenda for sports communication scholars in the years to come.

Experiencing 2020 through the National Pastime

As both a scholar and fan, I follow sport closely. From an academic perspective, I am a rhetorical critic who has focused on the relationships between politics and sport. My expertise especially lies in the symbolic construction of myths and ideologies that shape national identity and political culture (Butterworth, 2010, 2014, 2019). I am troubled by sport's commercial excesses, the contradictions between sport's claims to "meritocracy" and experiences of communities which it excludes, and sport's eagerness to serve as a stage for bombastic performances of patriotism and militarism. Nevertheless, I am compelled by sport's athleticism and aesthetic beauty, the inherent drama found in athletic competitions, and the legitimate pathways sport facilitates for personal and community identification.

Nothing better captures these contradictory feelings for me than baseball, the sport which I follow most closely and about which I have dedicated more academic writing than any other. To engage more carefully with the issues of 2020, then, I begin with some reflections on my experiences with the "national pastime." The year 2020 began with some ominous signs, including the impending impeachment of Donald Trump, wildfires in Australia, and global reports about the spread of COVID-19. Like many Americans, I was alert to these circumstances but naïve about how much the pandemic, in particular, would affect our lives. My family is one of the millions with children playing youth baseball. Our son was 10 years old at the beginning of 2020, preparing for a season of tournament play for an 11u (ages 11 and under) select team. I am ambivalent about this arrangement because select baseball is both a more competitive experience and a more expensive—and, therefore, exclusionary—endeavor than recreational sports. Like so many other children in school sports and youth leagues, one of his primary activities was suddenly gone (as was his sister's anticipation for her first season of high school marching band, which is inextricably bound to football in Texas).

Our family's disappointment over lost youth games was compounded by the disruption of spring break plans in March. We had never gone to spring training baseball games, and we had planned a one-week road trip to Phoenix where we would watch our beloved Chicago Cubs in two locations. That trip was to begin on March 14, and we held out hope for our plans even as the news grew more grim each day. Ultimately, we canceled, only days before new travel restrictions would have forced us to do so anyway. The missed spring training games were only the beginning, of course, as Major League Baseball's (MLB) Opening Day on March 26 came and went while the ballparks remained silent. Sports media already had lamented the lack of live events (Curtis, 2020), and the loss of baseball left an enormous gap in the sports calendar. Among the first leagues in the world to resume play was the Korean Baseball Organization (KBO) and ESPN televised live games from Korea to overnight audiences in the United States. If only for a brief moment, American fans discovered the art of the Korean bat flip (Kimes, 2016) and a bevy of "how to choose a favorite KBO team" features that helped create identifications based on presumed similarities with MLB clubs (McKeone, 2020; Weaver, 2020). I chose the NC Dinos, primarily because I found myself easily charmed by their dinosaur mascots.

In the subsequent weeks, MLB leadership and the MLB Players Association engaged in acrimonious negotiations about when and how to resume the season. A truncated, 60-game schedule began on July 23, with games played in empty stadiums only between teams located within close geographic proximity. Once again, I found myself in an ambivalent position. Although I was concerned about proceeding with a season in the midst of the pandemic, I frankly missed seeing MLB games. Even an empty Wrigley Field, I thought, might be better than not seeing games at all. When the season did begin in late July, the league echoed other major sports organizations by acknowledging the national conversation about race. Opening day pre-game ceremonies featured tributes to George Floyd, Breonna Taylor, and Ahmaud Arbery, as well as expressions of "unity" that became commonplace in U.S. sports during the season.

The opening game between the New York Yankees and defending World Series champion Washington Nationals aired live on ESPN. During the pre-game, the network featured a conversation between Hall of Fame Yankees pitcher Mariano Rivera and President Trump. In case the symbolism of conflating the presidency with the national pastime was lost on viewers, the segment also included a game of catch between Rivera and Trump on the White House lawn. Inside the stadium, the Nationals welcomed Dr. Anthony Fauci for the ceremonial first pitch. Fauci, arguably the most visible figure in the nation's response to COVID-19, had a visibly tense relationship with the president. Fauci's participation in the first pitch ritual stood in contrast to the less favorable reception given Trump when he had attended one of the games during the 2019 World Series (Dalton, 2020).

No team hosted the World Series in 2020, as it was held with limited fans at Globe Life Field in Arlington, Texas. The Los Angeles Dodgers won the 2020 championship, and their celebration provided a striking moment to encapsulate the challenge of the pandemic and the politics surrounding it. In the middle of the clinching game, the Dodgers' third baseman, Justin Turner, was suddenly removed from the game. Viewers found out later that a positive coronavirus test for Turner came back during the game, and MLB protocol required his removal. Yet in the midst of heated debates about social distancing policies and the merits of wearing masks in public, the freshly diagnosed Turner emerged from the dugout after the game to celebrate with his teammates. MLB officials expressed their frustration and launched an investigation into the team's lack of adherence to COVID-19 protocols. In the end, neither Turner nor the Dodgers were sanctioned (Burke, 2020).

Each of the above moments affected me as both a fan and an academic critic of sport. More importantly, they all point to the many ways sport is implicated in the study of communication. Nearly 72% of children between the ages of 6 and 12 in the United States participate in youth sports ("State of Play," 2019), placing our experience of missing out on baseball among the majority of Americans. More than channels for developing athletic skills, youth sports foster interpersonal communication, team building, and conflict resolution skills. They also prompt important questions for family communication, as do outings and trips that focus on attendance at live sporting events. Meanwhile, losing live content and inventing new forms of programming—H-O-R-S-E, anyone? (Clapp, 2020)—presented challenges for sports media industry and scholars alike. In addition, our understanding of race and advocacy has been advanced by athlete activists, and elected officials continue to provide evidence that sport has always been used as a political and patriotic symbol. In short, the nexus of events and discourses that defined 2020 invites sports communication scholars to assess its existing base of knowledge and seek new pathways for academic inquiry.

Sport, Racial Justice, and the 2020 Election

If baseball provides a suitable context for showing multiple issues in isolation, allow me to turn to two additional contexts to explore these issues more synthetically. In both cases, the symbolic importance of the pandemic, racial identity, and electoral politics are all brought into sharp relief through the lens of sport.

First, the suspension of sports in the spring raised immediate questions about the viability of the football season later in the year. In particular, college football became the subject of considerable speculation about the fall, especially because the sport is governed at multiple levels—the National Collegiate Athletic Association (NCAA), the athletic conferences, and the member institutions. In the spring, coaches such as Clemson's Dabo Swinney remained confident that the virus would be contained quickly enough to preserve their season. In April, Swinney invoked the myth of American exceptionalism to assure college football fans that the nation's historic greatness would serve present purposes:

> I mean, this is America, man. We've stormed the beaches of Normandy, we've sent a car and drove around on Mars, we've walked on the moon. This is the greatest country and the greatest people in the history of the planet. . . . Listen, we're going to rise up and we're going to kick this thing right in the teeth, and we'll get back to our lives. (Bromberg, 2020, para. 4)

By invoking military and scientific triumphs, Swinney implied that the nation could simply will itself through the pandemic because of its exceptionalist history.

Other coaches leaned into college football's role in boosting Americans' morale and, perhaps more importantly, economic prosperity. Louisiana State University coach Ed Orgeron told a live audience that "[f]ootball is the lifeblood of our country in my opinion. It gets everything going, it gets the economy going, the economy of Baton Rouge, the economy of the state of Louisiana" (Gardner, 2020, paras. 2–3), and Oklahoma State University's Mike Gundy offered:

> In my opinion, we need to bring our players back. They are 18, 19, 20, 21, and 22-years old and they are healthy and they have the ability to fight this virus off. If that is true, then we sequester them, and continue because we need to run money through the state of Oklahoma. (Scott, 2020, para. 5)

Later in the summer, Gundy found himself embroiled in controversy after musing about the allegedly apolitical nature of One America News Network (OAN) even as the channel transparently promoted a right-wing agenda and discredited the Black Lives Matter movement. The uproar led to criticism from the Cowboys' best player, Chuba Hubbard, and a public apology from Gundy (Harris, 2020). Significantly, both of Gundy's statements spotlighted the political symbolism of having an older, white, male authority figure in charge of a labor pool that is largely made up of young, Black players. Against the backdrop of racial justice activism, then, the insistence from coaches that college football players existed merely to serve local economies speaks to the many layers of meaning to be found within sport.

Coaches were not the only ones who took an interest in college football's return. After the Big 10 Conference announced a suspension of the fall season, elected officials publicly lobbied for the resumption of play. Senator Ben Sasse wrote an open letter pleading with university presidents, asserting that "[t]his is a moment for leadership. These young men need a season. Please don't cancel college football" (West, 2020). Vice President Mike Pence tweeted: "America needs College Football! It's important for student-athletes, schools, and our Nation" (Nocera, 2020, para. 9), and President Trump added simply, "Play College Football!" (Schlabach, 2020, para. 3). When the Big 10 eventually decided to proceed with a shortened schedule, the president took credit for the decision, using the first presidential debate to proclaim, "By the way, I brought back Big Ten football. It was me, and I'm very happy to do it and the people of Ohio are very proud of me" (Bailey, 2020, para. 3). Trump's dubious claim obviously attempted to appeal to voters in the critical swing states of the Midwest in the weeks just before the presidential election. No evidence exists to suggest that it affected the outcome in states such as Michigan and Ohio, but the effort serves as a clear reminder that politicians recognize the symbolic capital invested in sport.

If we lack reason to connect the outcome of the presidential election to sport, a Georgia Senate race may suggest something different. A surprise resignation in 2019 left a pending vacancy for one of the Georgia Senate seats, and Republican Governor Brian Kemp appointed marketing executive Kelly Loeffler to the position. Loeffler was an unexpected pick, but she was praised for her business ties and "outsider" status. She also happened to have an ownership stake in the Atlanta Dream franchise of the Women's National Basketball Association (WNBA). Despite her own background playing basketball and her role with the team, Loeffler followed President Trump's campaign lead, playing up her conservative credentials while stoking culture war fears and condemning Black Lives Matter activists (Buckner, 2020). Such maneuvering corresponded with the conventional wisdom about how to win an election in a deep South state, with Loeffler echoing the president's calls to play college football and praising his leadership in response to COVID-19 (Loeffler, 2020).

WNBA players had been among the first athletes to align with Black Lives Matter, even pre-dating Kaepernick's protest in 2016 (Lavelle, 2019). Thus, the criticisms from Loeffler were especially pointed for the members of the Atlanta Dream. In a public rebuke of their part-owner, Dream players, along with many others across the league, endorsed Loeffler's opponent, the Reverend Raphael Warnock. At the time, Warnock's poll numbers suggested that he was a significant underdog. Once WNBA players began wearing t-shirts declaring, "Vote Warnock," his exposure and fundraising took off. Although many factors surely led to Warnock's improved prospects, he acknowledged the support from the WNBA "was helpful. . . . It was one of the many turning points of the campaign" (Armour, 2020, para. 7). After a closely contested race in November, Warnock narrowly defeated Loeffler in a special election in January, 2021. In a year marked by the antagonistic politics associated with the pandemic and the elections, athlete activism on behalf of racial justice may have been the determining factor in swinging the U.S. Senate from one party to the other.

Forecasting Future Possibilities in Sports Communication

It is tempting to account for the many other ways these issues intersected in 2020 or to evaluate other dimensions of sports communication. Yet, the multiple points of emphasis in baseball and the conflation of issues present in college football and the WNBA make clear the range of communicative phenomena associated with sport. Based on the preceding discussions, consider the following ways scholars might evaluate these issues:

- The extent to which youth sports contribute to adolescent *socialization* (Kremer-Sadlik & Kim, 2007) and the effect on children of missing out on play.
- The ability to link *identification* with a sports team to attachment to a larger *social group* (Wann, 2006).
- The balance of positive psychological associations with a successful sporting outcome (*basking in reflected glory*) against negative psychological associations with sporting failures (*cutting off reflected failure*) (Cialdini et al., 1976).
- The varied responses by organizations to crises precipitated by COVID-19 and political activism can be understood in terms of crisis communication, especially through approaches such as *situational crisis communication theory* and *image repair* (Brown-Devlin & Brown, 2020).
- The choices made by sports media organizations about how to approach the intersection of sport and the pandemic or sport and racial activism invite discussions of *agenda setting* and *media framing* (Angelini & Billings, 2010).
- The choices made by sports media consumers invite discussions of *uses and gratifications* and *parasocial interaction* (Kassing & Sanderson, 2009).
- The representation of racial identity demands an accounting of *whiteness* (Griffin & Calafell, 2011) and *intersectionality* (Crosby, 2016).
- The pervasiveness of *nationalism* and *militarism* points to the ideological effects of sport and sports media (Butterworth, 2014).
- The resurgence of athlete activism serves as a reminder that sport is already a political context and may be a site of meaningful social change (Khan, 2021).

This list, as long as it may already be, is far from comprehensive. In other words, from the perspective of Communication, few contexts are as richly symbolic as sport.

Communication scholars will be assessing the messages and meanings that emerged over the course of 2020 for years to come. From the impeachment of President Trump, to the coronavirus pandemic, to the resurgence of racial activism, the critical events of the year profoundly affected and were affected by the world of sports. This chapter details only some of the ways those effects were felt, but it signals many possible directions for the future. As much as Sports Communication has grown as a subfield, we need more contributions in areas that overlap with subfields such as family, interpersonal, and organizational communication. As much quality work as we have seen in evaluating social media practices in sport, scholars would benefit from fewer thematic analyses of content and more critical assessments of that content's effects. Further, the convergence of sport and political interests demands a greater range of theoretical approaches that can evaluate the institutional, as well as ideological, implications of this relationship. Given the growth of Sports Communication scholarship and the impact sure to be felt long after 2020, little doubt remains of the opportunities that lie ahead.

Note

1. How best to name the subfield is a matter of continued conversation. Foregrounding "communication" gives primacy to the larger disciplinary conversation, whereas foregrounding "sports" suggests there is a particular context in which communication can be studied and understood. A related matter is the distinction between "sport" and "sports." The singular term tends to refer to the institutional collection of the interests at stake—not only the games themselves, but also the athletes, coaches, owners, fans, sponsors, and media. The use of "sports," then, typically references specific games or leagues. Although there is fluidity between these terms, I will generally use "sports communication" throughout this chapter. As for "communication," I trust we all can agree there is no "s" at the end!

References

Angelini, J., & Billings, A. C. (2010). An agenda that sets the frames: Gender, language, and NBC's Americanized Olympic telecast. *Journal of Language & Social Psychology, 29,* 363–385.

Armour, N. (2020, October 27). Opinion: By speaking out, WNBA players are altering Senate race in Georgia. *USA Today.* https://www.usatoday.com/story/sports/columnist/nancy-armour/2020/10/27/election-2020-wnba-players-make-impact-us-senate-race-georgia/6044477002/.

Bailey, A. (2020, September 29). President Donald Trump, during debate, declares, "I brought back Big Ten football". *USA Today.* https://www.usatoday.com/story/sports/ncaaf/bigten/2020/09/29/presidential-debate-donald-trump-i-brought-back-big-ten-football/3583550001/.

Billings, A. C. (2016). *Defining sport communication.* Routledge.

Bromberg, N. (2020, April 3). Coronavirus: Dabo Swinney has "zero doubt" football will be played in 2020. *Yahoo! Sports.* https://sports.yahoo.com/dabo-swinney-has-no-doubt-football-will-be-played-in-2020-170901639.html.

Brown-Devlin, N., & Brown, K. A. (2020). When crises change the game: Establishing a typology of sports-related crises. *Journal of International Crisis and Risk Communication Research, 3,* 49–70.

Buckner, C. (2020, August 29). How politics transformed Kelly Loeffler from hoops junkie to WNBA villain. *Washington Post.* https://www.washingtonpost.com/sports/2020/08/29/kelly-loeffler-wnba-black-lives-matter/.

Burke, M. (2020, November 7). Dodgers organization has 5 positive coronavirus tests days after World Series win. *NBC News.* https://www.nbcnews.com/news/us-news/dodgers-organization-has-9-positive-coronavirus-tests-days-after-world-n1246913.

Butterworth, M. L. (2010). *Baseball and rhetorics of purity: The national pastime and American identity during the war on terror.* University of Alabama Press.

Butterworth, M. L. (2014). Public memorializing in the stadium: Mediated sport, the tenth anniversary of 9/11, and the illusion of democracy. *Communication & Sport, 2,* 203–224.

Butterworth, M. L. (2019). George W. Bush as 'the man in the arena': Baseball, public memory, and the rhetorical redemption of a president. *Rhetoric & Public Affairs, 22,* 1–31.

Butterworth, M. L. (Ed.). (2021). *Handbook of communication and sport.* De Gruyter.

Cialdini, R. B., Borden, R. J., Thorne, A., Walker, M. R., Freeman, S., & Sloan, L. R. (1976). Basking in reflected glory: Three (football) field studies. *Journal of Personality and Social Psychology, 34,* 366–375.

Clapp, M. (2020, April 4). An NBA H-O-R-S-E competition on ESPN is in the works during the COVID-19 pandemic. *Awful Announcing.* https://awfulannouncing.com/espn/an-nba-h-o-r-s-e-competition-on-espn-is-in-the-works-during-the-covid-19-pandemic.html.

Crosby, E. D. (2016). Chased by the double bind: Intersectionality and the disciplining of Lolo Jones. *Women's Studies in Communication, 39,* 228–248.

Curtis, B. (2020, March 16). What do we do now? Sports media ponders the coronavirus. *The Ringer.* https://www.theringer.com/2020/3/16/21181180/coronavirus-media-espn-nba-utah-jazz-scott-van-pelt-jim-rome.

Dalton, K. (2020, July 21). Washington Nationals delivering brushback pitch to President Trump on opening day. *Sportscasting.* https://www.sportscasting.com/washington-nationals-delivering-brushback-pitch-to-president-trump-on-opening-day/

Gardner, S. (2020, July 14). LSU coach Ed Orgeron confident of college football's return: "Football is the life blood of our country." *USA Today.* https://www.usatoday.com/story/sports/ncaaf/sec/2020/07/14/lsu-ed-orgeron-vice-president-mike-pence-support-college-football-return/5439610002/.

Griffin, R. A., & Calafell, B. M. (2011). Control, discipline, and punish: Black masculinity and (in)visible whiteness in the NBA. In M. G. Lacy & K. A. Ono (Eds.), *Critical rhetorics of race* (pp. 117–136). New York University Press.

Harris, J. (2020, June 15). Oklahoma State coach Mike Gundy's OAN t-shirt spurs outrage from star players. *Los Angeles Times.* https://www.latimes.com/sports/story/2020-06-15/oklahoma-state-coach-mike-gundys-oan-tshirt-spurs-outrage-chuba-hubbard.

Kassing, J. W., & Sanderson, J. (2009). "You're the kind of guy that we all want for a drinking buddy": Expressions of parasocial interaction on Floydlandis.com. *Western Journal of Communication, 73,* 182–203.

Khan, A. I. (2021). The ethos of the activist athlete. In M. L. Butterworth (Ed.), *Handbook of Communication and sport* (pp. 161–178). De Gruyter.

Kimes, M. (2016, October 4). The art of letting go. *ESPN.com.* https://www.espn.com/espn/feature/story/_/id/17668845/korean-bat-flip.

Kremer-Sadlik, T., & Kim, J. L. (2007). Lessons from sports: Children's socialization to values through family interaction during sports activities. *Discourse & Society, 18,* 35–52.

Lavelle, K. (2019). "Change starts with us:" Intersectionality and citizenship in the 2016 WNBA. In D. A. Grano & M. L. Butterworth (Eds.), *Sport, rhetoric, and political struggle* (pp. 39–54). Peter Lang.

Loeffler, K. [@KLoeffler]. (2020, October 5). *COVID stood NO chance against @realDonaldTrump!* [Tweet]. Twitter. https://twitter.com/KLoeffler/status/1313201217309417478.

McKeone, L. (2020, May 4). Choosing a Korean baseball team to support. *The Big Lead.* https://www.thebiglead.com/posts/korean-baseball-teams-espn-support-01e7gbd56ctb.

McManus, J. [@janesports]. (2020, May 4). *Sports are the result of a functioning society, not the precursor. If you like sports so much, you should be pushing for a better response to the virus, not the de facto ritual sacrifice of some number of pro athletes and their kin* [Tweet]. Twitter. https://twitter.com/janesports/status/1257347739626754049.

Nocera, J. (2020, August 12). Big 10 defies money and politics to protect athletes. *Bloomberg.* https://www.bloomberg.com/opinion/articles/2020-08-12/covid-19-big-10-defies-money-and-politics-to-delay-football.

Schlabach, M. (2020, August 10). President Donald Trump voices support for #WeWant-ToPlay movement. *ESPN.com.* https://www.espn.com/college-football/story/_/id/29633809/president-donald-trump-voices-support-wewanttoplay-movement.

Scott, N. (2020, April 7). Mike Gundy dismisses coronavirus concerns, wants players to "run money through the state of Oklahoma". *USA Today.* https://ftw.usatoday.com/2020/04/mike-gundy-coronavirus.

State of play: Trends and developments in youth sports. (2019). *The Aspen Institute.* https://assets.aspeninstitute.org/content/uploads/2019/10/2019_SOP_National_Final.pdf.

Wann, D. L. (2006). The causes and consequences of sport team identification. In A. A. Raney & J. Bryant (Eds.), *Handbook of sports and media* (pp. 331–352). Erlbaum.

Weaver, L. (2020, May 7). "Which KBO team should I root for?" We have you covered, and then some. *The Athletic.* https://theathletic.com/1796118/2020/05/07/which-kbo-team-should-i-root-for-we-have-you-covered-and-then-some/.

West, J. (2020, August 10). Source: Ben Sasse to send letter urging Big Ten to hold football season. *Sports Illustrated.* https://www.si.com/college/2020/08/10/ben-sasse-letter-big-ten-hold-college-football-season-coronavirus.

SECTION III

Through Communication, We Can Transform What Has Been into What Can Be

17

ON BATS, BREATHING, AND *BELLA VITA VERDE*

Reflections on Environmental Communication during a Global Pandemic

Phaedra C. Pezzullo

Learning Objectives

1. Define environmental communication, including comparing ethics of crisis and care.
2. Understand what the more-than-human world (or an ecocentric or biocentric perspective) of COVID-19 might entail.
3. Identify the role naming and scapegoating play in public health discourses, as well as the ways systemic oppression intersects with public health.
4. Appreciate not only the importance of reactive crisis communication, but also storytelling that is speculative, imaginative, and future-oriented.

While each of us have lived through the COVID pandemic, we all have experienced it differently. My awareness of the virus came in waves. During the Fall semester of 2019, I was finishing a co-edited book with a colleague who was born and works in China, which focuses on not only how the United States and China differ but also overlap more than that might be expected through shared green values, practices, and ecosystems (Liu & Pezzullo, 2020). So, I was following the news about Wuhan. Hospitals were built seemingly overnight. My immediate family then contracted flu in January 2020 in Hawai'i on vacation while visiting Haleakalā National Park. We were tested earlier than most in the United States for COVID-19 and had contracted another strand of the flu with shared symptoms. The next wave hit when my relatives in Italy were quarantined; isolation has been hard to practice in a physically intimate and communal culture at church, in piazzas, and in homes. By March 26, 2020, when my governor declared a state of emergency, waves had turned into a flood. As I write, the COVID global pandemic has not ended.

DOI: 10.4324/9781003220466-20

I study environmental communication, which involves "the pragmatic and constitutive modes of expression—the naming, shaping, orienting, and negotiating—of our ecological relationships in the world, including those with nonhuman systems, elements, and species" (Pezzullo & Cox, 2021, p. 17). This research includes instrumental communication (e.g., "Vote" or "Wash your hands for twenty seconds with soap and water") and constitutive communication (e.g., what wearing a mask means to us). The "environment," in this context, is understood broadly through the environmental justice movement as "where we live, work and play" (Pezzullo & Cox, 2021, p. 7); it also is "[m]ore than a location" because "the environment *is what it does*"—it involves everything we do because we are part of the environment and it exceeds us (Pezzullo, 2008, p. 361, emphasis in original).

Robert Cox (2007) defined environmental communication as a *crisis discipline*. He suggested that we have a duty not only to study harm, but also an ethical responsibility to intervene to help bring about a more sustainable world. Considering a range of crises, such as wildlife habitat planning, toxic pollution, sacrifice zones, and climate change, Cox argued our goal should be "to enhance the ability of society to respond appropriately to environmental signals relevant to the well-being of both human civilization and natural biological systems" (p. 16).

In response, I have emphasized an appreciation of our field as a *care discipline*, one that also has the duty to honor and to cherish the people, species, and places we love (Pezzullo, 2017; Pezzullo & Cox, 2021; Pezzullo & de Onís, 2018). This ethic involves unearthing human and nonhuman interconnections, interdependence, biodiversity, and system limits. During the pandemic, the rhetoric of "care" has abounded:

> Care is having a moment. If neoliberalism is the zeitgeist of contemporary politics—championing hierarchies of capitalist individualism, hypermasculine competition, xenophobic border policing, white settler colonialism, anti-Black racism, fascist propaganda, petrochemical extractivism, and more—then care is the structure of feeling emerging in resistance. (Pezzullo, 2020)

Thinking about the COVID-19 pandemic, the interdependence of the ethics of crisis and care seems even more palpable. The pandemic itself became a crisis, causing illness and death, a loss of jobs, and a transformation of our whole way of life. It also became a moment to reaffirm our care work, such as how we depend on finding ways to check in with loved ones, even when we could not visit each other in person. Honoring essential workers. Protecting our neighbors. Adopting puppies.

In environmental communication, we engage these kinds of entanglements in our teaching, research, and public service. In this chapter, I consider three touchstones of my COVID experience: bats, breathing, and storytelling. Though not exhaustive, I hope to generate connections and conversations about what it means to do the work of environmental communication in these times.

On Bats

I think about physical scales and adaptation a lot—from how microscopic viruses spread to the role of climate chaos. Our goal in environmental communication is, in a sense, to try to help understand and to express how the world is interconnected and dynamic. What contact should we try to avoid (such as toxic chemicals and infectious diseases)? And what contact do we wish to foster (such as forest bathing, eating vegetables, and emotional support)? Some call this perspective "biocentric" or "ecocentric" one "motivated by care of a sentient being or ecosystem" (see Pezzullo & Cox, 2021, p. 29). While a philosopher might ask: "What is it like to be a bat?" (Nagel, 1974, p. 435), an environmental communication approach tends to seek more contextual questions about power and culture.

Have you spent much time caring about the habitat of bats and how the disease came to exist in their bodies? I have been thinking about the ecological relations entangled in the virus' anthropocentric (human-centered) origin story. Environmental communication is based in thinking about how humans and the nonhuman world are born, grow ill, thrive, and die together. Our journals and books are filled with stories of these interdependencies. As Milstein (2011) noted, even the act of pointing and naming a wild animal as "a bat" can enable "setting apart the named individual from the whole, or front-staging the entity and . . . in most cases, back-staging the ecology" (p. 4).

To bring ecology back into the foreground, a lack of adequate conservation to protect them from unsustainable human practices precipitated the risk of bats developing COVID-19 (Benvenuto et al., 2020; Quammen, 2012). Yong (2020) recounted an interview with Colin Carlson:

> [T]he biggest factors behind spillovers are land-use and climate change. . . . Our species has relentlessly expanded into previously wild spaces. Through intensive agriculture, habitat destruction, and rising temperatures, we have uprooted the planet's animals, forcing them into new and narrower ranges that are on our own doorsteps. Humanity has squeezed the world's wildlife in a crushing grip—and viruses have come bursting out.

Thinking about how ecological systems are threatened and how those transformations have unsustainable consequences is at the core of environmental communication research.

In addition to better understanding causes, environmental communication scholars also examine reactions. When asked how climate and COVID-19 relate, for example, the pattern in the disinformation playbook that Naomi Oreskes outlined is: "First, one denies the problem, then one denies its severity, and then one says it is too difficult or expensive to fix, and/or that the proposed solution threatens our freedom" (quoted in Edelman, 2020). Identifying misinformation (the sharing of false ideas knowingly or not) and disinformation campaigns (deliberate efforts to share false ideas), as well as the worldviews to which they become articulated or linked, remains significant, ongoing work (Bloomfield, 2019; Pezzullo & Cox, 2021).

In the United States, some politically scapegoated all of China for being the first country where the virus initially was shared with humans. Scapegoating "is the unmerited blaming of a particular person or action instead of addressing systemic or structural changes, as well as those most responsible" (Pezzullo & Cox, 2021, p. 26). In studying scapegoating discourses related to environmental communication, Schmitt (2019) argued that such efforts not only deflect but also distract by taking "potential attention from the more aggravating, complex, or unsolvable environmental challenges by instead offering an immediately satisfying morality tale" (p. 160). There are, of course, better ways to respond.

Experts in risk communication in conservation contexts, for example, have found that messages highlighting the benefits of species are more effective than merely focusing on potential harms. One study, for example, found that risk-benefit messages about bats with rabies in U.S. parks worked better at changing human behavior than no messages, or ones solely focused on risk (Lu et al., 2016). This research illustrates one of the many ways environmental and health communication overlap (Pezzullo & Cox, 2021).

On Breathing

Thinking back to the early days of the pandemic—and then the long, drawn-out months that followed—I also spent a lot of time caring about breathing: Avoiding the breath of those living outside my home, finding masks, researching designs to sew masks, and filtering the air in my home. The spread of COVID appeared to pivot more on air than on touch; masks, ventilation, and going outside all came to matter as precautionary acts to protect public health throughout the pandemic (Miller, 2020). Having a predisposition to respiratory issues comprised an increased risk; difficulty in breathing constitutes a symptom, and long-term health complications for those who have survived the pandemic include shortness of breath as well as coughing. I stocked up on my child's and my own asthma inhalers.

Early in the global pandemic of COVID-19, perhaps the least productive act of naming was "social distancing." Social and physical distance are not the same. Research on the interpersonal theory of suicide illuminates the importance of distinguishing between "social distancing/" and "physical distancing," especially for those with access to media that can provide social connections even when we are physically isolated (Christensen et al., 2013; Tucker et al., 2018). Without media access, physical distance becomes torture through its capacity to socially isolate. This need for contact with other humans is why the National Communication Association (2010) has strongly condemned extended solitary confinement. Humans require a sense of connection to thrive.

The idea of "social distancing six feet" to avoid spreading the virus through breathing on each other further caused confusion. Different government agencies and privately owned business tried to make the more abstract idea of six feet more concrete by showing images of arrows, cows, and more. Once again, nonhuman animals stood in as cultural signifiers of public health messages. Perhaps no one was more creative than the U.S. National Park Service by showing two picnic tables, moose antlers, a national park sign, a grizzly bear, and a bison. Officials sought to use these icons to make the abstract concrete across language communities and cultural norms. Each symbol chosen to illustrate "six feet" with presumably identifiable, cultural icons. However, the symbols did not carry the same meanings for everyone. A friend and Spanish language access advocate, for example, quickly pointed out that the Colorado symbol of skis was much less universal than a bed. Skis might be better marketing for tourism, but that was not the highest priority at the time.

Cultural norms matter across human differences as well. As "I Can't Breathe" became a Black Lives Matter slogan in 2014, environmental justice advocates immediately made the connection between the literal chokehold Eric Garner was placed in by a New York City Police officer and the disproportionate burden placed on BIPOC (Black, Indigenous, and People of Color) communities by our unsustainable patterns of pollution. The ironic cut even deeper when the public realized Garner's job working for the Horticulture Department of Parks and Recreation in the city (Gay, 2015). The slogan "I Can't Breathe" resurfaced in June 2020 with the killing of George Floyd, sparking new protests.

Asthma and other respiratory ailments have made some more susceptible during the pandemic. Pointing out the white violence against Asians and Asian Americans, as well as disproportionate cases and deaths, the NAACP produced a report early in the pandemic, emphasizing that, while COVID has impacted us all, it has not impacted all of us evenly (Patterson, 2020). The NAACP already had been thinking about the disproportionate impact of disasters, and, therefore, much of the inequities did not feel "new" or unprecedented, though each repetition of these cycles has performed differently (Steinchenv & Patterson, 2018).

My research has focused on environmental and climate injustices. Two questions that are central to my work are: Who is imagined as disposable, and how can we hold the people who make such decisions accountable? "There exists," as I have argued previously, "both a psychological and geographical distance between dominant public culture and the cultures of those who live in places where both waste and people are linked together as unnecessary, undesirable, and contaminating" (Pezzullo, 2007, p. 5). Basic human needs, such as clean air and drinking water, remain denied for too many unable to breathe or drink as taken for granted rights. In the context of COVID, we might extend this research to consider: Who is "essential?" and do those workers considered "essential" always mean that their labor is necessary or that their lives are more disposable to do necessary tasks, such as farmwork and grocery deliveries?

For the United States, as opposed to, for example, New Zealand, COVID-19 has more aptly been experienced as a *syndemic*: clustering with pre-existing conditions and driven to spread through political and racial crises (Horton, 2020;

Mendenhall, 2020). Consider the state of Colorado: during the summer of 2020, we experienced the largest wildfire season known in its history while we were still navigating the pandemic. The sky was orange midday and irritated our eyes, noses, throats, and lungs. By March 2021, the University of Colorado-Boulder had already suspended spring break because officials did not want to make time for people to travel and potentially spread the virus more. We all had Zoom fatigue. Over the past year, I missed three funerals of kin, attended a virtual memorial, and celebrated my dad's 80th birthday virtually. We were tired, and then, the day I received my first vaccination shot, a mass shooting with a semi-automatic rifle occurred a few blocks from my home at our neighborhood grocery store. Many of us expressed feeling simultaneously heartbroken and numb: when the reverse 9–1–1 alerts informing of us the need for another lockdown went off inside my home (which also was my workplace and my child's school space at the time), the myth of a self-isolated "pod" once again was exposed.

The events since the COVID-19 syndemic began have once again traumatically exposed the devaluation of the sanctity of life by elites in power, as well as—particularly in the United States—the costs of a lack of basic social welfare infrastructures of care, including universal healthcare, mental health support, clean drinking water, broadband access, and more. Inequalities persist in the vaccine distribution. (Consider, e.g., how prisoners have been more at risk, but not prioritized in the rollout.) The inequities of the United States reflect broader global inequities of vaccine distribution globally and, sadly, share company with other countries as well. The weight of the ongoing and multiple crises of the early 2020s can feel overwhelming at times, even if this year seems to promise more hope than last. Given the interconnected relationship between crisis and care, not surprisingly, breathing during the pandemic became envisioned as a risky act for spreading the contagion and as a practice for taking breaks from the anxiety the pandemic was causing. Kin remind each other: "Drink water and breathe."

On Bella Vita Verde—Or Storytelling to Make Another World Possible

A common protest chant has occurred repeatedly at climate and other global political gatherings for decades now: "Another World is Possible." That claim may seem obvious at first and, yet, if we use all our time reacting to decisions that others make, we may forget our role as producers of futures, speculative painters, imaginative community builders. To conjure another future requires effort. Practice. Relationship maintenance. Meetings. Listening. Failing. It is much easier to fall into habits and the paths laid out for us by dominant culture.

Our stories, if told well, must account for culture and power—that is, the ways we share common and uncommon experiences of the pandemic, as well as the ways those possibilities were shaped by social structures. "Storytelling," as Betasamosake Simpson (2011) observed, "is an important process for visioning, imagining, critiquing, the social space around us" (pp. 33–34). She noted that this practice occurs today not only through Indigenous oral storytelling, but also through the diverse range of human expression: "the written word, spoken word, theatre, performance, art, visual art, music and rap, film and video" (p. 34). Whether we imagine a possible role in the future as someone who builds infrastructure for clean renewable and efficient energy, provides expertise in critical areas of research, creates art, grows and distributes food, works in public services (supporting health, elections, communication systems), or some other path, the *stories* that each of us tell and retell about the future will have an impact on what is possible—or not.

Our everyday environments were transformed during the pandemic. Surviving became a central and immediate focus for most of us, as everyday acts like cleaning took on greater significance. Since public health officials discouraged travel, many of us also spent more time in the space we call "home," trying something new, such as baking or cooking more time-intensive recipes, walking more deliberately outside, gardening, homeschooling, training in a new job to find better work, and so on. Some of us also organized, donated, and volunteered for mutual aide, public health access, and public education.

Though the frenetic pace of life while enduring multiple crises during the first few years of the 2020s has been exhausting, during this time, many of us have thought more deeply about what constitutes *"the good life"/La Vita Bella/Buen Viver*. As Roy (2020) wrote:

> Historically, pandemics have forced humans to break with the past and imagine their world anew. This one is no different. It is a portal, a gateway between one world and the next. We can choose to walk through it, dragging the carcasses of our prejudice and hatred, our avarice, our data banks and dead ideas, our dead rivers and smoky skies behind us. Or we can walk through lightly, with little luggage, ready to imagine another world. And ready to fight for it. (para. 47–48)

Fight is exactly what many of us have been working toward. The Hawai'i State Commission on the Status of Women (2020) created a COVID-19 recovery plan that foregrounds feminist and decolonial voices. The environmental nonprofit 350.org lead an effort in 2020 to articulate "Just Recovery Principles" (see: https://350.org/just-recovery/#signletter). A U.S. coalition emerged in April 2021 for the Thrive Agenda, which supports legislation

> to revive our economy while addressing these interlocking crises of climate change, racial injustice, public health, and economic inequity with a plan to create dignified jobs for millions of unemployed workers and support a better life for the millions more who remain vulnerable in this pivotal moment. (https://www.thriveagenda.com/)

Internationally, similar movements sought to mobilize publics. Of particular interest to me has been the advocacy of Enrico Giovannini, former Italian minister of labor (2013–2014) and head of the Italian National Institute of Statistics, a Spokesperson for the Italian Alliance for Sustainable Development. While the common Italian adage for "La Vita Bella" long has been embraced by tourists, connoting romantic notions of Italian life, Giovannini has been advocating for a greener, healthier future to become part of that imaginary—creating good paying jobs, revitalizing the economy, and acting faster and more aggressively to improve environmental regulations, including climate action. Instead of "bouncing back" to life before COVID-19, Giovannini (2021) argued:

> After the economic blow delivered by COVID-19, Italy can't afford to keep pumping public money into polluting industries. Instead, we must redirect that capital to create high-quality jobs in sustainable sectors—especially for young people and women, the groups hit hardest economically by the crisis. By channeling its long-standing innovative and engineering prowess, Italy can secure *la bella vita verde*. (para. 13)

Imagine a future in which we designed places where we live for all the species that we need to sustain life, one that fostered biodiversity instead of trying to address it as an afterthought. In 2020, a Costa Rican suburb granted rights of nature for bats. Called "Ciudad Dulce" (Sweet City), the city of Curridabat's "urban planning has been reimagined around its non-human inhabitants." As Edgar Mora, the mayor who granted bees, bats, hummingbirds, butterflies, and more citizenship status, has argued pollinators are the key to productivity:

> Pollinators are the consultants of the natural world, supreme reproducers and they don't charge for it. The plan to convert every street into a biocorridor and every neighbourhood into an ecosystem required a relationship with them. (Greenfield, 2020, para. 3)

Likewise, during the 2021 confirmation hearing of the first Indigenous U.S. Secretary of the Interior, Rep. Deb Haaland (Laguna Pueblo) responded when asked why she co-sponsored a bill to protect Montana grizzly bears: "I imagine, at the time, I was caring about the bears." With these ecocentric perspectives, any planning of infrastructure (transportation, buildings, media), as well as decisions about water and energy access and consumption, would need to begin by considering the habitat required to coexist.

Which of these stories of our future will unfold and which will be thwarted? Has the pandemic moved us to reconsider what or who has been missed most? If we no longer take our lives or mobility for granted, what might we resolve to do in the future? Although we might not all agree on what the answers are, ecological crises and care ethics inevitably are part of our responses. Whatever questions we have about culture and power today, we all are entangled ecologically—in ways that are both harmful and healing. Environmental communication will be vital to shaping how our relations develop.

References

Banerjee, A., Doxey, A. C., Mossman, K., & Irving, A. T. (2021, March 1). Unraveling the zoonotic origin and transmission of SARS-CoV-2. *Trends in Ecology & Evolution, 36*(3), 180–184.

Benvenuto, D., Giovanetti, M., Ciccozzi, A., Spoto, S., Angeletti, S., & Ciccozzi, M. (2020). The 2019-new coronavirus epidemic: Evidence for virus evolution. *Journal of Medical Virology, 92*(4), 455–459. https://doi.org/10.1002/jmv.25688.

Betasamosake Simpson, L. (2011). *Dancing on our turtle's back: Stories of Nishnaabeg re-creation, resurgence and a new emergence.* ARP Books.

Bloomfield, E. (2019). *Communication strategies for engaging climate skeptics: Religion and the environment.* Routledge.

Christensen, H., Batterham, P. J., Soubelet, A., & Mackinnon, A. J. (2013). A test of the Interpersonal Theory of Suicide in a large community-based cohort. *Journal of Affective Disorders, 144*(3), 225–234. https://doi.org/10.1016/j.jad.2012.07.002

Cox, J. R. (2007). Nature's 'crisis disciplines': Does environmental communication have an ethical duty? *Environmental Communication, 1*(1), 5–20.

Doucleff, M. (2021, March 29). The origins of COVID-19? WHO report points to a bat after all. All things considered. *NPR: National Public Radio.* https://www.npr.org/2021/03/29/982417629/the-origins-of-covid-19-who-report-points-to-a-bat-after-all

Edelman, G. (2020, March 25). The analogy between Covid-19 and climate change is eerily precise. *Wired.* https://www.wired.com/story/the-analogy-between-covid-19-and-climate-change-is-eerily-precise/

Gay, R. (2015). *A small, needful fact* [Poem]. https://www.splitthisrock.org/poetry-database/poem/a-small-needful-fact

Giovannini, E. (2021). How Italy can green 'La Bella Vita'. *Project Syndicate.* https://www.project-syndicate.org/commentary/italy-economy-green-transition-european-union-funding-by-enrico-giovannini-2020-11

Greenfield, P. (2020, April 29). 'Sweet city': The Costa Rica suburb that gave citizenship to bees, plants and trees. *The Guardian.* https://www.theguardian.com/environment/2020/apr/29/sweet-city-the-costa-rica-suburb-that-gave-citizenship-to-bees-plants-and-trees-aoe

Horton, R. (2020, September 26). Offline: COVID-19 is not a pandemic. Comment. *The Lancet, 396*(10255), 1731. https://doi.org/10.1016/S0140-6736(20)32000-6

Liu, J., & Pezzullo, P. C. (Eds.). (2020). *Green communication and China: On crisis, care, and global futures.* Michigan State University Press.

Lu, H., McComas, K. A., Buttke, D. E., Roh, S., & Wild, M. A. (2016). A one health message about bats increases intentions to follow public health guidance on bat rabies. *PLoS ONE, 11*(5). https://doi.org/10.1371/journal.pone.0156205

Mendenhall, E. (2020, October 22). The COVID-19 syndemic is not global: Context matters. Correspondence. *The Lancet, 396*(10264), 1731. https://doi.org/10.1016/S0140-6736(20)32218-2

Miller, S. (2020, August 10). How to use ventilation and air filtration to prevent the spread of coronavirus indoors. *The Conversation.* https://theconversation.com/how-to-use-ventilation-and-air-filtration-to-prevent-the-spread-of-coronavirus-indoors-143732

Milstein, T. (2011). Nature identification: The power of pointing and naming. *Environmental Communication, 5*(1), 3–24. https://doi.org/10.1080/17524032.2010.535836

Nagel, T. (1974, October). What is it like to be a bat? *The Philosophical Review, 83*(4), 435–450. https://www.jstor.org/stable/2183914

National Communication Association. (2010). *Resolution regarding extended solitary confinement and torture.* https://www.natcom.org/sites/default/files/pages/2010_Public_Statements_Resolution_Regarding_Extended_Solitary_Confinement_and_Torture_November.pdf

Patterson, J. (2020, April 3). *Ten equity considerations of the coronavirus* [Report.] NAACP. https://naacp.org/coronavirus/ten-equity-considerations-of-the-coronavirus-covid-19-outbreak-in-the-united-states-final/

Pezzullo, P. C. (2007). *Toxic tourism: Rhetorics of travel, pollution and environmental justice.* University of Alabama Press.

Pezzullo, P. C. (2008). Overture: The most complicated word. *Cultural Studies, 22*(3–4), 361–368.

Pezzullo, P. C. (2017). Environment. In D. Cloud (Ed.), *Oxford research encyclopedia of communication and critical studies* (19 pages). Oxford University Press. https://doi.org/10.1093/acrefore/9780190228613.013.575

Pezzullo, P. C. (2020). Resisting carelessness. Book review. *Cultural Studies.* https://doi.org/10.1080/09502386.2020.1855455

Pezzullo, P. C., & Cox, R. (2021). *Environmental communication and the public sphere* (6th ed.). SAGE.

Pezzullo, P. C., & de Onís, C. M. (2018). Rethinking rhetorical field methods on a precarious planet. *Communication Monographs, 85*(1), 103–122. https://doi.org/10.1080/03637751.2017.1336780.

Quammen, D. (2012). *Spillover: Animal infections and the next human pandemic.* W. W. Norton & Co.

Rasmussen, A. L. (2021). On the origins of SARS-CoV-2. *Natural Medicine, 27*(9), https://doi.org/10.1038/s41591-020-01205-5

Roy, A. (2020, April 3). The pandemic is a portal. *Financial Times.* https://www.ft.com/content/10d8f5e8-74eb-11ea-95fe-fcd274e920ca

Schmitt, C. R. (2019). Scapegoat ecology: Blame, exoneration, and an emergent genre in environmental discourse. *Environmental Communication, 13*(2), 152–164.

Steinchenv, L., & Patterson, J. (2018). *In the eye of the storm: A people's guide to transforming crisis and advancing equity in the disaster continuum* [Report]. NAACP. https://www.naacp.org/climate-justice-resources/in-the-eye-of-the-storm/

Tucker, R. P., Hagan, C. R., Hill, R. M., Slish, M. L., Bagge, C. L., Joiner, T. E. Jr., & Wingate, L. R. (2018, January.). Empirical extension of the interpersonal theory of suicide: Investigating the role of interpersonal hopelessness. *Psychiatry Research, 259,* 427–432. https://doi.org/10.1016/j.psychres.2017.11.005

Yong, E. (2020, September). How the pandemic defeated America. *The Atlantic.* https://www.theatlantic.com/magazine/archive/2020/09/coronavirus-american-failure/614191/

18

HEALTH COMMUNICATION, GENDER VIOLENCE, AND INEQUALITY DURING COVID-19

A Critical Feminist Health Communication Perspective

Leandra Hinojosa Hernández

Learning Objectives

1. Discuss how racialized and minoritized bodies of color have been disproportionately impacted by COVID-19.
2. Analyze the relationship among intersectionality, racial capitalism, and critical health communication.

Migrant health at the Mexico–U.S. border has dominated recent news headlines, given the rapid spread of COVID-19 in the United States. A cursory glance at American news headlines of migrant health at the border illustrates several health concerns, including but not limited to sexual abuse, violence, and poor access to healthcare. As Hernández and De Los Santos Upton (2019) described, migrants often occupy a precarious position in the American imaginary. According to Basok and Rojas Weisner (2018), "They live in overcrowded houses and are subject to abuse and exploitation by employers in shady economies and denied access to education and health care. Furthermore, fearful of detention and deportation, they are susceptible to stress and anxiety," among other acts of violence (p. 1274). Such conditions have become exacerbated with the rise of COVID-19 in the United States, as policies of the homeland security state have held migrants at the border in detention camps and then overturned detention policies to deport migrants in the interest of maintaining and protecting American public health. In April of 2020, news outlets reported that the United States "aggressively" deported thousands of migrants because of COVID-19 concerns (Dickerson & Semple, 2020). Dickerson and Semple asserted:

> In March, ICE completed 17,965 removals, according to agency records. Total deportations have declined so far in April, however, with 2,985

DOI: 10.4324/9781003220466-21

removals of foreign nationals from all countries" (para. 7). Of those deportations, "A total of 95 minors traveling without their parents were deported to
Guatemala in March, up from 16 in January, before the border closure began,
according to figures provided by the Guatemalan government. A total of 92
were deported to Guatemala during the first half of April. (para. 9)

In June of 2020, more than 1,400 migrants tested positive for COVID-19, yet this
estimate is likely higher, given that ICE (Immigration Customs and Enforcement)
reported testing fewer than 12% of detainees (Human Rights Watch, 2020). As
a critical feminist health communication scholar, I use the backdrop of violence
against migrants at the Mexico–U.S. border to highlight the intersections of critical health communication, gender violence, and reproductive injustices during the
time of COVID-19. In this chapter, I will discuss my own personal and political
experiences during COVID-19 that have shaped (and continue to shape) my health
communication research and activism and conclude a discussion of how COVID-19
will fundamentally shape the future of critical health communication scholarship.

COVID-19 through the Eyes of a Critical Health Communication Researcher

COVID-19 and other events that transpired during 2020 radically affected the
lives of individuals in both the United States and across the globe. In March 2020,
I was teaching two undergraduate health communication courses, and I remember vividly the conversations that we had in class the week before the world essentially shut down, and classes were unexpectedly moved online. Students asked, in
both a concerned and inquisitive manner, whether COVID-19 was "just another
flu," whether the world was "overreacting," and whether it would be gone within
a matter of a few weeks. I had no idea that Thursday afternoon in mid-March
of 2020 would be the last time that I would see them (or any other students, for
that matter) in person to this day. COVID-19 presented many challenges for me,
as it has for many others. It exacerbated my anxiety radically, and the transition
to solely online teaching with the additional interpersonal isolation was an uphill
battle. I feared for the lives of my parents and family elders, given their age, fears
that were exacerbated when I saw posts on social media about my dear friends'
parents and family elders succumbing to COVID-19. Then, in May of 2020
when George Floyd was murdered, my anxieties skyrocketed for several reasons:
1) I was the only woman of color in my department (and one of very few women
of color across my institution, which is largely white), which meant I struggled finding solidarity with allies, advocates, and other faculty of color; 2) I was
enrolled in a university global/intercultural certification program with a domi-
nantly white faculty member base, and the murder of George Floyd prompted
challenging conversations with other white faculty members predicated upon
white tears and white guilt (Hernández & Munz, 2021), and 3) I struggled to find

solidarity with other BIPOC individuals in my community, given that I live in a predominantly white state. Moreover, the emotional exhaustion and racial battle fatigue experienced when mentoring students of color and facilitating diversity, inclusion, and equity conversations—challenging conversations, to say the least— with a predominantly white student body often felt like it was too much to bear in our current sociopolitical and racial moment. However, my pandemic anxieties and stressors paled in comparison to those experienced by other academics with young children and no childcare assistance, individuals who are immunocompromised, and communities struggling with health disparities, disproportionate levels of healthcare access, and human rights violations. One such group includes migrant laborers and migrants detained at the Mexico–U.S. border.

Critical Health Communication and the Mexico–U.S. Border

For the past several years, utilizing intersectional, feminist, and critical health communication frameworks, I have dedicated my research and activist energies to addressing reproductive in/justice and migrant violence at the Mexico–U.S. border (Hernández, 2019; Hernández & De Los Santos Upton, 2018, 2019, 2020). Although it is outside the scope of this chapter to fully explicate historical and contemporary international relations between the United States and Latin America, I acknowledge here that America, as a world superpower, has long exploited countries throughout Latin America from a violence and industrialization perspective, an exploitation that has directly resulted in several migration catastrophes and the border militarization that we see in our present day. As an extent of such interventionist policies, through its racial gaze, homeland security perpetually treats Latinos and Latin Americans as suspect outsiders and foreigners, a particular framing accompanied by more concerns as it intersects with class and citizenship status (De Genova, 2007; Gonzales, 2013). As De Genova (2009) noted, the last several U.S. presidential administrations have created "an ever more dismal horizon of rightlessness" for Latinos and Latin Americans alike (p. 445). Their right-less status as foreigners has significantly problematic and lethal implications for racialized death and public health, as I will discuss in this chapter.

Violence against Migrants

One of the most pressing migrant health concerns pertains to violence against migrants within larger structural contexts of family-child separation, sexual abuse, and physical violence (Hernández, 2019; Hernández & De Los Santos Upton, 2019; Valencia, 2017). Over the past several years, scholars have detailed abuse and violence that migrants have long endured at the Mexico–U.S. border; however, many of these injustices were either overshadowed in news discourses during COVID-19 or not covered at all. Within a family context, families have been disintegrated with the separation of children from their parents. According to the

American Civil Liberties Union (ACLU), in June of 2020, "U.S. District Court Judge Dana Sabraw issued a preliminary injunction that ordered the government to return all children under 5 years old to their parents within 14 days and within 30 days for the rest" (para. 1). The ACLU asserted that over 2,600 immigrant children have been separated from their families because of immigration policies enforced by the Trump administration. Other reports have indicated that as many as 5,000 children have been separated from their families at the Mexico–U.S. border. ("More than 5,400 children split at border, according to new count," 2019.) Of these children, 2,363 were discharged from the Office of Refugee Resettlement custody, and 125 children decided with family members (who were since deported) to stay in the United States and pursue asylum. As I argued in a previous publication, migrant family separation is a form of extreme reproductive violence (Hernández, 2019). Hernández and De Los Santos Upton detailed:

> Within the context of immigration from Latin America, the Trump Administration's migrant violations include but are not limited to the following: migrant adults and children have been kept in cages (Barry, 2018; Raff, 2018), migrant children have been both physically and sexually abused (Honarvar, 2018; Neuman, 2018), migrants have been forced to sleep under bridges because cages and detention centers have reached full capacity (Romero, 2019), and migrant women have been sexually abused, with no concrete understanding of just how many migrant women have been assaulted while on their journey or upon arriving at the U.S.-Mexico border. (p. 2)

Such reproductive violence and injustice operates at multiple levels. From a sociocultural and ecological perspective, journalists and politicians often frame asylum seekers as criminals and threats to the American social order, which "justifies the creation and endorsement of American laws to separate families with the worst possible outcomes" (Hernández, 2019, p. 132). Moreover, according to Hernández, from a reproductive justice perspective, in addition to detainment procedures and reports of abuse,

> there is no mention of any sort of reparation for the mental health injustices and traumatic experiences which separated migrant children currently face and might face as they grow older and which were instigated and inflicted at the hands of the American government and its immigration officials. (p. 132)

In addition to reproductive injustices perpetrated against migrant children at the border, migrant women and girls have also been subjected to various forms of abuse at the Mexico–U.S. border (Centeno, 2019; Fernandez, 2019). Fernandez asserted:

> On America's southern border, migrant women and girls are the victims of sexual assaults that most often go unreported, uninvestigated and

unprosecuted. Even as women around the world are speaking out against sexual misconduct, migrant women on the border live in the shadows of the #MeToo movement. The stories are many, and yet all too similar. Undocumented women making their way into American border towns have been beaten for disobeying smugglers, impregnated by strangers, coerced into prostitution, shackled to beds and trees and—in at least a handful of cases—bound with duct tape, rope or handcuffs. (para. 4–5)

Taken together, health concerns at the Mexico–U.S. border have been characterized by a confluence of several factors, such as the rapid spread of COVID-19, family separation and deportation policies, and violence against women and children. Scholars contend that health communication efforts and scholarship can and should combine several theoretical and methodological approaches—intersectionality. feminist theory, critical health communication, and border studies—to address gender violence, assist marginalized populations, and resist human rights health violations at the Mexico–U.S. border (Hernández, 2019; Hernández & De Los Santos Upton, 2019).

Migrant Violence in Labor Contexts during COVID-19

Migrant communities at the border have not been the only ones impacted by COVID-19; however, migrant laborers and bodies of color in service positions have also been disproportionately impacted by COVID-19 with little justice or retribution for their illnesses. In the midst of the COVID-19 pandemic in the United States, citizens across the country were urged to quarantine in the interest of public health and public safety. However, lower-class individuals, often individuals of color, were unable to quarantine and work remotely, particularly those who worked in service-based industries (Team & Manderson, 2020; Williams et al., 2020). Take, for instance, the death of a janitorial services employee (a man of color) at the University of Texas who was diagnosed with COVID-19 and died in July of 2020. This custodial employee (whose name was not released to the media) contracted COVID-19 within a transmission cluster of 11 other custodial services employees, and his death was the university's first-related COVID-19 fatality. His story—a racial capitalism fatality, indeed—is one of many that characterizes the fate of service workers who have no other choice but to continue working in spite of pandemic fears about virus transmission and infection. Indeed, their very work enables capitalism to proceed, as many narratives of hospital and university janitorial staff have made clear. Moreover, such pandemic risk-management strategies highlight the class-based and race-based limitations of current public health models, particularly considering that people of color remain more highly disproportionately affected by COVID-19 infection rates than their white counterparts.

The term *racial capitalism* explores the intersections of race and violence that allow capitalism to flourish (Ralph & Singhal, 2019). Within a public health perspective, a racialized capitalism framework attends to the role of racial violence in the spread of COVID-19. As McClure and colleagues (2020) argued, the most salient commonality among workplace and service-based spaces that spread COVID-19 was, indeed, the race of the workers (i.e., Black and Brown individuals). However, as McClure et al. stated, "the greatly amplified transmission risk occurring in these settings is not because of an inherent vulnerability of Black, Brown, or immigrant workers" (p. 1245). Rather, "a system of racial capitalism that preceded the pandemic structurally concentrates exposures and exacerbates COVID-19 risk for these worker populations, through replication of historical inequities and state-supported corporate neglect of worker protection" (p. 1245).

Thus, the use of a racial capitalism framework during the COVID-19 pandemic illustrates how laborers of color are expendable, particularly in meat packing, agricultural labor, service labor, construction, and assisted living contexts. McClure and colleagues (2020), for example, observed a concentration of COVID-19 exposure and cases in low-wage and essential-worker populations which are disproportionately comprised of racial and ethnic minorities and immigrants. They asserted that health researchers (those in public health more broadly and those in health communication, more specifically, for the purposes of this chapter) should "question the ways in which we recreate racism through our study designs, information collection, research questions, and data-analysis methods" (p. 1250), a conclusion similar to Hernández and De Los Santos Upton's (2019) research on critical health communication methods at the Mexico–U.S. border. In other words, building on Ford and Airhihenbuwa's (2010) model of critical race theory and public health, scholars assert that a critical lens must be utilized during the COVID-19 pandemic to call attention to systemic, structural, and racial inequities, lest we "absolve industries and government leaders of their responsibility for equitable health protection" by ignoring and misrepresenting the root causes of such inequities (McClure et al., 2020, p. 1250).

Racial capitalism defines the nature of COVID-19 risk and crisis management strategies in the Americas, evidenced most glaringly in the labored expectations and forced requirements of im/migrant day laborers and laborers of color, particularly in the United States. Coronavirus has been reported in more than half of Latino meat and poultry workers in 21 states. Of nearly 10,000 COVID-19 cases, more than half (56%) were Hispanic workers (Gamboa, 2020). As Gamboa illustrated, "The latest CDC data, published Tuesday [during July 2020], reinforces alarms raised as meat and chicken facilities and their surrounding communities have become COVID-19 hot spots, and deaths among workers have mounted this year" (Ibid, para. 2) In total, almost 9 in 10 new COVID cases (87%) occurred among racial and ethnic minority workers.

Such racial/ethnic disparity rates reveal racial capitalism at play—workers left unsafe, vulnerable, and, in migrant cases, unable to advocate for themselves. According to Gamboa (2020), a coalition of civil rights advocates, human rights advocates, and food worker advocates filed a civil rights complaint in early July 2020 with the U.S. Department of Agriculture against Tyson Foods Inc. and JBS USA, asserting that "for the purpose of maximizing profits and processing capacity, these companies treat plant floor workers as sacrificial" (Ibid, para. 6). While the term "sacrificial" might appear to be hyperbolic, it encapsulates how the poor working conditions at poultry and meat plants render laborers to be nothing more than a capitalistic means to an end: workers cannot maintain social distance, as they often toil in closed and cramped quarters and share work, transportation, and housing spaces, thus rendering social distancing and quarantine recommendations practically impossible. In other words, in this current moment both characterized by and exacerbated by COVID-19, employers treat racialized and minoritized bodies as expendable means to an end, both suffering from a global pandemic and serving as some of its first (and continued) fatalities.

2020 and Critical Health Communication Futures

If but nothing else, the events that transpired in 2020 (and that are still transpiring now)—the COVID-19 pandemic, violence against Black and Brown bodies, gender violence, and cultural activism—have highlighted the gaps in traditional health communication scholarship and illuminated the ever-pressing need for intersectional, borderlands, feminist approaches to health communication. As Hudak (2020) described, the history of health communication in our discipline has long favored quantitative, post-positivist scholarship; as such, publishing queer, feminist, and critical health communication scholarship continues to confront many challenges, what Hudak referred to as "intense scrutiny" (p. 1). Hudak's research revealed that critical (read: feminist, intersectional, queer, borderlands) health communication scholarship struggles to find a home, and my own experiences mirror this chasm.

Although my PhD is in health communication, I strayed from the National Communication Association (NCA) Health Communication Division for a decade because reviewers constantly told me that my work did not fit, that it was too critical, that it would be best suited for other divisions or outlets, and—similarly to feedback Hudak (2020) has received—that communities of color and queer communities are no longer marginalized (read: we need more research on straight white communities). For these reasons, I have long called the Latina/o Communication Studies Division, the La Raza Caucus, and the Feminist and Gender Studies Divisions my academic home spaces. In 2020, however, a member of the NCA Health Communication Division asked me to consider running for the division's executive committee because the division was committed to supporting scholars of color and intersectional health communication scholarship. As a queer Chicana feminist who utilizes intersectional and borderlands approaches to study health communication topics, I was understandably hesitant to accept the nomination; however, now a year later, I am the division's Vice-Chair Elect, and I have dedicated my energies to supporting more diverse and equitable approaches to health communication for scholars and activists alike.

Scholars—such as Dutta (2010), Lupton (2012), Hudak (2020), and Hernández and De Los Santos Upton (2019)—have explained that critical health communication research focuses on the power structures that both create and perpetuate inequalities in healthcare. Critical health communication research "recognizes that truth and knowledge are both constructed and reinforced by power relations and we should, therefore, be skeptical of those claims" (Hudak, p. 1). Critical health communication scholars and activists challenge dominant health frameworks, work with communities to advocate for those who are most disenfranchised, and advocate for more nuanced, critical, and multi-faceted approaches to the study of power, health, identity, and culture. Within this epistemological approach, the COVID-19 pandemic glaringly highlighted the necessity of an intersectional, critical, feminist approach to health communication. Such an approach calls our attention to the intertwined power matrices of racism, sexism, classism, nationalism, and health disparities that have disproportionately impacted the ways in which communities of color have been impacted by COVID-19. While post-positivist health communication research can provide valuable research and information on statistics associated with COVID-19, it does little to help us understand the cultural, community, and power forces at play that lend one person to be more susceptible to COVID-19 than another.

As we observed during 2020 in the United States, militaristic, masculinized, and individualistic perceptions of wearing a mask not only galvanized individuals to radically disavow the mask, but also sparked public acts of violence to vehemently defend their personal right to not wear a mask. Moreover, the white individualistic (read: masculine) national ideology espoused in the United States does not account for diverse, collectivistic family structures—those which have multiple family members living under one roof—or the fact that working-class communities of color are the backs upon which our country's labor both depends and thrives, even in and especially in the time of a pandemic. As Dutta (2008, 2010) has long discussed in much of his work, critical health communication scholarship helps us to reconsider and interrogate how health communication discourses position agendas of the status quo, how research and practice routinely re/circulate dominant ideologies, and what possibilities and avenues exist for resistance. Although all three areas are valuable, the COVID-19 pandemic has truly highlighted the importance of resistance, whether it be through challenging dominant assumptions of universality; advocating for intersectional, feminist, critical health communication scholarship (Hudak, 2020); organizing with local communities to provide care and services (Hernández & De Los Santos Upton, 2019), and working with various organizations to eradicate health disparities and lessen the impact of COVID-19 in our communities.

References

American Civil Liberties Union. (2020). *Family separation by the numbers*. https://www.aclu.org/issues/immigrants-rights/immigrants-rights-and-detention/family-separation

Barry, D. (2018, July 14). Cleaning toilets, following rules: A migrant child's days in detention. *New York Times*. https://www.nytimes.com/ 2018/07/14/us/migrant-children-shelters.html

Basok, T., & Rojas Weisner, M. (2018). Precarious legality: Regularizing Central American migrants in Mexico. *Ethnic Racial Studies*, *41*, 1274–1293. https://doi.org/10.1080/01419870.2017.1291983

Centeno, R. (2019, August 30). What the border patrol doesn't want you to know about their abuses. *Medium*. https://zora.medium.com/what-the-border-patrol-doesnt-want-you-to-know-about-their-abuses-3adef7988cad

De Genova, N. (2007). The production of culprits: From deportability to detainability in the aftermath of "homeland security". *Citizenship Studies*, *11*(5), 421–448.

De Genova, N. (2009). Conflicts of mobility, and the mobility of conflict: Rightlessness, presence, subjectivity, freedom. *Subjectivity*, *29*(1), 445–466.

Dickerson, C., & Semple, K. (2020). U.S. deported thousands amid Covid-19 outbreak. Some proved to be sick. *New York Times*. https://www.nytimes.com/2020/04/18/us/deportations-coronavirus-guatemala.html

Dutta, M. J. (2008). *Communicating health: A culture-centered approach*. Polity.

Dutta, M. J. (2010). The critical cultural turn in health communication: Reflexivity, solidarity, and praxis. *Health Communication*, *25*, 534–539.

Fernandez, M. (2019, March 3). 'You have to pay with your body': The hidden nightmare of sexual violence on the border. *New York Times*. https://www.nytimes.com/2019/03/03/us/border-rapesmigrant-women.html

Ford, C. L., & Airhihenbuwa, C. O. (2010). Critical race theory, race equity, and public health: Toward antiracism praxis. *American Journal of Public Health*, *100*(S1), S30–S35.

Gamboa, S. (2020, July 8). Coronavirus reported in over half of Latino meat, poultry workers in 21 states, CDC says. *NBC News*. https://www.nbcnews.com/news/latino/coronavirus-reported-over-half-latino-meat-poultry-workers-21-states-n1233192

Gonzales, A. (2013). *Reform without justice: Latino migrant politics and the homeland security state*. Oxford University Press.

Hernández, L. H. (2019). Feminist approaches to border studies and gender violence: Family separation as reproductive injustice. *Women's Studies in Communication*, *42*(2), 130–134.

Hernández, L. H., & De Los Santos Upton, S. (2018). *Challenging reproductive control and gendered violence in the Américas: Intersectionality, power, and struggles for rights*. Lexington Books.

Hernández, L. H., & De Los Santos Upton, S. (2019). Critical health communication methods at the US-Mexico border: Violence against migrant women and the role of health activism. *Frontiers in Communication*, *4*(34), 1–12.

Hernández, L. H., & De Los Santos Upton, S. (2020). Insider/outsiders, reproductive (in)justice, and the US-Mexico Border. *Health Communication*, *35*(8), 1046–1050.

Hernández, L. H., & Munz, S. M. (2021). Autoethnography as assessment: Communication pedagogies as social justice activism. *Communication Teacher*, 1–18.

Honarvar, A. (2018, July 27). A 6-year-old girl was sexually abused in an immigrant-detention center. *The Nation*. https://www.thenation.com/article/six-year-old-girl-sexually-abused-immigrantdetention-center/

Hudak, N. (2020). Navigating publishing critical health communication research. *Frontiers in Communication*, *5*, 1–5.

Human Rights Watch. (2020, June 4). *US: Suspend deportations during pandemic.* https://www.hrw.org/news/2020/06/04/us-suspend-deportations-during-pandemic

Korte, L. (2020, July 7). UT custodian dies from coronavirus in Austin. *Austin American-Statesman.* https://www.statesman.com/story/news/coronavirus/2020/07/07/ut-custodian-dies-from-coronavirus-in-austin/42477657/

Lupton, D. (2012). *Medicine as culture: Illness, disease and the body* (3rd ed.). SAGE.

McClure, E. S., Vasudevan, P., Bailey, Z., Patel, S., & Robinson, W. R. (2020). Racial capitalism within public health—how occupational settings drive COVID-19 disparities. *American Journal of Epidemiology, 189*(11), 1244–1253.

More than 5,400 children split at border, according to new count. (2019, October 25). *NBC News.* https://www.nbcnews.com/news/us-news/more-5-400-children-split-border-according-new-count-n1071791

Neuman, S. (2018, August 3). Allegations of sexual abuse surface at Arizona shelters for migrant children. *NPR.* https://www.npr. org/2018/08/03/635203037/allegations-of-sexual-abuse-surface-at-arizonashelters-for-migrant-children

Raff, J. (2018, September 7). The separation was so long. My son has changed so much. *The Atlantic.* https://www.theatlantic.com/politics/archive/2018/09/trump-family-separation-children-border/569584/

Ralph, M., & Singhal, M. (2019). Racial capitalism. *Theory & Society, 48,* 851–881.

Romero, S. (2019, March 29). Migrants are detained under a bridge in El Paso. What happened? *New York Times.* https://www.nytimes. com/2019/03/29/us/el-paso-immigration-photo.html

Team, V., & Manderson, L. (2020). How COVID-19 reveals structures of vulnerability. *Medical Anthropology, 39*(8), 671–674.

Valencia, Y. (2017). Risk and security on the Mexico-to-US migrant journey: Women's testimonios of violence. *Gender, Place & Culture, 24*(11), 1530–1548.

Williams, J. C., Anderson, N., Holloway, T., Samford III, E., Eugene, J., & Isom, J. (2020). Reopening the United States: Black and Hispanic workers are essential and expendable again. *American Journal of Public Health, 110,* 1506–1508.

19

COLLAPSING CONTEXTS

Reconciling Technology Amplification and Human Agency in an Era of Surveillance Capitalism

Prashant Rajan

Learning Objectives

Readers of this chapter will learn about the following theoretical terms:

1. **Context Collapse**: Context collapse is a key concept in the literature on computer-medicated communication that is typically presented as a challenge for users communicating with different audiences while online. I chose this concept because my personal experiences suggest that context collapse may not only be inevitable for users communicating in the 2020s, but also that users might consider planning ways to intentionally collapse their contexts in order to communicate in ways that are authentic to changing professional and personal circumstances. Through my personal narrative about teaching online from home, I make the case that being authentic during communication is a way to enact agency, a concept I further discuss in light of the Capability Approach.

2. **Amplification thesis for information and communication technologies**: Drawing on Kentaro Toyama's (2015) amplification thesis, I contradict the solutionist assumption that simply using new or more technologies helps democratize human activity in productive ways. Reflecting on my efforts to use technology for teaching online again, and other experiences with COVID-19 testing, I note that technology tends to exacerbate existing inequities and cannot substitute for appropriate institutional capacity and benign human intent.

3. **The Capability Approach (CA)**: The Capability Approach is a theoretical framework that can be effectively used by Communication students and scholars to study human agency as people's freedom to choose to do and be

DOI: 10.4324/9781003220466-22

in ways that are meaningful to them. I recount experiences in this past year to discuss how the capability approach has informed my everyday interactions especially in the classroom. I also make the case that using CA can help communication students and scholars engage in meaningful conversations with colleagues in development studies, economics, and sociology around a variety of topics that are broadly concerned with social change and human welfare. Specifically, I connect CA's definition of agency with on-going conversations among technical and professional communications scholars about the need to initiate critical action that amplifies the agencies of underrepresented and disadvantaged groups.

"Daddy, can I say hello to your class?"

I was not quite sure how to respond. It was my first time teaching synchronously online. I felt nervous seeing all the tiles, each representing a student in my class. Why weren't any of them turning their cameras on? Was it appropriate for me to ask them to turn their cameras on?

And why wouldn't my child leave the room so I could teach?

I tried to gently direct her attention away, a futile attempt that only made her come and sit on my lap. My camera was turned on. My students could all see my daughter sitting on me. I could feel my heart rate rising at a steady clip. How was I going to appear professorial with a 5-year-old grinning at the class?

And then, something surprising happened. One by one, the students started turning their cameras on. Every face was smiling. I had a feeling that they were not smiling at me out of excitement for learning about t-tests and standard deviations. Before I could say a word, Aisha began to wave at the screen, and students started waving back.

Just like that, my 5-year-old had done something that any instructor likely knows is both important and incredibly difficult to achieve—something I had so often struggled to do—break the ice in a natural and authentic manner. In fact, Aisha had gone a step further. It felt like she had nurtured a feeling of warmth by spreading smiles on the first day of class.

It was not over though. Aisha wanted to know what we were going to be learning. So I told her and the students that we were going to be learning today about the ways that a social scientist would ask questions about the world. Ever focused on the present moment, Aisha responded: "So, tell us papa!"

"Oh, but I wasn't going to do that right away!"

"So, what were you going to do now, papa?"

"I was going to greet everyone and spend some time introducing myself."

"Then do that papa!"

And so I did. I smiled through the embarrassment and started talking through my slides for the first day of class. Several students cooed when they saw the photo of Aisha from when she was just a year and a half old. Aisha giggled, and promptly wandered off into another room. The class period went well.

In the sections that follow, I reflect on the theoretical significance of such melding between the personal and the professional. To do so, I first employ the concept of context collapse to describe pedagogical tensions that arose from the involuntary and often simultaneous negotiation of multiple social contexts by students and myself as their teacher. Second, I draw on the technology and development literatures to discuss how embracing context collapse helped me develop a more empathic approach to teaching in mediated settings. Specifically, I locate concepts such as context collapse and technology amplification within the framework of the capabilities approach to reflect on how my teaching and research efforts can be better integrated. Finally, I suggest ways in which Communication teachers and researchers can develop more symmetric accounts of how communication technology use shapes and is shaped by human agency.

Context Collapse

A scholar of communication and technology use would inform me that I had just experienced a context collapse. Context collapse occurs when people find themselves having to concurrently negotiate different social contexts (Davis & Jurgenson, 2014; Marwick & boyd, 2011). Each social context is grounded in a different set of norms, making the task of responding simultaneously challenging with high probability of the speaker struggling to make themselves understood (Gil-Lopez et al., 2018). Think about running into a workplace colleague while attending a rock concert or rushing to get to the checkout line at the grocery store on Sunday.

Gil-Lopez et al. (2018) suggested that context collapse imposes costs on the communicator. After all, we have different goals when communicating with students versus when we are communicating with family. Therefore, it is harder to frame messages that are simultaneously relevant to audiences that belong to different non-overlapping subsets of our social networks.

Wang et al. (2016) asserted that context collapse can have a dampening effect on self-disclosure online. We tend to want to share less often and less detail when communicating across contexts. Indeed, young adults and teens might argue that it is best if we employ dedicated channels to communicate with different audiences. Many young people use Finstas or Fake Instagram accounts, for example, to communicate candidly with close friends (Dewar et al., 2019).

However, I learned from my daughter's intervention about communicating while teaching online in 2020 and 2021 that sometimes letting contexts collapse has value. We have a small home. I did not have much of a choice when it came to preventing my family from breaching the boundary separating professional and personal. A locked door means little to a child that is intent upon getting in.

So, we developed a little ritual. Aisha would come in at the beginning of class and say hello to everyone. She could hang around longer if she wanted, but she was not allowed to interject in the lecture or discussion. It did not always work out, and I needed to be rescued a couple of times by my spouse or the nanny.

As fazed as I might be, my students began to take Aisha's presence for granted. On days that she did not show up, I could see that they were waiting for her. I felt compelled on occasion to explain her absence. Lunch, a visit to the dentist, a strep infection—my daughter's itinerary began to become a small part of classroom conversation. I began to feel guilty. Was I wasting valuable class time or perhaps using my gregarious child to seem more affable in class?

These misgivings cleared when both of my children fell ill in October 2020. We could not invite any help because they were sick. My partner was breastfeeding non-stop while teaching online and mandatory on-campus labs. I was falling behind on grading. At this time, I chose to share my circumstances with my students. In a synchronous classroom session, I apologized to them for being late on returning their assignments. It was an emotional moment, in part because I had not had a chance to sleep the night before. In my sleep-deprived state, I owned up to my fallibility and showed without trying that I was a human, just like them.

Having shared my helplessness with students in a vulnerable moment, I found myself reflecting later on their circumstances. We were in a pandemic with no known end. Business could not be as usual for a variety of reasons. I knew that I would struggle to take 18 credits and work part time for FedEx or Doordash as many of my students did. It could not be easy to stay focused on coursework while isolating or living at home with family as a 20-something.

How could I invite the students to talk about their experiences isolating? Sure, I was not a licensed counseling psychologist or social worker. However, did I really need diplomas to recognize that a student might be suffering or in pain? The evidence was unequivocal about a mental health crisis predating and accompanying the COVID-19 pandemic (Curtin & Heron, 2019; Pfefferbaum & North, 2020).

I began to include short reflective exercises inviting students to describe their experiences learning during the pandemic. I was stunned to learn about the breadth of experiences. Many of my students worked during the day. Others stayed home, babysitting for younger siblings, cousins, nieces, and nephews, so adult family members in essential and frontline occupations could go to work. Still others found themselves sharing space with family members that they could not bear to try and get along with but had to find a way to do so, given COVID constraints.

Several shared stories of trouble seeking medical attention and medication for their anxiety and other health conditions. All of them expressed a longing for a return to campus life. They missed their friends and had no idea if and when things would return to normal or what normalcy might mean in a post-pandemic era. An election year did not do much to assuage frayed relations between politically opposed family members, with no idea of when the forced cohabitation would end.

Multiple students contacted me and expressed gratitude for giving them a chance to pen their thoughts on what was going on outside of class. Just the act of writing about their hybrid life made it a little easier to deal with. Reading their poignant submissions, I recalled Amartya Sen's (1992) capability approach

(CA) that illustrated the difference between capabilities, defined as the freedom to choose to be and do in meaningful ways to the person(s) making choices. A person who is starving for lack of money and a person who is fasting for Lent or Ramadan are both depriving their body of nutrition. The difference remains that calorie deprivation comprises a choice for only one of them.

Technology Amplification and Agency

I thought of the role that technologies play in enabling and constraining choices and human agency to make choices freely—a topic that I have studied for the past decade. When I teach courses on technology, organizing, innovation, and information diffusion, I strive to help my students recognize that technologies are not only material objects, but also the mechanisms and methods of managing activity (King & Frost, 2002). Such mechanisms and methods include technical artifacts, social norms, organizational forms, institutions, and narratives about how these all are configured in relations of relative equity.

Equally, my effort in the classroom and in the field involves explaining how new technology is not always a tool of societal transformation through the democratization of access. More often than not, technology functions as an amplifier of existing inequity. The starting slide of my research presentations often tends to be a single quote from Toyama's (2015) book *Geek Heresy*, asserting that technology amplifies rather than substitutes for human intentions, abilities, and efforts. Toyama's amplification thesis suggests that human agency is shaping and shaped by technology. How then did technologies work as amplifiers in the context of expanding and constraining my students' freedoms to choose and live life in meaningful ways?

Questions of agency are also fundamental for contemporary technical and professional communication scholarship. Scholars in this field have increasingly advocated for amplifying the agency of underrepresented and disadvantaged populations of users (Jones & Walton, 2018), with agency being defined here in a way that echoes Sen's capability approach: the realization of "preferred goals" (Grabill, 2001, p. 163). My students faced several contingent challenges despite their collective privilege in enjoying access to higher education, requiring me to reassess my teaching in light of modes of learning that might be preferred by them.

I decided to listen more carefully. I regularly invited their feedback on the organization and workload for each module, using their comments to modify readings and assignments in ways that I aimed to be enjoyable and doable given the constraints faced by students. I began to realize how obtaining commitment from most of my students to read 20 pages in a week could help their learning experience more than imposing an arbitrary benchmark for rigor by demanding they read say, 50–100 pages.

Rather than outlining a single, linear path to completing the course and achieving a high grade, students wanted the freedom to choose multiple paths to the grade outcome. For instance, some students performed better in groups and sought team-based learning opportunities. Others preferred to go it alone because they felt more comfortable not seeking to coordinate work with members in online teams. I developed assignments for both categories.

My students also offered an honest repudiation of solutionist arguments that rely on improving access to technology; they plainly desired to use fewer technologies. An anecdotal survey in the class suggested that many students employed more than a dozen technologies to simply access course content and meet across just five courses in a single semester.

I dropped my plans to use snazzy tools that I had imagined would increase interactivity in the online classroom. To implement a team-based learning protocol, I worked with just two technologies—a communication platform and another learning management system. Yet, I struggled alongside the students with glitches that ate up valuable class time and made me to want to drop the protocol altogether.

When I asked students to share their thoughts, several opined that team-based learning efforts could be helpful if we split the work between asynchronous and synchronous components. Again, I listened to them and found that the technology became a lot less cumbersome when I used it with the intention of listening to students and implementing their feedback, than as a tool to implement my predetermined syllabus.

My students missed the regularity and structure of pre-pandemic classes. Neither were they enthused about meeting twice or thrice a week. So I held weekly mindfulness meetups wherein we would meditate together for two to three minutes and then spend 15–20 minutes on lecture with the remaining time used to work together on the class material. In this way, my students could find me consistently every week and in a space that allowed them to be comfortable yet vulnerable, without feeling compelled to show up and participate only because their grade depended on it.

Over the three semesters that I taught during COVID-19, I learned that I did not need students to turn on their cameras. My discomfort had little to do with them and a lot to do with how uncomfortable I felt and how out of water that I feel when teaching online. By giving students the freedom to share about their pandemic experiences, I learned to respect that student circumstances might preclude them from turning on their cameras.

Sen's (1992) capability approach, Toyama's (2015) amplification thesis, and the notion of context collapse perhaps make an odd theoretical triad for making sense what has been a decidedly strange couple of years. Each of these perspectives, however, does represent a conceptual linkage to the field of Communication. CA renews the potential for scholars to move beyond work done during the modernization era (e.g., Rogers, 1976; Schramm, 1964; Singhal & Rogers, 2002). CA also provides a lens for understanding the role of communication in aiding social change projects at the micro-level as illustrated by my reflections about teaching. For instance, applying CA in planning course delivery helped me move away from an in-person or online to a hybrid model of instruction that gives each student the choice to join either in-person or online for the lecture. Students were, thus, free to choose the modality in which they received instruction. At the same time, CA can also be used to rebuild Communication's status as a key element of macro-level development (Jacobson, 2016).

For example, I have found CA and the amplification thesis helpful in studying whether and to what extent communication technology infrastructures helped increase the freedoms of below-poverty-line households to choose when, where, and how they access food (Rajan et al., 2016). The capability approach can similarly be used to study how human agency relates to participatory communication processes in diverse organizational forms including educational organizations, rural communities, government agencies, and non-profits (Backhaus, 2020; Jacobson, 2016).

Looking Ahead: Conceptual Tools for Pedagogy, Scholarship, and Praxis

Agency constitutes a key part of calls by technical and professional communication scholars to move toward critical action and away from critical analyses (Jones & Walton, 2018). In order for critical action to be undertaken, we must learn the circumstances in which technology-amplified agency can be beneficial. Equally, we must ask who benefits from the use of technology, inquire into the nature of the labor that is needed to amplify agency, and the cost of performing such labor. Finally, we should investigate whether increased participation offers sufficient proof of agency by examining which identities that perform the labor of implementing and using technologies are actually benefited by amplification.

Such questions can be answered through fieldwork in rural India, the Eastern Cape of South Africa, or Appalachia. The reflections noted here suggest that questions such as those listed earlier can equally be raised in the classroom especially in light of the inexorable move in universities toward hybrid modes of content delivery. Regardless of the site where such questions will be asked, context collapse can prove useful in helping educators and researchers document their reflexivities when engaging with the broader macro-social conditions circumscribing individual experiences with micro-level social contexts.

The study of communication technology by Communication researchers will likely continue to accelerate as researchers, teachers, and practitioners increasingly rely on communication technologies as the focus and tools for conducting their work. More-and-more, Communication scholars acknowledge the late 20th-century error in assuming that technologies impact society and that the beneficiaries of such impact can be increased merely through the expansion of technology access (e.g., Castells, 1996). Across different Communication sub-disciplines, I anticipate continued criticism of technological determinism and greater acknowledgment of the roles that institutional capacities and human intentions play in rendering technologies benign *and* harmful in society.

We can see these changes, for instance, through studies of monopolistic technology platforms (e.g., Gillespie, 2010; Zhang, 2021). Other topics of high policy, public, and scholarly interest in other disciplines that can be fruitfully studied by Communication scholars using CA and technology amplification include net neutrality (e.g., Becker & Bode, 2018), algorithmic bias in the representation of historically disadvantaged social identities (Velkova & Kaun, 2021), human moderation of objectionable content on social media platforms (Roberts, 2019), and surveillance of prospective and payroll workers by employers and recruiters (Berkelaar, 2017).

Each of these topics instantiates the surveillance capitalism that characterizes work and life in the 2020s. Typically, surveillance capitalism involves large privately owned technology platforms extracting and selling digital traces of human behavior and communication to enterprise customers (Zuboff, 2015). Without adopting or eschewing a predetermined critical perspective, CA and technology amplification present the opportunity for scholars and practitioners to construct symmetric accounts of technology that explain not only what is made possible but also what is erased, made un-possible, and often elided through the design and use of technological artifacts.

References

Backhaus, B. (2020). Tuning in: Identity formation in community radio for social change. *International Journal of Communication, 14*, 4646–4661. https://ijoc.org/index.php/ijoc/article/view/14421/3208

Becker, A. B., & Bode, L. (2018). Satire as a source for learning? The differential impact of news versus satire exposure on net neutrality knowledge gain. *Information, Communication & Society, 21*(4), 612–625.

Berkelaar, B. L. (2017). Different ways new information technologies influence conventional organizational practices and employment relationships: The case of cybervetting for personnel selection. *Human Relations, 70*(9), 1115–1140.

Castells, M. (1996). *The information age.* Blackwell Publishers.

Curtin, S. C., & Heron, M. (2019). Death rates due to suicide and homicide among persons aged 10–24: United States, 2000–2017. NCHS data brief, no 352. Hyattsville, MD.

Davis, J. L., & Jurgenson, N. (2014). Context collapse: Theorizing context collusions and collisions. *Information, Communication & Society, 17*(4), 476–485.

Dewar, S., Islam, S., Resor, E., & Salehi, N. (2019). Finsta: Creating "fake" spaces for authentic performance. *Extended Abstracts of the 2019 CHI Conference on Human Factors in Computing Systems,* 1–6. https://doi.org/10.1145/3290607.3313033

Gillespie, T. (2010). The politics of 'platforms'. *New Media & Society, 12*(3), 347–364. SUNY Press.

Gil-Lopez, T., Shen, C., Benefield, G. A., Palomares, N. A., Kosinski, M., & Stillwell, D. (2018). One size fits all: Context collapse, self-presentation strategies and language styles on Facebook. *Journal of Computer-Mediated Communication, 23*(3), 127–145. https://doi.org/10.1093/jcmc/zmy006

Grabill, J., T. (2001). *Community literacy programs and the politics of change.* SUNY Press.

Jacobson, T. L. (2016). Amartya Sen's capabilities approach and communication for development and social change. *Journal of Communication, 66*(5), 789–810. https://doi.org/10.1111/jcom.12252

Jones, N. N., & Walton, R. (2018). Using narratives to foster critical thinking about diversity and social justice. In A. M. Haas & M. F. Eble (Eds.), *Key theoretical frameworks: Teaching technical communication in the twenty-first century* (pp. 241–267). Utah State University Press.

King, J. L., & Frost, R. L. (2002). Managing distance over time: The evolution of technologies of dis/ambiguation. In P. J. Hinds & S. Kiesler (Eds.), *Distributed work* (pp. 3–26). MIT Press.

Marwick, A. E., & boyd, d. (2011). I tweet honestly, I tweet passionately: Twitter users, context collapse, and the imagined audience. *New Media & Society, 13*(1), 114–133.

Pfefferbaum, B., & North, C. S. (2020). Mental health and the Covid-19 pandemic. *New England Journal of Medicine, 383*(6), 510–512.

Rajan, P., Chopra, S., Somasekhar, A. K., & Laux, C. M. (2016). Designing for food security: Portability and the expansion of user freedoms through the COREPDS in Chhattisgarh, India. *Information Technologies & International Development, 12*(3), 1–18.

Roberts, S. T. (2019). *Behind the screen*. Yale University Press.

Rogers, E. M. (1976). Communication and development: The passing of the dominant paradigm. *Communication Research, 3*(2), 213–240.

Schramm, W. (1964). *Mass media and national development: The role of information in the developing countries* (Vol. 65). Stanford University Press.

Sen, A. (1992). *Inequality reexamined*. Clarendon Press.

Singhal, A., & Rogers, E. M. (2002). A theoretical agenda for entertainment—education. *Communication Theory, 12*(2), 117–135.

Toyama, K. (2015). *Geek heresy*. PublicAffairs.

Velkova, J., & Kaun, A. (2021). Algorithmic resistance: Media practices and the politics of repair. *Information, Communication & Society, 24*(4), 523–540. https://doi.org/10.1080/1369118X.2019.1657162

Wang, Y.-C., Burke, M., & Kraut, R. (2016). *Modeling self-disclosure in social networking sites*. Proceedings of the 19th Association of Computing Machinery Conference on Computer-Supported Cooperative Work & Social Computing, San Francisco, CA.

Zhang, Z. (2021). Infrastructuralization of TikTok: Transformation, power relationships, and platformization of video entertainment in China. *Media, Culture & Society, 43*(2), 219–236. https://doi.org/10.1177/0163443720939452

Zuboff, S. (2015). Big other: Surveillance capitalism and the prospects of an information civilization. *Journal of Information Technology, 30*(1), 75–89. https://doi.org/10.1057/jit.2015.5

20

PANDEMIC REFLECTIONS

Precarity, Solidarity, and Global Inequities in Organizational Communication Research

Mahuya Pal and Beatriz Nieto-Fernandez

Personal Narratives (Mahuya)

I have been living in the United States for almost two decades, first as a graduate student and then as a professor. I left India in 2003, and, over time, I embraced a hybrid identity navigating between what I consider my two home countries—the United States and India. Since then, for every experience, I have had two prominent reference points—culturally, economically, and politically. Comparing the lived realities in my two home countries was more innocuous in my early years. Yet, as I grew into a postcolonial scholar studying organizations and organizing in the aftermath of colonialism, I came to understand the differences in the lived experiences in and within these two countries more from a sociocultural, political, and historical perspective. I also learned to reflect on the stark disparities between and within the countries in more humanistic and theoretical ways. The global COVID-19 pandemic then hit in 2020, opening up a whole new world of thinking and realization. In this chapter, I reflect on two specific events that I consider to have been defining moments for me—the conditions of migrant workers in India during the COVID-19 pandemic and the collapse of India's health system during the second wave of the pandemic. These events are interconnected and have implications for the global order.

In March 2020, India announced its first 21-day complete lockdown to contain the COVID-19 pandemic (Vyas, 2020). My middle-class friends and family were negotiating their inconveniences—the boredom of social isolation, not having the help of maids with household work, no weekend parties or eating out, and having to switch from the joys of buying fresh produce from neighborhood farmers' markets to online grocery procurement. Some more serious concerns involved not having caregivers for older family members; as daily commuters,

DOI: 10.4324/9781003220466-23

these caregivers were not available for their daily morning and night shifts for lack of transportation. On a happier note, with barely any vehicles and people on the roads, many began to enjoy the less-polluted blue sky and birds and the bees.

However, the problems of the middle-class paled into insignificance when compared to the crisis of the daily-wage earners, who are mostly migrant workers. The lockdown was a death knell for them with their source of income gone overnight. The migrant workers mostly come from the historically disenfranchised communities, and much of India's infrastructure rely on their labor (Chatterjee, 2020). They are construction and factory workers, porters, rickshaw pullers, rag-pickers, and daily-wage laborers in the unorganized economies. When the Indian government announced the lockdown and public transportation came to a halt, the migrant workers living in Indian metropoles such as Delhi, Kolkata, Bangalore, and Mumbai had only one choice—return to their villages by foot (Alam & Zaini, 2021). For me, the most enduring image of the pandemic has been the picture of these millions of migrant workers trekking arduously to their villages, walking for days and nights. The tragedy grabbed international headlines and struck a chord with many citizens within and beyond borders (Slater & Masih, 2020).

Another major crisis hit India at the time of the second wave in April 2021 when India's health system completely collapsed with insurmountable COVID-positive cases and hospitals running out of oxygen, mostly from a sense of complacence that India had defeated the pandemic in the first wave (Biswas, 2021). The situation had started to look remarkably different in this part of the world at the time. I got my vaccine and could see some light at the end of the tunnel in the United States. However, rather than enjoying the moment, I felt what I would call a gnawing survivor's guilt. While I could think of some semblance of normalcy here in the United States, the pandemic was ravaging India, and my near and dear ones were battling to get the vaccine and survive. Around this time, I was reading and hearing a lot about a voluntary organization called the Red Volunteers—a group of youngsters who rose to the occasion. They are the youth brigade of the Leftist political party of the state of West Bengal in eastern India (Datta, 2021). They made a mark in my home state in India by reaching out to help people from all sections of the society. They responded to calls to deliver medicine, food, and oxygen cylinders and offered rides to the hospital, even organized funeral services. They stepped up when the state failed.

Personal Narrative (Beatriz)

I have been living in the United States for almost a decade as an international student. I came to the United States to pursue my undergraduate and graduate degrees, pushed by political and economic unrest in my home country, Venezuela. The hybridity of my position as an international scholar forces me to deal with straddling two cultures in both my home country and my new country, where I pursue education and work as a graduate teaching assistant. For many years, I have been a de-territorialized and displaced Venezuelan citizen, with little to no choice about whether I could return to my home country, very aware of the realities (lack of food, lack of healthcare, lack of freedom) that would incur if I ever chose to return. After a decade, I understand the United States as my "new country," where I have "acculturated" to the "American" way of life. My diasporic existence and feeling of belonging to the United States, however, has always been marred by my "Non-citizen Alien" status that brands me as a perpetual foreigner, and, as such, it has hindered my ability to fully see myself or my possibilities in this new country. This tension between belonging and not belonging to the United States never became more apparent than in the Summer of 2020, in the midst of the COVID-19 pandemic.

The beginning of the pandemic caught me in the United States. I am lucky enough to have some family in the neighboring city of Miami, which is considered a haven for the Latin American diaspora (Aranda et al., 2014). This support and feeling of community gave me some comfort during that summer where the collective feeling was that the world was ending. Throughout the first couple of days of the pandemic, the new reality of the virus and its ramifications glared at us in the face, and the air was stifling. As an Organizational Communication scholar, I had been used to examining labor and power in the workplace. However now, all of these issues were staring back at me. Like many Americans, I saw how businesses closed, how many workers were laid off, how people were forced to collect unemployment, and how life and economic livelihood for so many people became uncertain, while so many other people profit from this uncertainty, a clear example of precarity and inequity in the face of a pandemic. Suddenly, we saw the rise of a new category of worker in the United States, the "essential worker," whose labor was considered to be so essential that it warranted exposure to a deadly virus about which we knew nothing (Rogers et al., 2020).

In July of 2020, I saw my own livelihood and ability to remain in the United States in danger, with the passing of a new U.S. Department of Homeland Security rule that banned me, as an international student, from staying in the United States when taking online courses (Lemieux et al., 2020). Most universities had completely shifted to online-only modes of instruction, so this change meant that I would lose my status as a graduate teaching assistant, my ability to register for classes, and my possibility of graduating. As such, I would have to leave the United States in the middle of the pandemic, with nowhere to go because of Venezuela's borders being closed. For three weeks, I pondered on my options, feeling caught by my hybrid position, understanding the reality: it did not really matter how much I worked to stay in the United States, how much I "acculturated," how hard I tried to succeed, my success and my livelihood would always be in the hands of others; my non-Alien citizen status would come to haunt me; the realities of not having a clear pathway to citizenship would eternally hurt my chances of "making it" in the foreign country that I now called home. After three weeks, the Department of Homeland Security decided that this new ruling would only apply to incoming students, effectively exonerating me (U.S. Immigration and

Customs Enforcement, 2020). I was able to stay in the United States and not lose my position as a graduate teaching assistant. Even though I was in a comfortable position as a graduate teaching assistant of the University to which I was lending my labor, the sudden possibility of losing funding and my work, scrapping my three years of schooling, and not being able to get a degree became a reality overnight. The fear and the hurt of those three weeks of uncertainty still linger. The feeling of precarity, of being disposable, of being "non-essential" remains. I consider myself incredibly lucky and privileged to be in an academic setting, working for a University, which, in the end, protected me from many of the realities of living and working in a pandemic. Still, this experience changed how I saw my workplace, my relationship to my work, my understanding of labor, bringing to light the disposability and precariousness of my position as tied to citizenship.

Throughout 2020, my diasporic and hybrid position gave me insight about how the pandemic was being handled across territory lines and the inequalities that in many cases existed regarding resources. I was able to live the pandemic from the perspective of the United States (as I lived there), and I understand how it was being experienced in both Venezuela (where my father and most of my extended family still lived) and Spain (where my mother and siblings lived, forced out of Venezuela). These three ways of understanding the pandemic guide my reflection.

Despite my capacity for solidarity, the reality is that I live in a position of privilege. In the middle of the pandemic, I lived in a country of privilege. When vaccines were distributed in the United States, I (working from home) got to vaccinate first before my best friend, a fellow Venezuelan immigrant, an "essential worker" in healthcare who is working in a COVID-19 Intensive Care Unit in Colombia. I became the first person in my nuclear and extended family to get vaccinated. I got vaccinated earlier than my 93-year-old grandmother living in Venezuela and earlier than my Spanish 82-year-old grandmother with a heart condition, all because of my position, geo-locality, and close proximity to privilege. For the rest of 2020, life became an uncertain dance:

Soon, things started to open up for me in the United States. Life became more "normal."

My family and friends in Venezuela, the very few that are left, still have not been able to access the vaccine.

My American university lifts the mask mandate.

Every day, I get bad news of family friends and acquaintances getting sick and dying of COVID-19 because of lack of resources.

I go to a Tampa outdoor bar with some friends. I am the only one wearing a mask.

When my dad got sick from COVID in Venezuela, we held on to his every word, knowing that, if things became more complicated, it would be difficult to find him help. He pulled through. With Venezuelan borders being closed, my family eventually managed to find him safe passage to Spain where he received care for his post-COVID side effects, which have become a chronic condition. He is one of the lucky ones.

Back in the United States, a couple of my students boast about going to "COVID parties," to see who gets sick and gets to skip school, as some type of Russian roulette game. Some politicians in the state still call COVID-19 a "flu."

These different realities bring to mind not only the differences between Global North and Global South and how pandemic experiences might differ depending on geo-localities, but also the difficult tensions that exist between countries and their transnational relationships. The "re-opening" of Europe and North America comes at the cost of millions of lives in the developing world, as vaccines have become a commodity and privilege of wealthier nations (Harman et al., 2021). While the Global North re-opens and rebuilds their stunted economies, the Global South has never stopped producing to satisfy the world's supply chains and ongoing demands, without receiving the same type of access to vaccination and healthcare (Free & Hecimovic, 2021). While the Global North gets to "forget" about COVID and its realities focused on a "new way of living," the Global South still lives it.

Future Studies in Organizational Communication Work and Precarity

From the perspective of Organizational Communication, the pandemic allowed us to see a transformation in how work is and can be conceptualized. COVID-19 has changed the way in which we work and live. Physical spaces have become less important, and work from home has suddenly become mandatory for many employees across the world (Savić, 2020). This sudden shift to work from home for a large section of population is driving the digital transformation of the workforce and the work environment at an unprecedented speed. Mass adoption of telecommuting and enhancement of technologies have become a vital business change since the outbreak of the virus. As Savić asserted, this change is here to stay.

The pandemic resulted in the working population being divided between those privileged enough to be able to work remotely and retain their jobs, those considered essential and working outside of homes, and those deemed nonessential and, hence, laid off (Loustaunau et al., 2021). Working conditions changed dramatically, and low-wage essential workers and those laid off faced greatest precarity. According to Loustaunau et al., while low-wage essential workers negotiated the choice between putting their families' lives at risk or being unable to pay their bills, those deemed nonessential were not left with any choice whatsoever but to fend for themselves.

We note that, in the context of globalization, the labor of migrant workers in India is connected to the global network of production and permeates the borders in several ways. Hence, focusing on such conditions of work is extremely relevant. The conditions of the migrant workers from India or the Global South demonstrate the extreme vulnerability and precarity of people living at the margins of civil society and extend discussions on precarity of labor. While Südkamp and Dempsey (2021) discussed precarity in the field in the realm of uncertain work conditions, unpaid labor, and disposability of labor, the migrant worker situation in India underscores that it constitutes an economically and politically induced condition in which certain bodies suffer disproportionately (Butler, 2004). The failure of the local and global institutions distributes precarity unequally and exposes a section of the society to violence, death, and forced migration. As such, the dominant organizations render certain workers disposable, while making others privileged (Arora & Majumder, 2021).

Solidarity and Civic Mobilization

Slater and Masih (2020) reported in the *Washington Post* that the mass exodus of migrant workers comprised the largest since the India–Pakistan partition after India's independence in 1947. Academic theorizing seems inadequate when thinking about extreme difficulties such as the conditions of these migrant workers. The plight of these migrant workers represents the struggles faced by vulnerable communities across the world. How do we make sense of these conditions as academics and practitioners? Primarily to address this question in the context of marginality, we advance the concept of solidarity in Organizational Communication (Beverley, 2004; Pal, 2014). The logic of solidarity creates a space for academics to serve the interests of underprivileged communities. Solidarity suggests that it is our ethical responsibility to think of what we can do for and with the vulnerable communities, who are on the opposite side of the position of privilege of the author/academic. Solidarity creates more reflexive openings and allows us to ask questions such as: How can we build infrastructure better?

The idea of solidarity, we believe, has been central to civic mobilization. For instance, individuals founded the Red Volunteers as a voluntary organization amid the pandemic and the oxygen crisis in eastern India early in 2021. Its Facebook page shows that it has almost 135,000 members currently (https://www.facebook.com/groups/RedVolunteersWB/about). The Red Volunteers are flooded with distress requests according to media reports (Datta, 2021). An initiative of this scale requires massive leadership and administration skills. Many such civil society organizations emerged in the face of the pandemic across the world for humanitarian aid delivery (Brechenmacher et al., 2020).

We call for Organizational Communication scholars to engage with these kinds of civic organizations that emerge organically and add to existing scholarship on volunteering and civil society partnerships (Ganesh & McAllum, 2012). What is their potential for impacting far-reaching socioeconomic reforms? When the arms of the state showed abject apathy, the ordinary people showed empathy and care. How does this phenomenon of communicative care help us to think about large-scale organizational transformation?

Global Inequities

The differences in the ways in which people experienced the pandemic in the Global North and the Global South also forces us to pay attention to transnational labor practices and the ways that they might have been affected by the disruption between supply and demand (Aday & Aday, 2020; Mollenkopf et al., 2021). The disruptions and disparate labor conditions also force us to ask about global inequities, differential access to healthcare when facing a global crisis, and the international responsibilities of powerful countries toward countries that have been historically exploited and colonized and now find themselves struggling to handle the realities of a pandemic (Chowdhury & Jomo, 2020). Addressing these issues, Organizational Communication scholars also should respond to the call for grappling with the full potential of globalization (see Ganesh et al., 2005). Solidarity in this case also means a wider understanding of the pandemic. Organizational Communication scholars should examine the ramifications of the pandemic in the developing world and interrogate vaccine apartheids and lack of global infrastructures of health (Byanyima, 2021; Newman et al., 2021).

We should seek solidarity that understands the pandemic and the socioeconomic and political struggles that it brought, not as one chapter in the history of the United States, but as an event of global ramifications that makes us well aware of the existing systems of domination.

References

Aday, S., & Aday, M. S. (2020). Impact of COVID-19 on the food supply chain. *Food Quality and Safety*, 4(4), 167–180.

Alam, M., & Zaini, S. H. R. (2021). COVID-19 and the plight of the migrant worker in India. *Community, Work & Family*, 1–5. https://doi.org/10.1080/13668803.2021.1975651

Aranda, E. M., Hughes, S., & Sabogal, E. (2014). *Making a life in multiethnic Miami: Immigration and the rise of a global city*. Lynne Rienner.

Arora, S., & Majumder, M. (2021). Where is my home? Gendered precarity and the experience of Covid-19 among women migrant workers from Delhi and National Capital Region, India. *Gender, Work & Organization*. https://doi.org/10.1111/gwao.12700

Beverley, J. (2004). *Subalternity and representation. Arguments in cultural theory*. Duke University Press.

Biswas, S. (2021, April 19). Covid-19: How India failed to prevent a deadly second wave. *BBC News*. https://www.bbc.com/news/world-asia-india-56771766

Brechenmacher, S., Carothers, T., & Youngs, R. (2020, July 10). *Civil society and the coronavirus: Dynamism despite disruption*. Carnegie Endowment for International Peace. https://carnegieendowment.org/2020/04/21/civil-society-and-coronavirus-dynamism-despite-disruption-pub-81592

Butler, J. (2004). *Precarious life: The powers of mourning and violence*. Verso.

Byanyima, W. (2021). A global vaccine apartheid is unfolding: People's lives must come before profit. *UNAIDS*. https://www. unaids.org/en/20210203_oped_guardian

Chatterjee, P. (2020, April 12). The pandemic exposes India's apathy toward migrant workers. *The Atlantic*. https://www.theatlantic.com/ideas/archive/2020/04/the-pandemic-exposes-indias-two-worlds/609838/

Chowdhury, A. Z., & Jomo, K. S. (2020). Responding to the COVID-19 pandemic in developing countries: Lessons from selected countries of the global south. *Development*, 63(2), 162–171.

Datta, R. (2021, May 22). The Red allies: The Left's youth wing steps up in a major way in Bengal to provide Covid-19 support. *India Today*. https://www.indiatoday.in/magazine/cover-story/story/20210531-the-red-allies-the-left-s-youth-wing-steps-up-in-a-major-way-in-bengal-to-provide-covid-support-1805333-2021-05-22

Free, C., & Hecimovic, A. (2021). Global supply chains after COVID-19: The end of the road for neoliberal globalisation? *Accounting, Auditing & Accountability Journal, 34*(1), 58–84.

Ganesh, S., & McAllum, K. (2012). Volunteering and professionalization: Trends in tension? *Management Communication Quarterly, 26*(1), 152–158. https://doi.org/10.1177/0893318911423762

Ganesh, S., Zoller, H., & Cheney, G. (2005). Transforming resistance, broadening our boundaries: Critical organizational communication meets globalization from below. *Communication Monographs, 72*(2), 169–191. https://doi.org/10.1080/03637750500111872

Harman, S., Erfani, P., Goronga, T., Hickel, J., Morse, M., & Richardson, E. T. (2021). Global vaccine equity demands reparative justice—not charity. *BMJ Global Health, 6*(6504), 1–4.

Lemieux, M., Colazo, J. M., Kienka, T., & Zhakyp, A. (2020). A basis to be here: Stories from international graduate students in the United States. *Cell Reports Medicine, 1*(6), 100100.

Loustaunau, L., Stepick, L., Scott, E., Petrucci, L., & Henifin, M. (2021). No choice but to be essential: Expanding dimensions of precarity during COVID-19. *Sociological Perspectives, 64*(5), 857–875. https://doi.org/10.1177/07311214211005491

Mollenkopf, D. A., Ozanne, L. K., & Stolze, H. J. (2021). A transformative supply chain response to COVID-19. *Journal of Service Management, 32*(2), 190–202. https://doi.org/10.1108/JOSM-05-2020-0143

Newman, P. A., Guta, A., & Black, T. (2021). Ethical considerations for qualitative research methods during the COVID-19 pandemic and other emergency situations: Navigating the virtual field. *International Journal of Qualitative Methods, 20*, https://doi.org/10.1177/16094069211047823

Pal, M. (2014). Solidarity with subaltern organizing: The Singur movement in India. *The Electronic Journal of Communication, 24*(3, 4). http://www.cios.org/EJCPUBLIC/024/3/024343.html

Rogers, T. N., Rogers, C. R., VanSant-Webb, E., Gu, L. Y., Yan, B., & Qeadan, F. (2020). Racial disparities in COVID-19 mortality among essential workers in the United States. *World Medical & Health Policy, 12*(3), 311–327.

Savić, D. (2020). COVID-19 and work from home: Digital transformation of the workforce. *Grey Journal (TGJ), 16*(2), 101–104.

Slater, J., & Masih, N. (2020, March 27). In India, the world's biggest lockdown has forced migrants to work hundreds of miles home. *The Washington Post*. https://www.washingtonpost.com/world/asia_pacific/india-coronavirus-lockdown-migrant-workers/2020/03/27/a62df166-6f7d-11ea-a156-0048b62cdb51_story.html

Südkamp, C. M., & Dempsey, S. E. (2021). Resistant transparency and nonprofit labor: Challenging precarity in the Art+ Museum wage transparency campaign. *Management Communication Quarterly, 35*(3), 341–367. https://doi.org/10.1177/0893318921993833

U.S. Immigration and Customs Enforcement. (2021, July 6). *SEVP modifies temporary exemptions for Nonimmigrant Students taking online courses during Fall 2020 Semester*. https://www.ice.gov/news/releases/sevp-modifies-temporary-exemptions-nonimmigrant-students-taking-online-courses-during

Vyas, M. (2020). Impact of lockdown on labour in India. *The Indian Journal of Labour Economics, 63*(1), 73–77.

21

THE END OF THE WORLD AS WE KNEW IT

Strategic Communication in the 2020 Pandemic

Deanna D. Sellnow

Learning Objectives

1. Define the fundamental tenets of Strategic Communication theory.
2. Describe how instructional communication is a form of strategic communication.
3. Apply the IDEA model to explain [in]effective risk communication during the COVID-19 pandemic.
4. Justify the value of strategic communication as a means by which to enact positive change in the world.

On February 14, 2020, I sat on an airplane with Tim (my spouse) eagerly anticipating our upcoming adventure with colleagues and students at Uganda Christian University. Our colleagues there were launching a new master's program in strategic communication, and we had volunteered to team-teach the Strategic Communication Theory course. While there, we would also do follow-up research regarding deadly mudslides in the Bududa District. Our ultimate goal was to help enhance safety through improved strategic communication among farmers and government officials. By the time we returned to the United States and finished hosting our annual International Crisis and Risk Communication Conference (March 9–11), the year would take a dramatic turn from "business as usual" to a "new normal" spurred by the COVID-19 global pandemic. On March 12, 2020, "America shut down" (McCaskgill, 2020). As it so happens, March 12 is also my birthday—a birthday that signaled the end of the world as we knew it—at least for me.

As a scholar who studies strategic instructional communication as it occurs in risk and crisis contexts, I describe March 12th as a cosmology episode that, in turn, triggered myriad secondary crises in industries ranging from health to business to entertainment to education. A cosmology episode occurs when a chaotic

DOI: 10.4324/9781003220466-24

crisis event elicits a sudden loss of meaning regarding what to do now or how to proceed (Weick, 1993).

For college professors and students, remote course delivery (albeit synchronous, asynchronous, or some combination) quickly usurped "business as usual" traditional pedagogies. In this sense, COVID-19 also triggered a crisis in higher education (Miller et al., 2020). Going forward, my birthday will now also serve as a reminder of the moment when learning management systems (e.g., Blackboard, Canvas) and video conferencing (e.g., Zoom, Skype) shifted from being optional to essential (Miller et al., 2020).

Over the course of the months that followed, I found myself challenged personally living in the midst of a life-threatening global pandemic. Professionally, however, I found myself constantly examining the strategic communication choices being made by leaders at all levels of government, medical sciences, and public health. Although I was not surprised at the negative consequences of poor communication choices, I was frustrated not as much at them as at myself and my colleagues. Clearly, we had not done due diligence to convey what we know from research to the on-the-ground professionals doing the work. In 2020, I realized we must do better at translating our work in ways that truly inform the work of on-the-ground spokespersons.

The following paragraphs describe my epiphany as it unfolded over the course of the year. I do so by describing how the IDEA model functions as strategic communication and how it played out in COVID-19 communication throughout the year. I close with a call to action to my colleagues and me to develop and implement a strategic communication plan to broaden the reach of our work. In this small way, I believe that we can and must use what we have learned from failed strategic communication in 2020 as a learning opportunity. We must practice what we preach—that is, to communicate more effectively with the audiences that can truly use what we know to save lives.

Strategic Communication

Technical jargon pervades all academic disciplines, including Communication. Moreover, debates are ongoing among theorists and practitioners regarding the [un]necessary role it plays (Gozali et al., 2017). I agree with the theorists that jargon is critical to distinguish among specific phenomena that function uniquely in various fields. However, I also agree with the practitioners that jargon is useless unless all involved parties understand its meaning. Thus, this section deconstructs the meaning of Strategic Communication theory as it occurs in instructional risk situations and crisis events using the IDEA model as a framework.

Standard dictionary definitions of *strategic* can be summarized as both identifying overall goals and developing cogent plans for achieving them (e.g., Thorson, 2018). *Communication* constitutes the process of conveying them (through verbal/nonverbal symbols, signs, behaviors) to create shared meaning. A *theory* describes, interprets, and/or predicts and explains relationships among phenomena. Finally, *instructional* is a form of strategic communication that manifests a clearly articulated goal and plan intended to improve learning (a.k.a. affective, cognitive, behavioral). Thus, strategic communication theory focuses on research-informed goals and clearly articulated implementation plans carried out and adapted based on ongoing assessment. Consequently, strategic communication that is not informed by a clearly articulated goal and plan is destined to fail. One could argue that, for this reason alone, strategic communication during the 2020 pandemic was doomed from the start (Sellnow & Sellnow, 2020b). One model originally designed to guide spokespersons in effective strategic communication, particularly in terms of instruction during times of risk and crisis, is the IDEA model.

The IDEA Model of Strategic Communication

The Communication discipline is comprised of myriad subfields, ranging from health to interpersonal to organizational communication. The IDEA model is one theoretical framework for understanding how instructional communication functions strategically to reduce harms and save lives in times of risk and crisis (Sellnow & Sellnow, 2019). Grounded in experiential learning theory (Dewey, 1938), effective strategic communication results in learning, which is measured based on affective (perceived relevance/value), cognitive (comprehension/cognition), and behavioral (performance) outcomes. Notably, these outcomes are receiver-oriented in that they measure "what a learner knows or can do as a result of learning" (Otter, 1992, p. i). This receiver orientation differs from many theoretical frameworks that focus on what the sender (a.k.a. teacher) intends to teach rather than what the receiver (a.k.a. student) actually achieves (Eisner, 1979). For example, effective strategic communication in the form of earthquake early warnings (EEW) is measured according to whether target audiences *pay attention to* the alert (affective), *understand* that dangerously strong shaking is coming (cognitive), and *take appropriate actions* for protection (behavioral) (D. Sellnow et al., 2019).

IDEA is an acronym for the four components in the model. This acronym was strategically conceived to make the elements easy to remember, even when time is of the essence (Sellnow & Sellnow, 2019) (see Figure 21.1). The following paragraphs explain each element as applied to strategic communication in the United States during the 2020 COVID-19 pandemic.

"I" stands for *internalization*. According to the model, effective strategic communication must motivate people to both pay attention to and thoughtfully consider the message (Sellnow & Sellnow, 2019). To do so, messages must clarify how individuals and those they care about are affected/impacted by the topic (e.g., health, safety, personal wellbeing, prosperity) and to what degree. In terms of crisis response, internalization is fairly easy to attain due to clear imminent threat and short response time (Hermann, 1963). In the case of an earthquake, for instance, people may have only minutes or even just seconds to respond. Effective

FIGURE 21.1   The IDEA Model

strategic communication regarding risk is more challenging because it is characterized by uncertainty, potential threat, and extended response time (Sellnow &
Sellnow, 2020a). In the case of a tropical storm that may (or may not) grow into
a life-threatening hurricane, motivating people (that may or may not actually end
up in the danger zone and that have become desensitized based on previous experiences) to pay attention and, ultimately, to engage in recommended protective
actions is more challenging (Herovic et al., 2020).

"D" stands for *distribution*. Simply put, which communication channel(s) will
most likely reach target audiences? Because accessibility to and perceived credibility of various channels and information sources vary widely among people
and groups, strategic communication is most effective when stakeholders convey a consistent master narrative via a variety of sources and through multiple
communication channels (Sellnow & Sellnow, 2019). People more likely believe
and comply when they receive a convergent message across channels and sources
(Anthony et al., 2013). Moreover, different people and groups tend to rely on different channels and sources when seeking information (Burke et al., 2010). When
people get competing (divergent) messages from different sources and channels,
credibility and believability wane. Moreover, some of these divergent messages
may be based on mis-information, dis-information, or mal-information and actually result in misunderstandings that lead to negative consequences. For example,
the successful outcomes of the 2013 porcine epidemic diarrhea virus (PEDv), a
novel virus that emerged quickly and "was killing as many as 100,000 piglets each

week," were achieved in large part to strategic message convergence across channels and sources (T. Sellnow et al., 2019, p. 125).

"E" stands for *explanation*. First, providing lots of information and lots of links to websites where one can go to find more information does not constitute strategic communication. Information is only one of three content elements required in effective strategic communication. Content must also motivate people to pay attention in the first place and to act appropriately as a result (Sellnow & Sellnow, 2019). That said, the information also must be explained accurately and translated intelligibly. Too often, communicators fail to translate scientific details and technical jargon in ways that are intelligible to non-experts. For example, when explaining how strong earthquake shaking is likely to be, an "8" may be intelligible to earthquake professionals but not necessarily to various target audiences. "Very strong shaking" is more likely to be understood (D. Sellnow et al., 2019).

Perhaps one of the most common mistakes made regarding explanation is transparency. It is vital to share both what is known and what is not yet known, what is being done now and being done to learn more, and when/how often to expect updates. When communicating about an impeding hurricane, for instance, the expected point of landfall and possible wind speeds are likely to change as the storm develops. An effective strategic communicator will be clear about the shifting nature of hurricanes as they travel, the need to monitor regularly, and when/where to expect regular updates (Vanderford et al., 2007).

"A" stands for *action*. The critical questions to answer here include what to do (or sometimes NOT do) to mitigate harm and protect health and safety of self and others. This step differs from communicating information about what authorities and others are doing (explanation). Rather, action focuses on specific instructions for receivers to do or not to do. To clarify, explaining an industry's efforts to halt the distribution of contaminated food is important information but does not instruct the receiver: (a) how to determine whether they purchased the contaminated product, (b) what to do with contaminated products they may have purchased, or (c) what to do if they or someone they know ate the contaminated product (D. Sellnow et al., 2017). A second critical consideration involves reducing ambiguity about what are the specific action steps. For example, in the case of agricultural biosecurity, telling farm employees to "shower in and shower out" is ambiguous; however, showing a short video demonstration of the process is both specific and cogent (T. Sellnow et al., 2017).

Ultimately, effective strategic communication addresses all four of these elements Sellnow & Sellnow, 2019). Failure to consider any one or more reduces the chances for success as measured by affective, cognitive, and behavioral learning. The following section applies the IDEA model to strategic pandemic communication in the United States. In doing so, the 2020 pandemic strategic communication failures can be used as learning opportunities to do better next time a pandemic strikes, which most specialists know is not an "if" but a "when."

The IDEA Model and COVID-19

Experiencing communication during the pandemic as a community member and academic strategic communication scholar was surreal. I don't know if it is more accurate to describe the feeling as an ongoing in- and out-of-body experience or as a living nightmare. Maybe it was a bit of each. The following paragraphs apply the IDEA model to strategic communication as it occurred during four general phases of the pandemic.

1. <u>Calm Before the Storm</u> (12/2019–3/2020)

When the United States began reporting on the COVID-19 outbreak in China, very few Americans were worried because the crisis event was occurring halfway around the world. One way to motivate people to pay attention (internalization) is to address proximity. People are more likely to pay attention when they perceive a risk to be close to their home or the homes of their loved ones. Had more reports illustrated how quickly the virus could spread from Asia to the countries where we live, perhaps more would have taken the risk seriously earlier. For years, scientists have been using simulations to illustrate how quickly a disease may spread and its potential impact on those not yet feeling the effects (Merrill et al., 2019). Risk simulations could have been used to motivate people in the United States to take COVID-19 seriously sooner, as well.

Failure to address internalization was exacerbated by misinformation (explanation) regarding how the virus spread. Not only did experts focus almost entirely on washing hands and disinfecting surfaces (action); they even went so far as to claim the virus was not spread through the air (explanation). Hence, they argued that only healthcare professionals needed to wear masks (action) (Farmer, 2020; Lapook, 2020). We later learned that the experts did not yet know for certain all the ways in which the novel virus could spread, and were attempting to deal with the fact that N95 surgical masks were in short supply (and needed most by healthcare workers at the time) (Feng & Cheng, 2020).

These examples of failed strategic communication early on contributed to additional communication challenges in the months that followed. Had they followed the IDEA model guidelines for explanation more comprehensively, some of the problems and challenges they faced later could have been reduced or even avoided altogether. To clarify, had they admitted that COVID-19 was a novel (a.k.a. new) virus and that they could not say with certainty how it is spread, compliance to safety measure recommendations may not have suffered at the time, as well as later when they tried to change the narrative to acknowledge that it was an airborne virus and that mask wearing could mitigate spread (Farmer, 2020). Instead, they could have recommended precautions to take (including mask wearing and social distancing) while they continued to conduct research to find out how the virus spreads. They could have alerted us to when and where regular updates would be published/broadcast/shared. Had best practices for communicating strategically been followed, I believe that we could have reduced the number and severity of harms to people and communities. Consequently, effective strategic communication could have helped reduce the spread of COVID-19 and save lives.

2. **Cosmology Episode** (3/2020–6/2020)

Cosmology refers to the scientific study of the origins of the universe and an example of a cosmology episode is the *big bang* theory. However, Communication scientist Karl E. Weick (1993, 1995) transformed the meaning of cosmology episode to represent the sudden loss of meaning that comes from chaotic crises events. Whereas *déjà vu* describes a feeling that we have been here and done this before, *vuja de* refers to the point at which we realize we have never been here before and have no idea what to do now. What happened in March 2020 as a result of COVID-19—not only in the United States but also around the world— was surely a cosmology episode. I argue that effective strategic communication again could have helped reduce the number and severity of harms to people and communities during this period.

In terms of internalization, reports focused on the severity of harms on older people and those with compromised immune systems (WHO, 2020). Since the potential impact on young adults was dismissed, spring break travels and parties went on as usual throughout the month of March. Unmasked spring breakers flooded crowded beaches across the south. Regarding explanation, misinformation that began during the calm before the storm continued to confuse Americans as the master narrative framed as the truth (rather than the truth based on what is known at this point) kept changing. Now, we were being told to wear masks to protect ourselves and others. If we did not want to do it for ourselves, the campaigns pleaded, do it for those around you (Prager, 2021). The challenges that began in the first period persisted as medical scientists, public health officials, and trusted agencies like the WHO and CDC attempted to convince publics to trust their changing narrative regarding the nature of the virus (explanation), potential impact on people and publics (internalization), and actions to take for protection of self and others (action). It is far more difficult to maintain credibility when the master narrative keeps changing.

To make matters worse, various public figures shared competing narratives across social media platforms, among different media outlets, as well as from federal to state officials, from state-to-state, and among state and local officials. Moreover, many of these competing narratives were rooted in politics as presidential and congressional campaigns intensified. For instance, decisions about whether to wear/not wear a mask became based on politics rather than public health. Competing narratives are difficult to counter. Competing narratives rooted in politics are even more difficult to counter (Gulyas, 2016). Competing narratives rooted in politics that go viral over social media are almost impossible to counter, in part, because they operate as echo chambers where participants can choose what to believe/not believe as true or false. Echo chambers are essentially environments where one encounters information and opinions that reflect and reinforce their own beliefs and, as such, they provide fruitful arenas for mis-, dis-, and mal-information to thrive (Barberá et al., 2015).

3. Not Your Ordinary Crisis (7/2020–12/2021)

As the year went on, COVID-19 and the secondary crises in healthcare, in business and industry, in education, and in personal relationships struggled as we tried to stay sane while staying safe and staying home. The pandemic caused so many crises in so many contexts that mental and emotional well-being suffered. In terms of strategic communication, weary Americans became complacent as we became more and more disenfranchised about what we were missing out on as we continued to isolate ourselves from friends and families. Postponed or cancelled wedding celebrations, lost opportunities to be with loved ones, and missed chances to share in other important occasions such as births, christenings, graduations, and deaths were taking a toll. Personally, among other things, I struggled with missing both our son's wedding and the birth of our grandson.

During this time, strategic communication needed to be expanded to acknowledge the emotional toll lost opportunities were having on people and encouraging perseverance in spite of them. Instead, leaders had to remain vigilant in their focus on countering competing narratives that confused people with mis-, dis-, and mal-information. In terms of internalization, people needed to be acknowledged for their resilience and encouraged to keep going while scientists were getting ever closer to finding a safe and effective vaccine. In terms of explanation and action, people longed for assurance that our efforts were helping, that scientists were making progress, and that the prolonged confinement would come to an end soon. Unfortunately, the demands of countering mis-, dis-, and mal-information about the nature of the virus, how it is spread, the severity of it (ranging from illness to death to long-hauler symptoms), and actions to take made it impossible to expand the strategic communication in these important ways.

4. Living in the New Normal (2021–?)

With the new year came new hope as the Food and Drug Administration (FDA) approved several vaccines as safe and effective for emergency use. The foreboding challenge at that time was to generate enough vaccine to inoculate as many people as possible, as quickly as possible (*AJMC,* 2021). By mid-January of 2021, however, public health officials (and some politicians) blamed a chaotic rollout without a strategic plan complicated by confusion resulting from mis-, dis-, and mal-information, as well as frustration over technological difficulties in registering to get the vaccine and the number of vaccine doses being trashed at the end of each day throughout the country (McCormick, 2021).

By mid-February of 2021, the vaccine became increasingly available to American adults over the age of 18; however, a Gallup poll revealed a dramatic difference on intentions to vaccinate based on political affiliation (Brenan, 2021). According to Brenan, 91% of Democrats and 51% of Republicans planned to be vaccinated when it became available to them. The political divide that emerged during the presidential campaign regarding self-protection before the development of vaccines (e.g., washing hands, social distancing, avoiding crowds, wearing a mask) appears to be shifting to also include anti-vaccination (Milligan, 2021).

By July, nearly 50% of American adults had been fully vaccinated, but these rates vary dramatically by state, region, and political affiliation (*Our World in Data*, 2021). The fact that the compliance percentages vary so dramatically even when approved as safe and efficacious vaccines are readily available suggests much more needs to be done to counter mis-, dis-, and mal-information that dominated legacy and social media throughout 2020. Clearly, Strategic Communication scholars should share our expertise regarding effective communication theories, models, and strategies with on-the-ground professionals to shift the course of public opinion back to trusting research, science, and experts over counter-narratives that continue to prove deadly as the COVID-19 variants sicken and kill unvaccinated victims (Mahtani et al., 2021).

Conclusion

On June 2, 2021, Tim and I started our 10-day trip to visit loved ones that we had not seen since the initial lockdown on my birthday on March 12, 2020. Although we were concerned about traveling, we performed all the recommended health and safety guidelines set forth by the CDC. We were fully vaccinated *and* maintained social distancing *and* wore our masks when in public (outdoors or indoors) in addition to washing hands regularly and using hand sanitizer often. We also visited only those that had also been fully vaccinated. I am sad to say, however, that we were clearly in the minority except in areas where federal law mandated wearing masks. Even in those locations, however, many people acted in defiance by wearing their masks only around the neck or covering only their mouth. By the time we returned home, in mid-July, our experiences led us to make a strategic decision to return to the safety practices that we had been enacting throughout 2020. Unless strategic communication can effectively counter the mis-, dis-, and mal-information being communicated across states, regions, and political party lines, we have no doubt that 2021 will be another challenging year as more variants emerge and more unvaccinated people (and potentially vaccinated people) continue to succumb to the wrath of SARS-CoV-2 (a.k.a. COVID-19).

As I alluded to in the introduction, this chapter serves as my call to action to those of us that study communication to make strategic plans to communicate our knowledge not only in academic conferences and journals but also in venues that reach practitioners and disparate publics. Such outlets include, for instance, newspapers, magazines, and radio/tv, as well as social media platforms ranging from Facebook to Instagram and YouTube (see, e.g., our one-minute summary of the IDEA model at: https://www.youtube.com/watch?v=H8XsJl5K6Dg). Communication research is important work. Let us make it our mission to ensure that we go beyond sharing what we know among ourselves to share it in ways that literally operationalizes what Nelson Mandela once said: "Education is the most powerful weapon which you can use to change the world." Let us now accept the challenge to use our expertise to help do so.

References

AJMC. (2021, February 15). What we're reading: UK variant potentially deadlier; partisan gap in vaccine hesitancy; efforts to curb rising drug prices. *AJMC*. Retrieved July 10, 2021, from https://www.ajmc.com/view/what-we-re-reading-uk-variant-potentially-deadlier-partisan-gap-in-vaccine-hesitancy-curbing-rising-drug-prices

Anthony, K. E., Sellnow, T. L., & Millner, A. G. (2013). Message convergence as a message-centered approach to analyzing and improving risk communication. *Journal of Applied Communication Research*, 41(4), 346–364. https://doi.org/10.1080/00909882.2013.844346

Barberá, P., Jost, J. T., Nagler, J. Tucker, J. A., & Bonneau, R. (2015). Tweeting from left to right: Is online political communication more than an echo chamber? *Psychological Science*, 26(10), 1531–1542. https://doi.org/10.1177/0956797615594620

Brenan, M. (2021, February 10). Two-thirds of Americans not satisfied with vaccine rollout *Gallup*. Retrieved July 5, 2021, from https://news.gallup.com/poll/329552/two-thirds americans-not-satisfied-vaccine-rollout.aspx

Burke, J. A., Spence, P. R., & Lachlan, K. A. (2010). Crisis preparation, media use, and information seeking during Hurricane Ike: Lessons learned for emergency. *Journal Emergency Management*, 8(5), 27–37.

Dewey, J. (1938). *Experience and education*. Kappa Delta Pi.

Eisner, E. (1979). *The educational imagination*. Macmillan.

Farmer, B. M. (2020, April 3). March 2020: Dr. Anthony Fauci talks with Dr. Jon Lapook about Covid-19. *60 Minutes Overtime*. https://www.cbsnews.com/news/preventing-coronavirus-facemask-60-minutes-2020-03-08/

Feng, E., & Cheng, A. (2020, March 16). COVID-19 has caused a shortage of face masks. But they are surprisingly hard to make. *National Public Radio*. https://www.npr.org/sections/goatsandsoda/2020/03/16/814929294/covid-19-has-caused-a-shortage-of-face-masks-but-theyre-surprisingly-hard-to-mak

Gozali, C., Claassen Thrush, E., Soto-Peña, M., Whang, C., & Luschei, T. F. (2017). Teacher voice in global conversations around education access, equity, and quality. *Forum for International Research in Education*, 4(1), 32–51.

Gulyas, A. J. (2016). *Conspiracy theories: The roots, themes and propagation of paranoid political and cultural narratives*. McFarland.

Hermann, C. F. (1963). Some consequences of crisis which limit the viability of organizations. *Administrative Science Quarterly*, 8, 61–82.

Herovic, E., Sellnow, T. L., & Sellnow, D. D. (2020). Challenges and opportunities for pre-crisis emergency risk communication: Lessons learned from the earthquake community. *Journal of Risk Research, 23*(3), 1–16. https://doi.org/10.1080/1366987 7.2019.1569097

Lapook, J. (2020, March 8). Coronavirus: How U.S. hospitals are preparing for Covid-19, and what leading health official say about the virus. *60 Minutes.* https://www.cbsnews.com/news/coronavirus-containment-dr-jon-lapook-60-minutes-2020-03-08/

Mahtani, M., Macaya, M., Wagner, M., Alfonso II, F., & Rocha, V. (2021, July 15). July 15 coronavirus news. *CNN.* https://www.cnn.com/us/live-news/coronavirus-pandemic-vaccine-updates-07-15-21/index.html

McCaskgill, N. D. (2020, March 12). America shuts down. *Politico.* Retrieved June 20, 2021, from https://www.politico.com/news/2020/03/12/coronavirus-shutdowns-across-country-127018

McCormick, A. (2021, January 25). COVID-19 vaccine frustrations are mounting in Pennsylvania. *ABC Action News.* https://6abc.com/philadelphia-pa-covid-philly-covid19-vaccine-pennsylvania-coronavirus-us/10008358/

Merrill, S. C., Moegenburg, S., Koliba, C. J., Zia, A., Trinity, L., Clark, E. Bucini, G., Wiltshire, S., Sellnow, T., Sellnow, D., & Smith, J. M. (2019). Message delivery method, information certainty and infection risk influence willingness to comply with biosecurity in livestock facilities: Evidence from experimental simulations. *Frontiers in Veterinary Science, 6,* 156.

Miller, A. N., Sellnow, D. D., & Strawser, M. G. (2020). Pandemic pedagogy challenges opportunities: Instructional communication in remote. *HyFlex,* and *BlendFlex* courses. *Communication Education.* https://doi.org/10.1080/03634523.2020.1857418

Milligan, S. (2021, July 23). A deadly political divide: Two Americas are on display as political conversations turn to vaccines and election results. *U.S. News and World Report.* https://www.usnews.com/news/the-report/articles/2021-07-23/coronavirus-vaccines-highlight-a-deadly-political-divide

Otter, S. (1992). *Learning outcomes in higher education: A development project report.* ERIC document-ED354397

Our World in Data. (2021). *Statistics and research: Coronovirus (COVID-19) vaccinations.* Retrieved July 16, from https://ourworldindata.org/covid-vaccinations?country=USA

Prager, D. (2021, April 6). Scientific evidence supports the use of face masks to reduce COVID-19 spread, mainly by preventing infectious liquid particles from reaching uninfected people *Health Feedback.* https://healthfeedback.org/claimreview/scientific-evidence-supports-wearing-a-face-mask-to-reduce-covid-19-spread-mainly-by-preventing-infectious-liquid-particles-from-reaching-other-people/

Sellnow, D. D., Jones, L. M., Sellnow, T. L., Spence, P., Lane, D. R., & Haarstad, N. (2019). The IDEA model as a conceptual framework for designing earthquake early warning (EEW) messages distributed via mobile phone apps. In J. Santos-Reyes (Ed.), *Earthquakes—Impact, community vulnerability and resilience* (pp. 11–20). InTechOpen.

Sellnow, D. D., Lane, D. R., Sellnow, T. L., & Littlefield, R. (2017). The IDEA model as a best practice for effective instructional risk and crisis communication. *Communication Studies, 68*(5), 552–567. https://doi.org/10.1080/10510974.2017.1375535

Sellnow, D. D., & Sellnow, T. L. (2019). The IDEA model for effective instructional risk and crisis communication by emergency managers and other key spokespersons. *Journal of Emergency Management, 17*(1), 67–78. https://doi.org/10.5055/jem.2019.0399

Sellnow, D. D., & Sellnow, T. L. (2020a). Communication is . . . complex. In A. W. Tyma & A. P. Edwards (Eds.), *Communication is . . . perspectives on theory* (pp. 81–94). Cognella.

Sellnow, D. D., & Sellnow, T. L. (2020b). Effective communication in times of risk and crisis: The IDEA model for translating science to the public. *Research Outreach: Connecting Science with Society, 115,* 34–37. www.researchoutreach.org.

Sellnow, T. L., Parker, J. S., Sellnow, D. D., Littlefield, R. R., Helsel, E. M., Getchell, M. C., Smith, J. M., & Merrill, S. C. (2017). Improving biosecurity through instructional crisis communication: Lessons learned from the PEDv outbreak. *Journal of Applied Communications, 101*(4), COVC-COVC.

Sellnow, T. L., Parrish, A., & Semenas, L. (2019). From hoax as crisis to crisis as hoax: Fake news and information disorder as disruptions to the discourse of renewal. *Journal of International Crisis and Risk Communication Research, 2*(1), 122–142.

Thorson, K. (2018, July 25). Strategic communication. *Oxford Bibliographies.* https://www.oxfordbibliographies.com/view/document/obo-9780199756841/obo-9780199756841–0007.xml

Vanderford, M. L., Nastoff, T., Telfer, J. L., & Bonzo, S. E. (2007). Emergency communication challenges in response to Hurricane Katrina: Lessons from the Centers for Disease Control and Prevention. *Journal of Applied Communication Research, 3*(1), 9–25.

Weick, K. E. (1993). The collapse of sensemaking in organizations: The Mann Gulch disaster. *Administrative Science Quarterly, 38*(4), 628–652. https://doi.org/10.2307/2393339

Weick, K. E. (1995). *Sensemaking in organizations.* Sage.

World Health Organization. (2020, March 11). Coronavirus disease 2019 (COVID-19)—Situation Report 51. *World Health Organization.* https://www.who.int/docs/default-source/coronaviruse/situation-reports/20200311-sitrep-51-covid-19.pdf

22

COMMUNICATION STUDIES AND SOCIAL JUSTICE

25 Years and Counting

Amy Aldridge Sanford

Learning Objectives

1. Articulate the importance of communication skills in social justice scholarship.
2. Recognize the social justice concerns of Communication scholars in the past 25 years.
3. Identify key racial justice events in 2020 within the United States.
4. Set personal social justice goals related to Communication and activism.

For many people, 2020 is remembered as the Year of COVID-19, but that simple characterization does not fully capture the complexities of the political and social unrest in the United States during the year. Yes, the pandemic not only resulted in 375,000 U.S. deaths, but it also shined a spotlight on existing racial tensions within the country. For example, East Asians and Asian Americans were openly attacked after U.S. President Donald J. Trump dubbed COVID the "Chinese Virus" in a tweet (Kuo, 2020) and "Kung Flu" during a political rally (Yam, 2020). Additionally, Black people in the United States died of COVID-19 at twice the rates of white people (Scott & Animashaun, 2020). The untimely deaths tragically resulted from the disproportional numbers of Black folx[1] working in service industries, living in healthcare deserts, and lacking childcare options (Cabral, 2020; "Risks of exposure to COVID-19," 2020).

However, it was three non-COVID Black deaths—caused by current and former police officers—that took over social media and the 24-hour news cycle, beginning as a trickle in late February, building momentum by May, and lasting throughout the year. Dyson (2020) argued that the pandemic directly impacted people's heightened responses to the killings: "[COVID-19] forced us inside our

DOI: 10.4324/9781003220466-25

homes while forcing us deeper inside ourselves, deeper inside our thoughts about how we have lived, and deeper inside habits of mind or spirit that have nourished or harmed us" (p. 56). Similar police killings had happened before, but people did not have time to meditate on the injustice like they did during the first months of the pandemic.

Unquestionably, the targeting of Asian Americans and untimely deaths of minoritized people due to COVID-19, coupled with video proof of police brutality and activist responses to that brutality, made 2020 a Year of Racial Reckoning in the United States (Chavez, 2020). There were several social justice challenges that will be interrogated by Communication scholars and practitioners for years to come. In this chapter, I will define social justice and activism in the context of Communication Studies, examine the past 25 years of social justice scholarship in the discipline, highlight how 2020 was a year of racial reckoning in the United States, and consider the future of Communication Studies and social justice.

Definitions: Putting the *Social* in Social Justice

For this chapter, I define *social justice* as a commitment to promote a society in which diversity and difference are celebrated and not ignored or belittled (Sanford, 2020). Social justice, as a goal, is not about tolerance; it means fully embracing the identities and experiences of historically underrepresented and often excluded communities. Goodall (as quoted in Dempsey et al., 2011) asserted that communication and social justice are uniquely joined by an ethic of care and fairness and "a commitment to the use of communication in all of its forms to help coconstruct [sic] a better—and more just—world" (p. 257). Rodriguez (2006) argued that the constitutive nature of communication requires conversational partners, regardless of differences, be vulnerable to each other's humanity.

Abolitionist, activist, and communication practitioner Frederick Douglass (1857) infamously stated that "power concedes nothing without a demand" (para. 44). I define *activism* as direct actions (e.g., boycotting, rallying, canvassing) by people seeking change because of their commitment to social justice (Sanford, 2020). Douglass understood that very few decision makers would voluntarily end the oppressive practices, policies, etc. that benefitted their bottom lines. Huffman (2018) asserted that Communication practitioners and scholars are uniquely qualified to make social changes because of their abilities to persuade decision makers, build and maintain relationships, manage conflicts, facilitate group conversations, and speak to crowds. Crumley (2006) and Johnson (2017) argued that communication puts the *social* in social justice.

Currently, *social justice* and *activism* permeate Communication research, with 1,012 and 2,796 journal articles in the Communication Source database citing those terms, respectively. However, the scholarship was not always so bountiful.

25 Years of Calling Out and Calling in Communication Scholars

For the past 25 years, Communication scholars have both called out (publicly) and called in (privately) their colleagues regarding Communication's role in social justice scholarship and practice. The conversations have occurred publicly in journal articles, speeches, panel presentations, and newsletters, and, more privately, in faculty meetings, email exchanges, and in hallways of conference hotels. Initially, just a few persistent public voices spoke up, and most of them were white because the discipline was mostly white. However, over the past decade, as scholars have diversified in identities and experiences, the call outs have become more frequent and bolder.

The initial, most well-cited call out happened in the mid-1990s, when faculty from Loyola University Chicago urged colleagues across the country to expand and transform existing communication theories, methods, and pedagogical practices to promote "the engagement with and advocacy for those in our society who are economically, socially, politically and/or culturally underresourced" (Frey et al., 1996, p. 110). Wood (1996) responded defensively to the article, stating that research about social (in)justice [Wood's term] was already happening—pointing to her own gender scholarship dating to 1991 and other work related to sexual harassment, intimate partner violence, disability, ethnicity, and second language speakers. The Loyola scholars argued that Wood's examples privileged conversations among researchers and did nothing to improve the lives of the researched (see Pollock et al., 1996).

A couple of years later, a special issue of the *Journal of Applied Communication Research* was dedicated to Communication and social justice. One of the Loyola scholars wrote the response essay, stating that he hoped the articles would "legitimate the publication in front-line journals of the good work that many of us have been doing—much of which has been thought of (sometimes under the tutelage of editors and reviewers) as unpublishable" (Pearce, 1998, p. 272). The public admonishments (and subsequent attention) on the intersection of communication and social justice stopped for about a decade.

In 2007, Frey and Carragee edited the first of a three-volume book series titled *Communication Activism*. In the initial volume, the editors argued that early Communication scholars were overly concerned about legitimizing the discipline and, in turn, lost focus on societal issues and helping others. In 2008, Hartnett gave a keynote to the Rocky Mountain Communication Association where he chastised scholars for ignoring questions of race, class, gender, sexuality, and nationalism, unapologetically stating "Communication is still largely studied and taught not as a component of social justice but as a set of politically vacuous truisms or as tools for equipping would-be corporate warriors to make even more money" (Hartnett, 2010, p. 69).

In the 2010s, social justice became a common topic for research, teaching, and service in the Communication discipline. In 2011, Dempsey et al. archived a series of virtual café meetings, where eight scholars discussed the relationship between communication and social justice, ideas for how to engage in activism, and public scholarship. In 2013, Flores used her presidential address to the Western States Communication Association to highlight opportunities for social justice in the discipline, leaving the audience with three challenges: (a) more intentionality with hires, admissions, and recruitment; (b) commitment to inclusive excellence; and (c) embracing philosophy and practice. In 2014, the National Communication Association (NCA) established its Activism and Social Justice Division, and by 2021, the unit included 867 affiliated members and ranked as one of the largest divisions in the national organization.

In 2018, Chakravartty et al., in an article titled "#CommunicationSoWhite," rocked the discipline and its white allies with a critique of the systemic racism in the journal process. Chakravartty et al. advocated for increased non-white representation in editorial positions, authorship, and citation rates. The article put a mirror up to the discipline and its gatekeepers, including those woke, white folx who had called out their less woke colleagues for years. Chakravartty et al. exposed the lack of social justice *within* the discipline, not simply the lack of research and teaching *about* social justice. They saw performative allyship and named it.

In 2019, when I ended my time as Past President of the Central States Communication Association, I was humbled by "#CommunicationSoWhite" and what it exposed about a discipline in which I was deeply entrenched. In this state of humility and reflexivity, I offered my parting words:

> This is a call out and a call in of the privileged. . . . Our friends and colleagues in the margins are tired of carrying the burden of being uncomfortable and courageous for all of us. . . . To be a well-meaning ally is no longer enough; it is time to co-conspire. (Sanford, 2019, p. 679)

2020: A Year of Racial Reckoning in the United States

The tragic deaths of Ahmaud Arbery, Breonna Taylor, and George Floyd in 2020 forever changed the course of modern civil rights. The abbreviated timeline below begins on a Sunday afternoon in mid-February with Arbery taking a jog and extends through September when it was announced that none of the shooters in the killing of Taylor would be charged with her death.

* On February 23, Arbery, a 25-year-old aspiring electrician, jogged through a Brunswick, Georgia neighborhood. When he paused to look inside a house under construction, three neighborhood men chased him with their vehicles until he was trapped like a caged animal. Travis McMichael shot Arbery, who was unarmed, twice in the chest while McMichael's dad (a recently retired police officer) watched (Klibanoff, 2020–2021).

- Less than three weeks later, on March 13, police shot and killed Taylor, a 26-year-old hospital worker, in her Louisville, Kentucky, apartment when a no-knock warrant was served shortly after midnight. Three police officers—Myles Cosgrove, Joshua Jaynes, and Brett Hankison—blindly fired more than two dozen bullets into Taylor's apartment. The warrant was for her ex-boyfriend, who did not live at the address and had already been detained (Mofta, 2020).
- On May 4, officials released the initial video of Arbery's killing, and, on May 8 (his birthday), many people left their homes to jog 2.23 miles (his death date) to commemorate Arbery's life.
- On May 25, as the national news related to Arbery and Taylor ramped up, a police officer killed Floyd in Minneapolis, Minnesota, an incident that began with Floyd's the alleged use of a counterfeit $20 bill (Chavez, 2020, December 15). Teenager Darnella Frazier[2] recorded on her phone while Derek Chauvin put a knee on 46-year-old Floyd's neck for nearly nine minutes while Floyd begged for his life, face in the pavement, declaring "I can't breathe."

Frazier's video went viral, and the dam burst. Activists masked up and went to the streets, holding marches and rallies. In the following months, activists toppled Confederate statues and painted the moniker "Black Lives Matter" (BLM) on city streets; professional sports teams changed their mascots; municipalities renamed buildings and neighborhoods previously named for KKK members; and businesses rebranded products (Chavez, 2020). However, backlash also ensued. According to Chavez, in late June 2020, Mark and Patricia McCloskey pointed guns at anti-racism protestors in their St. Louis, Missouri, neighborhood. In September, Kentucky Attorney General Daniel Cameron announced that no officers would be charged for Taylor's death ("Breonna Taylor," 2020). Throughout the summer and fall, detractors spread misinformation about BLM-sponsored violence and looting, when in fact, 93% of BLM protests were completely nonviolent (Mansoor, 2020).

My 2020 Experience

At the end of 2019, my book, *From thought to action: Developing a social justice orientation*, was published, and I entered 2020 fully prepared to give talks about social justice, activism, and allyship. I planned some presentations at bookstores, universities, and conferences, but, when everything shut down in mid-March, we cancelled most original plans. I still gave talks, but they were far more organic and satisfying. A few days after the killing of Floyd, an acquaintance asked me to join her and some friends on Facebook Live to discuss how they, as Black folx, were handling twin pandemics—COVID and systemic racism. During the broadcast, we talked about self-care, direct action, and allyship. In the middle of June, a Latina friend interviewed me about social justice in front of a mostly Latina audience on YouTube.

These requests and subsequent interactions caused me to think differently about my responsibilities as an activist-scholar and white ally. I wanted to more strategically use my platform to better advocate for and partner with under-represented populations. When the local branch of the American Association of University Women—a group with many privilege identities—asked me to pre-sent a program in the early fall, I agreed to do it only if I could speak on BLM. They hesitantly said OK and ended up asking great questions. Not everybody was as receptive to my advocacy of Black communities though—including strangers responding to television interviews, a former colleague at a virtual panel, and even a few people at a Farmers Market during a (masked) book signing.

I became more immersed in the local Black community during 2020. In late May and early June, I attended BLM rallies and marches. By the end of August, I unexpectedly received an invitation from Black leaders to attend a "Black Lead-ership Meeting" with city officials. Today, I regularly meet with local Black lead-ers and have learned to listen more than I talk (a tough lesson for a full professor and university administrator). Additionally, the killings of Arbery, Taylor, and Floyd taught me that I had much to learn about policing specifically and systemic racism in general. I formed a book club with three former students—an assistant district attorney; a counselor married to a police officer; and an Emmy-award winning news broadcaster who lives life as a Black man. We met virtually for months to discuss *The end of policing* by Alex Vitale and engaged in some candid, somewhat difficult, and completely necessary conversations.

What We Learned from 2020: The Future of Communication and Social Justice

Flores (2013) reminded Communication practitioners and scholars that our spe-cific social justice responsibility is to change the conversation—both privately and publicly—when we encounter injustice. In the following section, I offer advice for how we can learn from the past 25 years of Communication scholarship and better advocate for social justice moving forward. Perhaps Frey and Carragee (2007) were right that early Communication scholars lost their way, but it is not too late to correct that misstep.

Practitioners

As students of communication, we all have a responsibility to be good practition-ers. To promote social justice in our communities, consider the framework of (a) self-reflection, (b) education, and (c) action (Sanford, 2020; see Figure 22.1).

Self-Reflection

Self-reflection requires a person to think about all their identities—both the priv-ileged and the marginalized—and includes race, ethnicity, sex, sexuality, ability

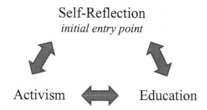

Self-Reflection
initial entry point

Activism ⟷ Education

FIGURE 22.1   Social Justice Framework

status, class, religion, geography, etc. (Sanford, 2020). It also allows the opportunity to inventory biases, implicit or otherwise. We must continually come back to self-reflection because it should never cease.

Education

We should learn from documentaries, college courses, books, podcasts, museums, webinars, journal articles, conference panels, etc. to become better versed in social justice causes and people's identities, avoiding reliance on people with lived experiences to be personal tutors. In time, authentic relationships will happen with individuals inside our communities if we seek to learn and serve.

Action

Many practitioners are good at self-reflecting and educating but never make the bold, necessary move to direct action. As a result, their interest in social justice comes across as performative and insincere. What Frederick Douglass (1857) taught more than 150 years ago still holds true today: oppressive systems will not change unless we directly ask, and decision makers feel a little heat[3]. In April 2021, the governor of Kentucky signed a law limiting the use of no-knock warrants like the one that resulted in Breonna Taylor's death (Treisman, 2021). This law happened because activists, including Taylor's family, were relentless in their fight for the legislation—taking over a Louisville city park, meeting with members of the legislature, and rallying across the country.

Scholars

It should not have taken the labor of BIPOC[4] scholars (see Chakravartty et al., 2018) to point out the decades-old racism on display in Communication journals. Too many white scholars were complicit in a system that rewarded complicity. Moving forward, *all* Communication scholars committed to social justice should recognize three major responsibilities: (a) promote a pipeline of BIPOC scholars and other folx (e.g., disabled, transnational, LGBTQIA+) who have been historically excluded; (b) increase research, theory, and pedagogy related to communication and social justice, and (c) commit to scholar-activism.

Pipeline of Historically Excluded Scholars

Increased diversity within the discipline will strengthen the discipline's relevance both inside and outside the academy. I join with Flores (2013) in calling for more intentionality with hires, admission decisions, and recruitment. Talented undergraduate students with underrepresented identities should consider pursuing graduate studies and the professoriate, and faculty mentors should encourage them to do so. Faculty can decrease systemic barriers for the students by offering regular affirmations, partnering on research, securing travel and research funding, co-traveling to conferences, and facilitating introductions of scholars who share the students' marginalized identities (see Sanford, 2019).

Research, Theory, and Pedagogy

Of course, we must build on the current momentum of original research, theory development and evolution, and pedagogical practices related to Communication and social justice. Additionally, degree plans across campuses should include social justice and activism courses and more textbooks need to be authored for those courses. Communication studies can be known as the discipline that brought social justice to the academy.

Scholar-Activism

Finally, more Communication scholars need to live as scholar-activists, not only studying and writing about social justice—but also living it. We should utilize our expertise to take public actions—writing op-eds for newspapers, organizing rallies, canvasing for progressive political candidates, and humbly joining practitioners on podcasts and social media events. Otherwise, our allyship with underrepresented communities and concern for social justice appears nothing more than performative.

Conclusion: Good Trouble

On July 17, 2020, during the midst of people demanding justice for Black lives, the great Black Civil Rights icon and congressman John Lewis passed at the age of 80. His last public act—just six weeks earlier—was an appearance in BLM Plaza in Washington, DC. In a letter that was printed posthumously, Lewis (2020) wrote:

> While my time here has now come to an end, I want you to know that in my last days and hours of my life you inspired me. . . . That is why I had

to visit Black Lives Matter Plaza. . . . I just had to see for myself that, after many years of silent witness, the truth is still marching on. (para. 2)

Lewis's attendance at BLM Plaza was a symbolic act of passing the torch and his affirmation of younger activists and their ways of seeking justice. The time has come in Communication Studies to do the same. The first generation of scholars dedicated to social justice are retiring and passing the torch to a younger, more diverse group of scholar-activists and practitioners, who will certainly have their own ways of advancing the work, and in the words of Lewis, will make "good, necessary trouble" in the advancement of the discipline.

Notes

1. The X is used to signify gender inclusion and the rejection of a binary.
2. Frazier was awarded a special citation by the Pulitzer Prize board in June 2021.
3. In April 2021, the governor of Kentucky signed a law limiting the use of no-knock warrants like the one that resulted in Breonna Taylor's death. This law happened because activists, including Taylor's family, were relentless in their fight for the legislation – taking over a Louisville city park, meeting with members of the legislature, and rallying across the country.
4. Black, Indigenous and People of Color.

References

Breonna Taylor: Police officer charged but not over death. (2020, September 23). *BBC*. https://www.bbc.com/news/world-us-canada-54273317

Cabral, A. (2020). *Allies and advocates: Creating and inclusive and equitable culture*. Wiley.

Chakravartty, P., Kuo, R., Grubbs, V., & McIlwain, C. (2018). #CommunicationSoWhite. *Journal of Communication, 68*(2), 254–266. https://doi.org/10.1093/joc/jqy003

Chavez, N. (2020, December 15). 2020: The year America confronted racism. *CNN*. https://www.cnn.com/interactive/2020/12/us/america-racism-2020/

Crumley, L. P. (2006). Social justice in interpersonal and family relationships. In O. Swartz (Ed.), *Social justice and communication scholarship* (pp. 175–192). Erlbaum.

Dempsey, S., Dutta, M., Frey, L. R., Goodall, H. L., Madison, D. S., Mercieca, J., Nakayama, T., & Miller, K. (2011). What is the role of the communication discipline in social justice, community engagement, and public scholarship? A visit to the *CM Café*. *Communication Monographs, 78*(2), 256–271. https://doi.org/10.1080/03637751.2011.565062

Douglass, F. (1857, August 4). *West India emancipation*. University of Rochester. https://rbscp.lib.rochester.edu/4398

Dyson, M. E. (2020). *Long time coming: Reckoning with race in America*. St. Martin's Press.

Flores, L. (2013). 2013 WSCA Presidential Address: Striving for social justice—The excellence of inclusion in education. *Western Journal of Communication, 77*(5), 645–650. https://doi.org/10.1080/10570314.2013.823514

Frey, L. R., & Carragee, K. M. (Eds.). (2007). *Communication activism: Vol. 1, communication for social change*. Hampton Press.

Frey, L. R., Pearce, W. B., Pollock, M. A., Artz, L., & Murphy, B. A. O. (1996). Looking for justice in all the wrong places: On a communication approach to social justice. *Communication Studies, 47*(1–2), 110–127. https://doi.org/10.1080/10510979609368467

Hartnett, S. J. (2010). Communication, social justice, and joyful commitment. *Western Journal of Communication, 74*(1), 68–93. https://doi.org/10.1080/10570310903463778.

Huffman, T. P. (2018). Paradigmatic tools for communication scholar-activists: Toward a pragmatic and relational epistemology. *Review of Communication, 18*(1), 19–36. https://doi.org/10.1080/15358593.2017.1405460

Johnson, A. (2017). A communication approach to social justice: Midwest college campus protests. *Howard Journal of Communications, 28*(2), 212–215. http://dx.doi.org/10.1080/10646175.2017.1283261

Klibanoff, H. (Host). (2020–2021). *Buried truths* [Audio podcast]. WABE. https://www.wabe.org/shows/buried-truths/

Kuo, L. (2020, March 17). Trump sparks anger by calling Coronavirus the 'Chinese virus'. *The Guardian.* https://www.theguardian.com/world/2020/mar/17/trump-calls-covid-19-the-chinese-virus-as-rift-with-coronavirus-beijing-escalates

Lewis, J. (2020, July 30). Together, you can redeem the soul of our nation. *New York Times*, A23(L). https://link.gale.com/apps/doc/A630986073/SCIC?u=txshracd2566&sid=bookmark-SCIC&xid=dc244bfa

Mansoor, S. (2020, September 5). 93% of Black Lives Matter protests have been peaceful, new report says. *Time.* https://time.com/5886348/report-peaceful-protests/

Mofta, L. (Producer). (2020). *The killing of Breonna Taylor* [Video]. Hulu. http://www.hulu.com

Pearce, W. B. (1998). On putting social justice in the discipline of communication and putting enriched concepts of communication in social justice research and practice. *Journal of Applied Communication Research, 26*(2), 272–278. https://doi.org/10.1080/00909889809365505

Pollock, M. A., Artz, L., Frey, L. R., Pearce, W. B., & Murphy, B. A. O. (1996). Navigating between Scylla and Charybdis: Continuing the dialogue on communication and social justice. *Communication Studies, 47*(1–2), 142–151. https://doi.org/10.1080/10510979609368470

Risks of exposure to COVID-19: Racial and ethnic disparities. (2020, December 10). Centers for Disease Control and Prevention. https://www.cdc.gov/coronavirus/2019-ncov/community/health-equity/racial-ethnic-disparities/increased-risk-exposure.html

Rodriguez, A. (2006). Social justice and the challenges for communication studies. In O. Swartz (Ed.), *Social justice and communication scholarship* (pp. 21–34). Erlbaum.

Sanford, A. A. (2019). Presidential spotlight: It's time for discomfort and change. *Communication Studies, 70*(5), 677–684. https://doi.org/10.1080/10510974.2019.1681701

Sanford, A. A. (2020). *From thought to action: Developing a social justice orientation.* Cognella Academic Publishing.

Scott, D., & Animashaun, C. (2020, October 2). Covid-19's stunningly unequal death toll in American, in one chart. *Vox.* https://www.vox.com/coronavirus-covid19/2020/10/2/21496884/us-covid-19-deaths-by-race-black-white-americans

Treisman, R. (2021, April 9). Kentucky law limits use of no-knock warrants a year after Breonna Taylor's killing. *NPR.* https://www.npr.org/2021/04/09/985804591/kentucky-law-limits-use-of-no-knock-warrants-a-year-after-breonna-taylors-killin

Wood, J. (1996). Social justice research: Alive and well in the field of communication. *Communication Studies, 47*(1–2), 128–134. https://doi.org/10.1080/10510979609368468

Yam, K. (2020, June 22). Trump can't claim 'Kung Flu' doesn't affect Asian Americans in this climate, experts say. *NBC News.* https://www.nbcnews.com/news/asian-america/trump-can-t-claim-kung-flu-doesn-t-affect-asian-n1231812

INDEX

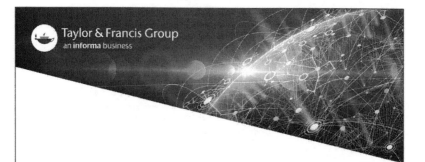